Looking for Dragon Smoke

Looking for Dragon Smoke

Essays on Poetry

ROBERT BLY

WHITE PINE PRESS / BUFFALO, NEW YORK

White Pine Press
PO Box 236
Buffalo, NY 14201
www.whitepine.org

Acknowledgments: Author/editor/translator of original publication Robert Bly unless
otherwise noted:

"Six Disciplines That Intensify Poetry" first appeared in *The Thousands, No. 1*, The Thousands Press, Minneapolis, MN, 2001.

"Looking for Dragon Smoke" first appeared in *The Seventies, No. 1*, Odin House, Madison, MN, Spring 1972. It was reprinted in *Leaping Poetry: An Idea with Poems and Translations*, Beacon Press, Boston, 1975, and in *American Poetry: Wildness and Domesticity*, Harper & Row, New York, 1990.

"The Work of Jane Hirshfield" first appeared in *The Thousands, No. 1*, The Thousands Press, Minneapolis, MN, 2001.

"Wallace Stevens and Dr. Jekyll" first appeared in *American Poets in 1976*, William Heyen, ed., Bobbs-Merrill, Indianapolis, IN, 1976. It was included in *A Little Book on the Human Shadow*, William Booth, ed., HarperOne, New York, 1988.

"My Doubts About Whitman" first appeared in *Walt Whitman: The Measure of His Song*, Jim Perlman, Ed Folsom and Dan Campion, eds., Holy Cow! Press, Minneapolis, MN, 1981. Revised essay published in second edition, 1996.

"Upward into the Depths" first appeared in *Tomas Tranströmer, The Half-Finished Heaven*, Graywolf Press, Minneapolis, 2001.

"Rilke and the Holy" first appeared in *Selected Poems of Rainer Maria Rilke*, Harper & Row, New York, 1981.

Acknowledgments continue on page 299

Publication of this book was made possible by the generous support of individuals who contributed to our Kickstarter Campaign.

Cover painting by Simon Xianwen Zeng. Used by permission of the artist.

Printed and bound in the United States of America.

ISBN 978-1-945680-26-7

Library of Congress number 2018947134

Contents

Introduction:
A Rebellious Originality: Robert Bly's Essays

Thomas R. Smith

For those readers who have followed the incandescent arc of Robert Bly's artistry and thought for the past five or six decades, this book packs the emotional satisfaction of a reunion of beloved friends — so many vivid speakers gathered at table, the conversation by turns fiery, lyrical, prophetic, reckless, intimate, generous, obscure or even esoteric. Nearly all offer the thrill of excess that has consistently made Bly one of our most colorful and daring poets. As he says in "Six Disciplines That Intensify Poetry," "To make poetry means that you need to go over the line, to be not sensible but arresting, not to be acceptable but to be unforgettable." Not only in his poetry but in his prose, Bly has succeeded in being unforgettable, which is why, for his long-time readers, these essays jar memories of our original encounters with such force of still-fresh revelation.

Looking for Dragon Smoke spans more than forty years, from the 1963 manifesto "A Wrong Turning in American Poetry" to the luminous appraisal of "James Wright's Clarity and Extravagance" from 2005. Part One throws down the gauntlet with passionate pronouncements on the intensity that has defined Bly's work from the beginning. Part Two, perhaps the most wonderful section of this book because the most abundant, celebrates ten poets, spiritual ancestors like Rilke and Machado and contemporaries like Tomas Tranströmer and James Wright, to whose work Bly has owed some debt. Part

Three focuses on matters of 20th century literary life in America and an illuminating and accessible discussion of Bly's translation process. And Part Four is devoted entirely to an extended meditation on one of Bly's most important American transcendentalist progenitors, Henry David Thoreau.

Bly has, perhaps cunningly, avoided chronology. How these essays are sequenced may loosely follow Yeats's principle of "countertruth," described by Bly in the Thoreau essay:

> We are given one truth, and the countertruth we have to develop. . . .
> The truth of the soul's interior abundance declared that we can have
> a love affair with the universe only if we decline to marry the world;
> that nature is the true friend of the soul; and the divine man is un-
> controlled by social obligation. The countertruth might be: society
> is a deeper friend of the soul than nature; a man or a woman grows
> only if he or she is willing to give up a solitary affair with a shrub
> oak; no solitary self can replace society, social sensibility, manners
> and institutions of Church and State. . . .

Developing the "countertruth" is not a contradiction of one's starting position, but an opening to a more complete consideration, much in the way Jung's "inferior function" complements or rounds out the one-sidedness of our dominant personality traits. Arriving at the countertruth can be seen as a necessary stage in the emotional and spiritual maturation of a human being. Bly's adoption of this line of thought is especially suggestive coming as it does in 1986, midway in the time range represented by these essays. Obviously it's an idea Bly has applied to himself, an indication or presentiment of some turning in his own life and views. As Bly says later in one of his ghazals, "Each sentence we speak to friends means the opposite / As well."

In fact, certain pairings of the essays in this book either intentionally or intuitively demonstrate this progression of truth-to-countertruth. I'll mention two areas in which we recognize this dynamic in play.

One of the major turnings in Bly's poetry in the 1980s was a new (or renewed) attention to form. In the political and cultural upheavals of the 1960s, Bly tended to minimize the importance of form, dismissing discussion of "craft" in poetry as unworthy of poetry's soul-task of bridging inner and outer worlds. One could assume from all but Bly's earliest published work an almost total lack of interest in form. Bly's rigorous friend Donald Hall commented in the 1970s, "If Bly could write his poems in amino acids or bird calls, he would just as lief; the spirit matters to him, and not the shoulders of consonants." (*Goatfoot Milktongue Twinbird*, p. 137) In Bly's work of that period, the image takes precedence over formal concerns, with the ability to "leap" swiftly from one area of the psyche to another most supremely valued among the several powers of poetry. This idea achieved its definitive expression in the landmark essay "Looking for Dragon Smoke," first published in 1967 and expanded in 1972.

Bly, who like others of his generation began as a formal poet under the spell of Yeats and Frost, in reality never abandoned form, though we could say that his work of the 1960s and 1970s followed a less conventional, more organic vision of form. He observes in "Six Disciplines," "Form is not a thing invented by human beings. . . . Each object you find on the beach or in the woods is a masterpiece of achieved form." Even so, Bly's 1981 collection *The Man in the Black Coat Turns* startled with its irregular Marianne Moore-like stanzas, which seemed novel or even foreign to his work. It was around this time too that Bly began to publish his *ramages*, an eight-line form he invented to explore the peculiar musical properties of the vowel-consonant combinations he has called "sound particles." The intricacies of form and sound-work figure fundamentally in his 1982 genius essay "The Eight Stages of Translation." That in 2001 Bly can list among "the six disciplines that intensify poetry" "obeying the form that is in nature" shows that he has developed his countertruth in relation to form on his own terms.

The second area of development I'll touch on is the growing care for community evident in Bly's thought from roughly the 1980s on. Of course Bly was deeply involved in many communities before that time, the American literary community and the 1960s anti-war community among them. Later experiments in the occasional communities of his Great Mother and men's conferences manifested Bly's gift for bringing together the talented, intellectually curious and spiritually adventurous under the Eros-tent of poetry and storytelling. At the same time he often espoused an uncompromisingly individualistic position toward the visionary imperative of the poet. That solitary note rings unmistakably in his admiration for Thoreau's acceptance of the loneliness demanded by his psychic and artistic development. Bly comments:

Courage is needed to withstand the melancholy and loneliness. . . .

for years nothing tangible will come from this inward and invisible swerving. No fruit will appear that [the artist's] family or the surrounding society can eat.

Bly knew from experience the lonely courage of which he spoke, having eked out years of post-Harvard poverty and isolation in New York City before publication elevated him from obscurity into international fame.

If solitude is Bly's original "truth," then the period of the mid-1980s that produced the Thoreau essay turns out to be something of a tipping point toward the countertruth of community, complementing Bly's original stance. By 1993, in praising William Stafford (temperamentally about as near as we'll find to Bly's polar opposite), he is able to affirm Stafford's care for our "mutual life":

[Stafford] offers his idea that the root of all cruelty lies in refusing to recognize what we all know as facts—that others are different from me, that we need to speak who we are, that one person "wandering" can have enormous harmful results.

Bly continues:

The artist owes language to the human community, but owes his or her breathing body to the animal community. Every poem we write, every day we live, we think about what we owe to each. By knowing what to take from the world of culture and what to give back, what to take from the world of animals and what to give back, we become adults. That awake people are aware of the two communities—the human beings and the animals—is assumed, and the decision between those two is not easy.

In an important way Stafford embodied what Bly needed in order to become a full member of the human community, i.e., an adult. A realized fruit of this development is Bly's 1997 collection *Morning Poems*, in which he not only allows some of Stafford's relaxed mood and understated humor into his work but adopts Stafford's practice of writing a poem each morning in the early hours before others are awake.

Not organizing *Looking for Dragon Smoke* chronologically allows Bly to juxtapose essays to make clear his movement in specific areas. An example is the pairing of "Some Rumors About Kabir" and "The Surprises in Ghalib." The Kabir essay, dating from 1977, displays Bly in his most confident wielding of far-flung ideas and influences, the bhakti tradition in one hand and Babylonian myth in the other. This is the kind of bravura thinking and writing that has earned Bly admiration from audiences far outside the poetry mainstream. Describing Kabir's energy, he says, "It is as if both thought and feeling fed a third thing, a rebellious originality, and with that tail the poem shoots through the water." We would have to look hard to find a more perfect description of Bly's own energy. Bly's tone in his 1999 piece on Ghalib is more measured, less excitable; here he becomes more soberly the teacher, helping Western readers grasp the intricacies of the ghazal form as practiced by Ghalib, though with his own inimitable flair for the image: "In a ghazal, it is as if the writer has thrown a group of handsome bones onto the field, and the reader has to put them together to make a dog. . . ." Contrasting the periods during which Kabir and Ghalib wrote (the 15th and 19th centuries respectively), Bly comments on Ghalib's more despairing mood: "Perhaps spiritual achievement becomes more difficult now." He may also be indirectly acknowledging the different energies of his own younger and older selves.

A final example of the emergence of a countertruth we might point to in *Looking for Dragon Smoke* is the stark tonal leap from 1963's passionate "A Wrong Turning in American Poetry," one of Bly's most defining early statements, to 1999's "When Literary Life Was Still Piled Up in a Few Places," an affectionate tribute to Paul Engle, who directed the graduate writing program in Iowa which Bly attended in the 1950s. In one insightful passage he notes: "I also found notes from a conversation I had had with Paul, in which I remarked, 'Paul's greatest need is precisely to be needed.' So he and I were much alike in that way." In fact this brief essay is so steeped in mature self-knowledge it makes one genuinely sorry that Bly has not produced a full-length memoir. If Bly's truth in 1963 is a Young Turk's judgment of elders, 1999's countertruth is an acknowledgment of gratitude toward those from whom he has learned. The distance between these two essays shows what thirty-six years can do in the life of someone for whom intellectual and emotional growth has not stopped. Bly, like Rilke, has indeed lived in his life "in growing orbits."

There are many more things I could say in praise of Bly's provocative essays, but an introduction should whet, not satisfy, the reader's appetite, which I hope by now has grown robust in anticipation of the feast within these pages. It should be evident that Bly has tended to move forward in his literary and personal life by way of oppositions and contraries. His ability to hold the tension of such opposition in poetry and prose is part of what accounts for the vital power and energy of both. Blake said, "Energy is eternal delight." Whether in opposition to others or himself, Bly accomplishes the movement that the heat of growth requires. As these essays amply demonstrate, Bly's work seen complete stands as a massive testimony to those who, like Rilke, "spend their lives trying to increase their store of consciousness." Like Machado, Bly is a matchless master instructor in "how to study the outer world without losing inward richness."

I
Looking for Dragon Smoke

Six Disciplines That Intensify Poetry

One could think of twenty skills or practices or disciplines that may help good writing turn into poetry. I've chosen these six out of many possibilities. Every veteran of the wars might choose a different six. The first I'll mention is the Delight of Metaphor.

We always have a choice between facts—I broke my knee when I was five, I have always been bad at math—and metaphor. A metaphor resembles a storm—it is a God-given gift to the countryside, it is a form of intensity like dancing; a good metaphor breaks open the stagnant mind and makes available the other mind's storehouse of raisins, macaroons, and jewels. When Pablo Neruda begins "Ode to My Socks," he opens with a couple of facts:

> Maru Mori brought me
> a pair
> of socks
> which she knitted herself
> with her sheepherder's hands. . . .

That's enough facts, and now he turns to metaphor:

> I slipped my feet
> into them
> as though into

two
cases
knitted
with threads of
twilight
and goatskin.
Violent socks,
my feet were
two fish made
of wool,
two long sharks
sea-blue, shot
through
by one golden thread,
two immense blackbirds,
two cannons:
my feet
were honored
in this way
by
these
heavenly
socks.

What blessings does metaphor give? It prevents the mind—the uneducated
or the educated mind—from going straight ahead down a railway of slum-
bering, half-interesting facts. Instead the metaphor stops the train, tells all
the literalists to get out. Finally they can see some open fields.

I slipped my feet
into them
as though into
two
cases
knitted
with threads of
twilight
and goatskin.

The metaphors open doors to weather, to knitting, to animals, to nature. The writer who insists on metaphor carries us out of our room, into the forest, where, Lorca says, all poems are found. Lorca remarked: "When I sit down, I always write with green ink, so that I don't frighten the wild animals. Gerald Diego claims that he uses red ink, but we all know that he lies about things like that." Lorca begins "Little Infinite Poem" this way:

> To take the wrong road
> Is to arrive at the snow
> And to arrive at the snow
> Is to get down on all fours for twenty centuries and eat the grasses
>   of the cemeteries.

Whether we can use metaphor with the swiftness and purity of the masters is not the point; even playfully climbing on metaphor, riding that horse, brings us into the kingdom of uncertainty, where a mouse can come along wearing King George's hat. Of course, we all know that simply using metaphors will not make the poem good in itself; the metaphors have to be fine.

A few years ago Don Hall and I gave a reading of our worst poems; we tried to trump each other and see who had written the worst poem. I offered this early poem.

> The green poet goes through the world
> Riding on the bark of a tree.
>
> He walks in the city streets meditating
> Like the fleece of a sheep.
>
> Or climbs on trains and buses
> With a tree growing from the sole of his foot.
>
> Alone at last he sits in his room,
> His face surrounded by leaves.
>
> And he carries inside
> Six tiny grains of mustard seed

And the seeds of wild strawberries,
And in his shirt the loaf of bread

Baked on the stormy day
When the Roman Empire ended at last.

The idea that sheep's wool does meditation is a doubtful proposition. I especially enjoy the idea of the writer climbing on a bus with a tree growing from the sole of his foot, which seems very cumbersome.

The genuine metaphor wakes the reader up abruptly. D. H. Lawrence in his tortoise-shell poem says:

I remember my first time hearing the howl of the weird amorous cats;
I remember the scream of a terrified, injured horse, the sheet-lightning,
And running away from the sound of a woman in labor, something
    like an owl whooing. . . .

The metaphor often opens the soul to the nonhuman world. Mary Oliver's "Sleeping in the Forest" goes this way:

I thought the earth
remembered me, she
took me back so tenderly, arranging
her dark skirts, her pockets
full of lichens and seeds. I slept
as never before, a stone
on the riverbed, nothing
between me and the white fire of the stars
but my thoughts, and they floated
light as moths among the branches
of the perfect trees. All night
I heard the small kingdoms breathing
around me, the insects, and the birds
who do their work in the darkness. All night
I rose and fell, as if in water, grappling
with a luminous doom. By morning
I had vanished at least a dozen times
into something better.

The poet, Jay Leeming, who hasn't published his first book yet, showed me a new poem of his the other day. His metaphors don't necessarily open you to nature, but they do something very swiftly.

> Trying to get rid of your ego
> Is like trying to get rid of your garbage can.
> No one believes you are serious.
> The more you shout at the garbage man
> The more your neighbors remember your name.

Here the metaphor does operations swiftly that it would take a Buddhist prose speaker hours to do.

Ananda Coomaraswami said something like: "To have lost the art of speaking in images is precisely to have lost the ability to touch the world of spirit and to have descended instead into the dry planes of philosophy."

Hart Crane said about Labrador:

> A land of leaning ice
> Hugged by plaster-grey arches of sky
> Flings itself silently
> Into eternity.

Hart Crane's "Voyages II" ends this way:

> Bind us in time, O seasons clear, and awe.
> O minstrel galleons of Carib fire,
> Bequeath us to no earthly shore until
> Is answered in the vortex of our grave
> The seal's wide spindrift gaze toward paradise.

The seal's "wide spindrift gaze toward paradise" reveals the deepest longing and the most ferocious secret of metaphor, namely that it can shift us, as no other gift can, to the plane of the divine, to the rooms of Paradise, to the roof beams of heaven.

The Ancient Friendships Between Sounds

When we sit down to write, we often imagine that thoughts are coming, or feelings are arriving. But actually what are arriving are syllables, each a marriage or affair of vowel and consonant. As we write along at our desk, we watch sometimes with amazement these little sound unit or particular love affairs coming along in their variety. They keep coming along, no matter what we do.

But it is another thing to take part in their arriving—to put out a call for sound friendships, to decide to encourage certain ones. Then we are awake by one more degree. To be awake as a writer is to take part in sound friendships and welcome them.

Let's take a small poem and look at it, keeping the repeating sounds in mind. This is a poem by Robert Creeley.

> Love comes quietly,
> finally, drops
> about me, on me,
> in the old ways.
>
> What did I know
> thinking myself
> able to go
> alone all the way.

The word "quietly" introduces the "ai" sound, and adds to it with "finally." "Quietly" also introduces an "ee" sound, which reappears twice as "me." But we also notice a few affairs that vowels have with "n"—"finally," "about," "on." With the word "old," something begins to shift, and the vowel "oh" begins to push its way in, dancing a bit with the earlier "ai" sound.

> What did I know
> thinking myself
> able to go
> alone all the way.

"Thinking" and "alone" honor the consonant "n"; and halfway through the stanza "ay" begins to enjoy itself. Nature loves repetition; and we could say that the little poem of Robert Creeley's has become an imperishable object of nature while pretending only to be art.

These tiny particles of spoken sound which are announced on paper as *in*, and *ar*, and *or* and *an* and *un* are lovely things! The language experts, who have very little sense of language, call them phonemes. Please forget that right away. Calling them sound particles is OK for now. Grasping these little sounds with the pincers of our ears is the most exciting process we can learn to do—it is like the study of Egyptian artifacts. They are really little creatures—*in* and *am* and *el* and *il* and *en*. A sound friendship, or a sound-urn contains the delicate, easily destroyed artifacts of music. A sound particle or being is the union of a heavily vieled vowel and a consonant, the one leaning on the other, so to speak, two friends who are never parted, who always sing the same little tune, no matter how it's spelled.

I've counted about eighty of these sound particles, or sound creatures, or sound friendships, in current spoken English. As we know if we have listened to Coleman Barks, strange sound particles flow out of the mouths of people in the Deep South, involving vowels that never pass New England lips. So we shouldn't be too Germanic and picky about how many sound particles there are in the many variations of the English language. One of the reasons I fell in love with *Lord Weary's Castle* when I was in college was because Lowell's ear is so receptive to *ar* and *in*. There's a great deal of pleasure in *Lord Weary's Castle*, which is really also the pleasure of sound. Here are the first five lines of "The Holy Innocents":

> Listen, the hay-bells tinkle as the cart
> Wavers on rubber tires along the tar
> And cindered ice below the burlap mill
> And ale-wife run. The oxen drool and start
> In wonder at the fenders of a car . . . .

You can see he's stretching things a little here and there in order to get "car," "cart," "tar," and "start" in succeeding lines, but that's what a musician does. He also brings in several *urs* and *ires*. He also honors the affairs *n* has with its lovers: uncle, cindered, run, oxen, wonder, fender. Finally it all seems right, or nearly right, because we are being fed at some deep level.

Let's give one more example of the way we can grasp these tiny sound particles with the pincers of our ears. Elsewhere in this issue we reprint Jane

Hirshfield's "The Envoy." She is talking of a rat and a snake who entered her room one winter. She associates them with "something" that entered her body that year.

> Not knowing how it came in,
> not knowing how it went out.
> It hung where words could not reach it.
> It slept where light could not go.
> Its scent was neither snake nor rat,
> neither sensualist nor ascetic.
>
> There are openings in our lives
> of which we know nothing.
> Through them
> the belled herds travel at will,
> long-legged and thirsty, covered with foreign dust.

The word "openings" is good. Those belled herds, travelling "at will," are superb side-steppings of the literal, and she offers the joy of metaphor.

Yet we notice that the metaphors retain some cunning power because she has paid careful attention to what we have called sound friendships, the friendships of vowel and consonant.

> Its scent was neither snake nor rat

Notice the en and the nye and the snay.

> Its scent was neither snake nor rat.

And now, while staying with sen, she adds ist and as:

> neither sensualist nor ascetic.

We can see why people who write poetry are traditionally associated with lovers. Who but a lover could honor these friendships of the shy vowel and the often ignored consonant. One would have to be—to love these friendships well—neither sensualist nor ascetic.

Marvell is a genius in sound friendships:

> Yet happy they whom grief doth bless
> That weep the more, and see the less:
> And to preserve their sight more true
> Bathe still their eyes in their own dew.

We notice first the *ear* and *air,* or *or* music—"preserve" comes forward, and merges toward "their" (three times), and "more" (two times). And we notice the *ay* sound—"happy they"—merging with "Bathe." "Weep," "grief," and "see" make a sound trio, and of course, encouraged by the rhyme, "true," and "dew," "bless" and "less." The old rhyme schemes did at least alert the writer to gain at least two resonances in a stanza, like an engagement party and a wedding that leads us to choose at least two gifts.

> Thus sung they, in the English boat,
> An holy and a cheerful note,
> And, all the way, to guide their chime
> With falling oars they kept the time.

He is one of the few poets who lift the *and* at the start of a line in such a way that in this poem it chimes nicely with "sung" and "an" and "English." *Ay* is chosen. And he lifts the *oh* sound up beautifully, with "boat" and "holy" and "note." There are many other chimings here we don't need to point out.

Perhaps we've said enough about sound particles. A skilled reader can tell instantly—within a half-line or so—whether the poet is conscious of this discipline, or just writing along, like a dog or cat going down the street. W. B. Yeats always emphasizes that, for the heart to take in a poem, the soul in us has to go into a slight trance; and that can't be done by assertion, nor image, for fact, nor meter. The music of the sound particles induces the trance. We can feel it deeply in "The Lake Isle of Innisfree."

Having mentioned "The Lake Isle of Innisfree," we might say a few words about what are called the long vowels. When it is "long," the sound itself is so strong, so penetrating, that it seemingly exists without any partners, something the way Queen Elizabeth reigned in court with no visible paramours.

In much ancient poetry, the main kinetic energies of the line, its feet, so to speak, rest in the long vowels. If you hear a Farsi speaker reciting Rumi or Hafez today, you find yourself swimming in a sea of long vowels, and the shorter vowels and their consonant companions are like little rafts. Attention to long vowels leads directly to dance. Pindar's poems were danced. Later both Sappho and Alcaeus developed more intricate dances, patterns of long and short vowels that were so satisfying that poets used them for centuries. As I mentioned, Tranströmer used them in 1962.

How many long vowels are there—those Queenly and Kingly vowels? Traditionally, seven. The seven we'll discuss here are *ay* as in "hay," *ee* as in "sea," *oh* as in "holy," *oo* as in "you," *ai* as in "tiny," *ah* as in "father," and *ohm* as in "home." It's possible that we have been responding physically to these vowels since we were in the womb. *The Secret Life of the Unborn Child* by Thomas Verny, for example, provides evidence, some gained by ultrasound experiments, that babies in the womb make motions that correspond to each of the long vowels.

Donald Hall, in his brilliant essay "Goatfoot Milktongue Twinbird," relates the joys of sound to mouth pleasure of the infant after birth. He calls the shameless enjoyment of vowels (which Dylan Thomas did so well) "milktongue," as if our love of poetry began while nursing, as if we remember the sensual joy at the nipple well into adult life. If the poet doesn't open his or her mouth wide enough at poetry readings, Don will accuse him or her of mouth-guilt. Several times he has accused me of this fault, which is not really a fault, but a simple characteristic of Midwestern farmers. It's clear from reading Dylan Thomas that he was a big nipple man. I'm afraid we're getting distracted here.

We won't spend a long time going over each vowel, but we might mention that some ancient gods had names made only of vowels. There was the old Mediterranean god Iao, which in our phonetic system probably would sound like Ai-ah-oh. The long vowel *ai* corresponds anciently to the sun. As for *ah* and *oh,* they are alpha and omega, the first and last letters of the Greek alphabet—so the name Iao could mean then Divine Sun Energy that Begins and Ends All Things. In many cultures *ah* is felt to be the strongest vowel of them all. We notice it appears once in our word "God," but twice in the Muslim word "Allah."

Goethe knew all of these ideas, and we can see from applying his knowledge to the poem "Wanderers Nachtlied II," or "The Second Song the Night Walker Wrote." He chooses the moment the sun begins to descend in the forest, and to bring that forward, he chooses the long vowel *oo*. I set the poem down first in English, simply for the meaning; and then in German for the meaning and the sound-work.

> Over all the hilltops
> Silence,
> Among all the treetops
> You feel hardly
> A breath moving.
> The birds fall silent in the woods.
> Simply wait! Soon
> You too will be silent.

In German the *oo* sound shines thorugh.

> Über allen Gipfeln
> Ist Ruh,
> In allen Wipfeln
> Spürest du
> Kaum einen Hauch:
> Die Vögelen schweigen im Walde.
> Warte nur! Balde
> Ruhest du auch.

Goethe offers the sound *oo* five times in eight short lines, two of them in the last line. By doing so, he affects the listener's body directly, and one falls into the sort of minor trance that allows one to take the "quiet" or "silence" or "stillness" into the heart.

Ancient traditions suggest that each of the seven long vowels tends to produce utterly different or distinct motions of the body. We won't go over those speculations here, but the reader can pronounce *oh* slowly, and see what his or her arms want to do. The sound *oh* apparently makes the body long for enclosure, devotion, holding, and the arms may move to suggest that.

Most ancient texts tend to declare that the seven major vowels symbolize "the primary sounds emitted by the seven heavenly bodies." The long *oh* as in holy is the sound of Saturn; *ai*, as we mentioned, is the sun, *ee* is the sound of Venus, and so on.

We recall that Rimbaud, who became aware of these old traditions, assigned in a sonnet written about 1870, colors to the vowels: *A*, noir; *E*, blanc; *I*, rouge; *U*, vert,; *O* bleu.

Finally, we must mention that many scholars in this field find that the long vowels can be associated fruitfully with one of the prime notes in our typical musical scale. Here we see how the colorful attention to long vowels leads directly and passionately to music, a connection that most contemporary poetry in America and Europe has utterly lost.

There is something delicious about playing with these seven vowels and noticing how one's own body wants to respond to them. Why do you need to study vowels? Because the chiming of sounds in poetry leads us out of the practical reason and into the joy of music. Sometimes in Africa you will hear in a ceremony a speaker pronouncing long vowels so slowly that the body has a chance to give its response.

If you're interested in this matter, you could read Joscelyn Godwin's book, a lively history of these speculations, from the Egyptians to the Celts, called *The Mystery of the Seven Holy Vowels*.

Soul Weight

For any clump of words to cease being good writing, and to become poetry, we notice the words have to have some psychic weight. Because the creative writing industry has a desire to graduate two or three hundred officially registered veterinarians—I mean poets—each year, a lot of bad poetry gets certified in this country. Hundreds of theses should be rejected by graduate writing programs each year on the grounds that the manuscripts have no discernable psychic weight.

This is a touchy matter, and we probably need someone with more tact than I to define psychic weight. When we call some writing "adolescent," we are usually referring to the lack of psychic weight, even though the work in question may have a lot of pain. When we call a school of poetry "witty," we usually signal that we are going to exempt those poets from the standards just mentioned. We enjoy reading poems that have no discernable psychic weight—that's a lot of fun, like going to the mall.

The weight of the soul is as important in fiction as it is in poetry. We probably all remember Kafka's tale about a son, who, disliked by his father, turned one day into a beetle and began to live under his bed. That single sentence has huge soul weight. We recall that the father returned unexpectedly and found his son—in beetle form—climbing up the wall. The father threw an apple at him, which permanently dented the son's back. This apple, which is apparently brought in from the Garden of Eden story, leads us to the conclusion that a detail drawn from mythology sometimes coincides in great art with psychic weight. Of course the presence of myth does not insure such a thing—mythology can be dished out in an academic, weightless way like anything else. But the soul weight which we feel in Homer and Horace and Rilke is indelibly associated with the mythologies they love. I'll set down a poem by the Spanish poet Antonio Machado; and you'll hear the weight and liveliness of mythology come into the last line.

> The wind one brilliant day, called
> to my soul with an aroma of jasmine.
>
> "In return for this odor of my jasmines,
> I'd like all the odor of your roses."
> "I have no roses; I have no flowers.
> All the flowers in my garden are dead."
>
> "Then I'll take the waters of the fountains,
> and the yellow leaves and the dried-up petals."
>
> The wind left. . . . I wept. I said to my soul,
> "What have you done with the garden entrusted to you?"

We notice the garden arrives with a small "g" first; then as we read the poem a second time, we sense a large "G." We have gone from a personal garden to a religious garden. Much recent confessional poetry fails to achieve psychic weight because it stays in the personal garden. Psychic weight does not require catastrophe.

Machado's friend, Juan Ramón Jiménez, simply contrasts the social personality with the "true"—great— personality, and it happens.

> I am not I.
>   I am this one

Walking beside me whom I do not see,
Whom at times I manage to visit
And at other times I forget.
The one who forgives, sweet, when I hate.
The one who remains silent when I talk.
The one who takes a walk when I am indoors.
The one who will remain standing when I die.

Scholars recently discovered a few "Round-Dances" associated with secret Christian worship in the third and fourth centuries in Rome. The discovery includes poems. Here are a few sequences that were apparently spoken by dancers:

I will wound, and I will be wounded.
I will be saved, and I will save.

The small "I" says "I will be saved," and the large "I" says, "I will save."

I will be begotten, and I will beget.
I will hear, and I will be heard.
I will adorn, and I will be adorned.
I will be watched, and I will watch.

The recent movement in the U.S. to adopt pills, and so move away from psychology and mythology is an ominous development, because it is psychology and mythology that has always led us along on the path from the small "I" to the large "I."

If we return to the Antonio Machado poem for a moment, we notice how little judgment there is in it. After Machado confesses that most of the flowers in his garden are dead, the wind doesn't judge him; it simply remarks that it will take the withered leaves and the yellow petals and the waters from the fountain. Machado does not judge himself either for having failed to tend the flowers that were entrusted to him. He simply asks himself: "What have you done with the Garden that was entrusted to you?"

Psychic weight often occurs when religious longings are taken seriously. Basho, whose garden lay near a Buddhist temple, said:

The temple bell bell stops.
But the sound keeps coming
out of the flowers.

Thoreau's writing often has terrific soul weight, perhaps because, like Basho, he is defending the religious quality of nature. You may recall that when Thoreau was dying, a visitor to his bed asked him how he stood with Christ. He said, "A snowstorm is more to me than Christ." When the Japanese poet Shiki died in the middle of winter, friends found his death poem under his pillow. It said:

I keep asking
how deep
the snow is now.

We notice little judgment in Van Gogh and almost none in Rembrandt. Even Judas is treated with tenderness by Rembrandt.

On the other hand, some judgment of a culture, if done fairly and with passionate dispassion, so to speak, can achieve soul weight. The last line of Robert Lowell's Boston poem reads:

A savage servility slides by on grease.

When a poem says things that we know need to be said, it has content; but often soul weight shows itself by things that do not need to be said. Sometimes we wish they hadn't been said, as when Robert Creeley says at the end of a poem:

Saith perversity, the willful,
the magnanimous cruelty,
which is in me
like a hill.

Psychic weight is one of the gifts given to a work of art by the poet's ability to grieve. We remember that the ancients admired so much in art the quality called gravitas. We can hear gravity in the word, and grave, and even the heaviness of pregnancy. These lines of Neruda have gravitas:

I walk through afternoons, I arrive
full of mud and death,
dragging along the earth and its roots,
and its indistinct stomach in which corpses
are sleeping with wheat,
metals, and pushed-over elephants

But above all there is a terrifying,
a terrifying deserted dining room. . . .
and around it there are expanses,
sunken factories, pieces of timber
which I alone know
because I am sad, and because I travel,
and I know the earth, and I am sad.

Rilke says:

Rejoicing has lost her doubts, and Longing broods on her error,
Only Grief still learns; she spends the whole night
Counting up our evil inheritance with her small hands.

Cesar Vallejo says:

They'll say that we have a lot
Of grief in one eye, and a lot of grief
In the other also, and when they look
A lot of grief in both . . .
Well then! . . . Wonderful! . . . Then . . . Don't say a word!

Have we said enough about soul weight? It often lifts ordinary writing into poetry. With some practice, one can develop a taste for psychic weight and for grief. The poetry of the United States has never been very welcoming to grief, and our culture in general avoids it. Television provides laugh tracks every 30 seconds. What we call "Language" poetry avoids the language of grief. American poets don't receive much encouragement in intensifying their poetry so that it goes over the line. But Mirabai and Hafez, Leopardi and Neruda, Vallejo and Akhmatova do give such encouragement. Jane Kenyon listened to Akhmatova, and wrote some great poetry. The enemy of psychic weight is fashion, but fashion doesn't last, grief does. The ones born after us will be interested in whether there is any grief in your poems.

Obeying the Urge to Form That Is in Nature

A nutty assumption which pervades much American thought about poetry is that form will hobble our free spirits. But once you've watched several thousand hours of television, one might ask, "What free spirit?"

In any event, nature looks at form differently. Form is something playful which actually increases one's chances of remaining alive in a dangerous world. Form is not a thing invented by human beings. On the contrary, nature seems always to be thinking about form. The clamshell makes its shape with a series of elegant repetitions. Each object you find on the beach or in the woods is a masterpiece of achieved form. Only creatures with achieved form live, whether it be a stingray or a hummingbird or some snake with elegantly repeated scales going on for ten feet.

Poets of my own generation were able to see the debate about form in poetry play out during the late 50s and the early 60s. There was so much chaos during the Second World War that I think it's no accident that a few poets beginning to publish as the war ended brought classical form back into their poems. Richard Wilbur would be an example. His first book, *The Beautiful Changes,* was persistent in form and grateful to form.

> One wading a Fall meadow finds on all sides
> The Queen Anne's Lace lying like lilies
> On water; it glides
> So from the walker, it turns
> Dry grass to a lake, as the slightest shade of you
> Valleys my mind in fabulous blue Lucernes.
>
> The beautiful changes as a forest is changed
> By a chameleon's tuning his skin to it;
> As a mantis, arranged
> On a green leaf, grows
> Into it, makes the leaf leafier, and proves
> Any greenness is deeper than anyone knows.

Your hands hold roses always in a way that says
They are not only yours; the beautiful changes
In such kind ways,
Wishing ever to sunder
Things and things' selves for a second finding, to lose
For a moment all that it touches back to wonder.

Robert Lowell published *Lord Weary's Castle* the same year, 1947. Its opening poem, "The Exile's Return," describes a German coming back to his occupied village.

There mounts in squalls a sort of rusty mire,
Not ice, not snow, to leaguer the Hôtel
De Ville, where braced pig-iron dragons grip
The blizzard to their rigor mortis. A bell
Grumbles when the reverberations strip
The thatching from its spire,
The search-guns click and spit and split up timber
And nick the slate roofs on the Holstenwall
Where torn-up tilestones crown the victor. Fall
And winter, spring and summer, guns unlimber
And lumber down the narrow gabled street
Past your gray, sorry and ancestral house
Where the dynamited walnut tree
Shadows a squat, old, wind-torn gate and cows
The Yankee commandant. You will not see
Strutting children or meet
The peg-leg and reproachful chancellor
With a forget-me-not in his button-hole
Where the unseasoned liberators roll
Into the Market Square, ground arms before
The Rathaus; but already lily-stands
Burgeon the risen Rhineland, and a rough
Cathedral lifts its eye. Pleasant enough,
V*oi ch'entrate*, and your life is in your hands.

Lord Weary's Castle exploded with chaotic energy; each poem was like a huge horse kept under some faint control by the iambic line.

A wise person said that form works best when it works in contrast to the content. Let's suppose that the form in a poem goes exactly right, and everything in the content, that is to say the poet's life and the world, goes exactly wrong. Here we see Robert Frost. His content is always out of control, on the edge of madness, but the form goes well. "The Draft Horse" is a good example:

> With a lantern that wouldn't burn
> In too frail a buggy we drove
> Behind too heavy a horse
> Through a pitch-dark limitless grove.
>
> And a man came out of the trees
> And took our horse by the head
> And reaching back to his ribs
> Deliberately stabbed him dead.
>
> The ponderous beast went down
> With a crack of a broken shaft.
> And the night drew through the trees
> In one long invidious draft.
>
> The most unquestioning pair
> That ever accepted fate
> And the least disposed to ascribe
> Any more than we had to to hate,
>
> We assumed that the man himself
> Or someone he had to obey
> Wanted us to get down
> And walk the rest of the way.

We could say that Robert Frost's madness was private and he could tame it and partly conceal it with meter. He did that all his life. But for many people who are a little younger, the madness—including the insanity of the Second World War—was social. By 1956, ten years after the end of the war, most of the poets in the "1962" generation—Hall, Simpson, Kennedy, Anthony Hecht, Adrienne Rich—had learned iambic pentameter well. The first anthology of that generation was *New Poets of England and America,* published in 1958. One of the editors, Louis Simpson, whose company was nearly wiped out at the Battle of the Bulge, remarked that the sort of experience that meant the most to him was simply not present in any of the poems he and the other editors received and published. In other words, iambic meter as it was used in 1958 took part in concealing dirt and madness. It acted for some as a screen and a filter, and very little hard reality got through.

It is a strange idea, that iambic meter can work to make a contrasting force to the power of private madness, or it can work so as to dull all disturbance and madness down.

A few years later many of these same poets were forced to make that social madness verbal and audible. What else could we do? Galway Kinnell wrote "The Bear," which is mad; Ginsberg wrote "America," which begins, "America, I've given you all and now I'm nothing... / I won't write my poem until I'm in my right mind . . . / I'm sick of your insane demands." Denise Levertov wrote:

> While the war drags on, always worse,
> the soul dwindles sometimes to an ant
> rapid upon the cracked surface . . .

Adrienne Rich said:

> Poetry never stood a chance
> of standing outside history.
> One line typed twenty years ago
> can be blazed on a wall in spray paint
> to glorify art as detachment.

Within a few years, almost every one of the American poets in *New Poets of England and America,* with the exception of John Hollander and Anthony Hecht, abandoned iambic meter. Why did that happen? It's possible we didn't want to follow nineteenth century England in using the iambic meter to diminish the madness. I remember in the early days of my own magazine *The Fifties* and *The Sixties* when we received poems that seemed excessively iambic, hide madness or deal with it —

we would send, instead of a rejection slip, a little card that said,
            This card entitles you to buy the next book
        of Alfred Lord Tennyson as soon as it is published.

We received many insulting responses to that, which we enjoyed deeply.

I think my own generation did make some headway in letting the madness be visible. That was true even in Anthony Hecht's case. He has said that his "cumulative sense of these experiences is grotesque beyond anything I could possibly write." In his poem, "More Light! More Light!", published in 1968, he shows that iambic pentameter can deal well with social madness:

> We move now to outside a German wood.
> Three men are there commanded to dig a hole
> In which the two Jews are ordered to lie down
> And be buried alive by the third, who is a Pole.
>
> Not light from the shrine at Weimar beyond the hill
> Nor light from heaven appeared. But he did refuse.
> A Luger settled back deeply in its glove.
> He was ordered to change places with the Jews.
>
> No light, no light in the blue Polish eye.
> When he finished a riding boot packed down the earth.
> The Luger hovered lightly in its glove.
> He was shot in the belly and in three hours bled to death.
>
> No prayers or incense rose up in those hours
> Which grew to be years, and every day came mute
> Ghosts from the ovens, sifting through crisp air,
> And settled upon his eyes in a black soot.

We could say the meter is whole and the content broken. In Robert Duncan's poem on the war, he adopts open form:

> Now Johnson would go up to join the great simulacra of men,
>   Hitler and Stalin, to work his fame

with planes roaring from Guam over Asia,
all America become a sea of toiling men
    stirrd at his will, which would be a bloated thing,
    drawing from the underbelly of the nation
    such blood and dreams as swell the idiot psyche
    out of its courses into an elemental thing
    until his name stinks with burning meat and heapt honors. . . .

this specter that in the beginning Adams and Jefferson feard and knew
    would corrupt the very body of the nation
and all our sense of our common humanity,
    this black bile of old evils arisen anew,
takes over the vanity of Johnson;
    and the very glint of Satan's eyes from the pit of the hell of
America's unacknowledged, unreprented crimes that I saw in
    Goldwater's eyes
    now shines from the eyes of the President
in the swollen head of the nation.

In Duncan, though the form is open, the madness of the Vietnam War shines through.

For those unclear about that decade, these details may help as a brief history. Our generation, or most of the poets in it, went to free verse in order to come closer to some madness that the iambic meter could not handle.

It's difficult in any century to find the right form. As I mentioned above, form is something playful which increases your chances of remaining alive in a dangerous world. How does one invent a form? Suppose one is not interested in iambic form but wants some form anyway? What can one do? I'll throw out an idea: If you are not counting anything in your poems, there is no form, no matter how much people talk about "open form." Marianne Moore counted syllables; she didn't care a bit about accents and the number of strong and weak accents; she counted syllables. That brought her poems closer to nature, which, I've said earlier in this essay, always counts.

Perhaps we could stop thinking of certain syllables as being stressed or unstressed; instead one could count them as so many whole notes and so many quarter notes and so many eighth notes. Sidney Lanier wrote about that form of counting, and I recommend his wonderful book, *The Science of*

English Meter.
Shakespeare writes:

That time of year thou mayst in me behold
When yellow leaves or none, or few, do hang
Upon those boughs that shake beneath the cold
Bare ruined choirs, where late the sweet birds sang.

It becomes clear that Shakespeare provides a long vowel in the fourth place and the tenth place in every line. He is definitely counting. The open vowels that we perceive are *year* and *hold*, *leaves* and *hang*, *boughs* and *cold*, *choirs* and *sang*. If we find a tune that fits this poem, we find it fits most of the sonnets that Shakespeare wrote. We might add that a tune helps us to count.

The Greek Alcaic meter, made popular in Greek by Alcaeus, and later brought into the Latin language by Horace, depends on the counting of three different lengths of vowels. Once more, these musical inventions become plausible when the sounds are spoken, or sung. Perhaps a form in English is impossible for those who do not memorize poems and recite or sing them. Tomas Tranströmer has successfully used Alcaic meter in Swedish; you'll find it in *For Levande och Döda*, "Alcaisk."

In the next years, I think we will receive much influence from the poetic forms in the Muslim culture. In classical Persian and Arabic and Urdu poetry, the relative lengths of all the vowels are counted. A Rumi or Hafez poem can be sung immediately. In hundreds of non-English languages, the poets count the long vowels, count the short vowels, count the number of syllables, count even interior rhymes. The small sound units such as *in* and *or* and *an* offer themselves for repetition and counting.

Perhaps I've said enough here to give the flavor of this discipline. The dead won't ask you which prizes you've received; they'll ask you if there is any form in your poems.

4 line stanza

Learning to Love Excess

We have the feeling that ancient poetry was always excessive. *Beowulf* could hardly be described as a moderate poem, following the middle way. Almost every human and non-human creature in its goes over the line on a

37

daily basis. Gilgamesh was out of line—he lacked social boundaries, we are told—and to cure him they brought in Enkidu who was even more excessive! In the *Iliad*, we find men who can kill fifty people out of simple hurt feelings. The dead have a great taste for excess.

In Eric Havelock's marvelous book *Preface to Plato*, he made a few remarks about the nature of a poetry reading in ancient Greece. He said that the Homeric poetry reading worked to bring such a huge presence of grief into the room that it took away grief.

He also observed that in a poetry reading the poet has to provide the initial charge of emotion and energy, and give that out of himself or herself even before the audience has given him or her anything back. That's how a poetry reading works. That's how story-telling works. The powerful Homeric meter, with its carefully registered beats and carefully provided pauses, worked so as to tie the grief into the heartbeat of the listeners. It's as if the mind couldn't reject the excess, because the excess was already in the body.

Perhaps someone should write a history of excess. Those who know Indian ecstatic poetry know that Mirabai is a great warrior against moderation. Jane Hirshfield has translated a poem of hers this way:

> When you offer the Great One your love,
> At the first step your body is crushed.
> Next be ready to offer your head as his seat
> To live in the deer as she runs toward the hunter's call,
> In the partridge that swallows hot coals for the love of the moon. . . .
> Like a bee trapped for life in the closing of the sweet flower,
> Mira has offered herself to her Lord.
> She says: The single lotus will swallow you whole.

Talking to the sort of people (her family) who urge her to reaccept a more ordinary householder's life, she says:

> I have felt the swaying of the elephant's shoulders, and now you
>   want me to climb on a jackass?
> Try to be serious.
>
>   (translated by RB)

Kabir, slightly older than Mirabai, speaks in the same immediate way:

38

The idea that the soul will join with the ecstatic
just because the body is rotten—
that is all fantasy.
What is found now is found then.
If you find nothing now,
you will simply end up with an apartment in the City of Death.
If you make love with the divine now, in the next life you will have
the face of satisfied desire.

(translated by RB)

This habit of excessiveness carries right through into the 19th century. Ghalib ends one of his poems:

The lightning that fell on Moses should have fallen on Ghalib.
You know we always adjust the quantity of the liquor to the quality
of the drinker.

(translated by RB and Sunil Dutta)

Because we are familiar now with Rumi's sweet overstatements, we might imagine that this art is particular to him; it has actually been a common form of speech among literature Shiites through the whole Muslim world for centuries. When we compare our sensible American poems, we are the ones who seem backward.

Hafez says:

Don't expect obedience, promise-keeping, or rectitude
From me; I'm drunk. I have been famous for carrying
A wine pitcher around since the First Covenant with Adam.

When we look at Shakespeare, we might ask: "Why do all the characters in Shakespeare's plays speak so wildly?" It is because he knew of this tradition. The Italians tell in *Orlando Furioso*, in Petrarch, in love sonnets, carried that speech of divine excess into France and England. The complicated syntax of the Renaissance actually supported that wildness. Even the minor characters in Shakespeare speak fabulously, outrageously, grandiloquently, rolling along in the delight of the immoderate.

The *Furioso* tradition began to dim in the 18th century; and during that century the popularity of Shakespeare fell sharply.

Samuel Johnson, an otherwise wonderfully intelligent man, is not very susceptible to excess. He's talking here of bad writing in general, but there's a sting in "invention":

> Why this wild strain of imagination found reception so long, in polite and learned ages, is not easy to conceive; but we cannot wonder, that, while readers could be procured, the authors were willing to continue it: For when a man had, by practice, gained some fluency of language, he had no farther care than to retire to his closet, to let loose his invention, and heat his mind with incredibilities; and a book was produced without fear of criticism, without the toil of study, without knowledge or nature, or acquaintance with life.

Pope is often belabored about his shoulders for writing this line:

> The proper study of mankind is man.

He probably deserved it. He went on:

> The bliss of man (could pride that blessing find)
> Is not to act or think beyond mankind;
> No powers of body or of soul to share,
> But what his nature and his state can bear.
> Why has not man a microscopic eye?
> For this plain reason, man is not a fly.

Well, that settles it. Jonathan Swift, like all the Irish, has secret stores of the unnameable, and he pays no attention to moderation. By the early years of the 19th century, English poetry still had not recovered the skill of excess. Blake stood out by his love for it, and that love is one reason so few Londoners would buy his paintings, or give honor to his poems. But he was unequivocal and unrepentent; he was in line with ancient literature.

> My mother groaned, my father wept,
> Into the dangerous world I leapt,
> Helpless, naked, piping loud
> Like a fiend hid in a cloud.

We know his aphorisms:

> The tigers of wrath are wiser than the horses of instruction.
> He whose face gives no light shall never become a star.
> The road of excess leads to the palace of wisdom.
> Drive your cart and your plow over the bones of the dead.
> The roaring of lions, the howling of wolves, the raging of the
>   stormy sea, and the destructive sword, are portions of
>   `eternity, too great for the eye of man.
> You never know what is enough unless you know what is more than
>   enough.

We can say that in the English language, Blake is, after Shakespeare, the greatest carrier of excess, and its greatest defender. Beautiful excess belongs to solitude and the company of geniuses.

> The Prophets Isaiah and Ezekiel dined with me, and I asked them how they dared so roundly to assert that God spoke to them; and whether they did not think at the time that they would be misunderstood, & so be the cause of imposition. . . .
> I then asked Ezekiel why he eat dung, & lay so long on his right & left side? he answer'd, "the desire of raising other men into a perception of the infinite: this the North American tribes practice, & is he honest who resists his genius or conscience only for the sake of present ease or gratification?"

In the U.S., both Emily Dickinson and Whitman stood up for the intemperate and the exhorbitant, for the inordinate and the overwrought. But during the 20th century it was in the Spanish language—both in Spain and in South America—that the longing to go beyond measure, to give more than enough, to "kill the slain," which was the character of much ancient literature, returned.

If you're looking for excess, Cesar Vallejo has it:

> Well, on the day I was born,
> God was sick.

He also began a poem:

> I will die in Paris, on a rainy day
> on some day I can already remember.

The purpose of powerful assertion at the beginning of a poem is so that one's deeper emotions will be called out. In our culture, flooded with mediocre art, it's perfectly possible to write poetry your whole life without ever being asked to bring forward the intense emotions that are somewhere inside of you—those emotions that love to be seen, those emotions we are each afraid of, those emotions that will curse us and poison us if we don't honor them by speaking them, those emotions that will bless us if we do speak them.

Some of us have a desire for life to end and the whole world to end and everything to die. We can watch Cesar Vallejo edge toward it:

> And what if after so many words,
> the word itself doesn't survive!
> And what if after so many wings of birds,
> the stopped bird doesn't survive!
> It would be better then, really,
> if it were all swallowed up, and let's end it!

He sometimes opens a poem with an assertion so outrageous that it can only be answered by intense emotion.

> I have a terrible fear of being an animal made of white snow.

If one begins a poem with that intensity, one can't go on later and be reasonable and complain about your parents. We want poets to tell the truth. But he is not trying to tell the truth. That is for writers. To make poetry means that you need to go over the line, to be not sensible but arresting, not to be acceptable but to be unforgettable.

My very insistence that excess is one of the qualities that distinguishes poetry from good writing is excessive itself. But still, I want to say that most of the greatest poetry in the twentieth century has kept the intemperate at its center. Here's Pablo Neruda, writing in 1933, a poem to which he gave an

English title, "Walking Around":

> It so happens I am sick of being a man.
> And it happens that I walk into tailorshops and movie houses
> dried up, waterproof, like a swan made of felt
> steering my way in a water of wombs and ashes. . . .
>
> It so happens I am sick of my feet and my nails
> and my hair and my shadow.
> It so happens I am sick of being a man.
>
> Still it would be marvelous
> to terrify a law clerk with a cut lily,
> or kill a nun with a blow on the ear.

It's the job of the poet to give the initial charge of emotion and energy at the start of the poem. Lorca says:

> To take the wrong road
> is to arrive at the snow
> and to arrive at the snow
> is to get down on all fours for twenty centuries and eat the grasses
>   of the cemeteries. . . .

He goes on:

> Dead people hate the number two,
> but the number two makes woman drop off to sleep,
> and since women are afraid of light,
> light shudders when it has to face the roosters,
> and since all roosters know is how to fly over the snow
> we will have to get down on all fours and eat the grasses
>   of the cemeteries forever.

He begins another poem:

> Get up,
> My friend, so you can hear the Assyrian hound howling.

Later in the poem he says:

> I loved a child for a long time
> who had a tiny feather on his tongue
> and we lived a hundred years inside a knife.

He wouldn't have arrived at that marvelous line about the feather on the tongue if the poem hadn't started with that high energy. The energy has to come in on the very first line.

The aim of poetry is to achieve an excess that is more interesting and more nourishing than truth. Eliot in "East Coker" says:

> The whole earth is our hospital
> Endowed by the ruined millionaire.

He is a worthy continuer of the old traditions we see first in *Gilgamesh*, Homer, and *Beowulf*. Among later poets, Ginsberg has made some true sallies into excess, as well as Thomas McGrath, and in a different mode Galway Kinnell. Lifting your writing up into poetry with the help of this discipline is not something which is easy to do. But English has so much energy in it now, that I think this lifting up is perfectly possible.

Talking in Such a Way That the Heart Can Hear

This particular skill seems to be open to beginners often, more often than professional writers. Children in the second or third grade are often geniuses in this sort of thing. As writers of my generation grew up, it was not a skill that was much admired among critics. What was admired was paradox, tension, multiple meanings, "the seven types of ambiguity," and the secret contrast between surface content and hidden content. Teachers could easily find these qualities in John Donne, in Yeats, in John Crowe Ransom, in Stevens and Pound. I still love those paradoxical complications, and the teachers' emphasis on them made us close readers of any text, and helped us to stay away a bit from the simple-mindedness that always seems to be a part of North American culture. But as poets we had to learn on our own about a quiet voice speaking to someone listening. Luckily, Chinese poetry has always modeled this skill well. The anthology of poetry by Robert Payne called *The White Pony* became a Bible for many of us. I'll recite to you one poem from that book.

Everyone knew there was a certain mountain, all solid stone, out of which a river flowed. In spring, one could see peach blossoms floating on that river. Li Po said:

> If you ask me why I dwell among green mountains,
> I would laugh silently; my soul is serene.
> The peach blossom follows the moving water.
> There is another heaven and earth beyond the world of men.

Emily Dickinson said,

> Poetry is all we know of heaven
> And all we need of hell.

We cannot imagine either of these poems being shouted. When we begin speaking of this skill, the voice naturally drops and we feel an achieved intimacy. Chinese poets have a genius for this tone. Perhaps the tone developed out of the circumstance that all classical Chinese poems were sung to a tune, so the mood was something like:

> Greensleeves are all my joy,
> And Greensleeves are my delight.

Songs are almost always directed at the heart. You can hear it in Leadbelly's song:

> Last Saturday night I got married
> Me and my wife settled down
> Now me and my wife are parted
> I'm going to take little stroll downtown
>
> Sometimes I live in the country,
> Sometimes I live in town,
> Sometimes I get a great notion
> To jump in the river and drown.

We also notice a beautiful playfulness often in poems aimed at the heart. Playful words are willing to live happily with some tune. Such songs are easy-going. Bob Dylan and Leadbelly and Li Po are all alike in that way.

In the west, Kenneth Rexroth was one of the poets who led the way out of the "seven types of ambiguity." Here is "Fifty":

> Rainy skies, misty mountains,
> The old year ended in storms.
> The new year starts the same way.
> All day, from far out at sea,
> Long winged birds soared in the
> Rushing sky. Midnight breaks with
> Driving clouds and plunging moon,
> Rare vasts of endless stars.
> My fiftieth year has come.

Gary Snyder learned it from him. Gary heard this old farm worker who was working with him say one day,

> "I first bucked hay when I was seventeen.
> I thought, that day I started,
> I sure would hate to do this all my life.
> And dammit, that's just what
> I've gone and done."

When *News of the Universe* came out, I dedicated the book to Rexroth, adapting a portion of a poem Machado wrote to his teacher: "One day the master imagined a new blossoming." Later I heard that a young poet brought the new book to Rexroth and gave it to him; when Rexroth read the dedication, tears came down his face. We understand that the community of poets is a genuine community.

Our subject is talking so that the other can hear. Ruth Stone, who is a little like Grace Paley, describes sitting with her daughter in a parking lot, having some doughnuts and coffee:

> We are silent.
> For a moment the wall between us
> opens to the universe;

then closes.
And you go on saying
you do not want to repeat my life.

A great master of this skill is Etheridge Knight. He said:

This poem
This poem
This poem / is / for me
     and my woman
     and the yesterdays
when she opened
     to me like a flower
     But I fell on her
     like a stone
I fell on her like a stone . . .

     4
And now—in my 40th year
     I have come here
to this House of Feelings
to this Singing Sea
and I and I / must admit
that the sea in me
has fallen / in love
     with the sea in you
because the sea
that now sings / in you
     is the same sea
that nearly swallowed you—
     and me too.

We know that American poets currently have great skill in this quality
which we call talking to the heart. Let's name a few others besides Etheridge
Knight: Galway Kinnell, Mary Oliver, William Stafford, James Wright,
Sharon Olds, and many more. A typical poem by Russell Edson will open:

"John, come on down here and hurt your father."

This ability to touch the heart is a gift of North and South America these days. One could say that French surrealism did considerable harm to the French poets' ability to talk to the heart. At this moment, poetry is in a low state in France, both in its writers and its readers; and the tendency of the French to become rhetorical and full of intellectual affects must have some responsibility here.

Some confessional poets in this country have missed the heart by going into the longing to judge. Both Sylvia Plath and Anne Sexton are constantly pointing out flawed people, parents, or country club types. By contrast, the contemporary Guatemalan poet Humberto Ak'abal, whose first book in English has now been printed, has, being Mayan, a thousand reasons to call down judgment on others, but he does not do so. He stays in the place where he can talk quietly. Here are three brief poems of his translated by Miguel Rivera:

> Poets are born old;
> with the passing of the years
> we make ourselves into children.

> *

> Shadow:
> little night
> at the foot of any tree.

> *

> In the high hours of the night
> stars get naked
> and bathe in the rivers.
> Owls desire them,
> the little feathers on their heads
> stand up.

This is the closest he gets to judgment:

> In the churches

you can only hear the prayer
of the trees
converted into pews.

One reason Rumi has become so popular in the U.S. is that Coleman Barks has put him into the "spoken American" that American poets have developed over the last fifty years; and the translated poems speak beautifully to the heart.

A night full of talking that hurts,
my worst held-back secrets. Everything
has to do with loving and not loving.
This night will pass.
Then we have work to do.

*

A chickpea leaps almost over the rim of the pot
where it's being boiled.

"Why are you doing this to me?"

The cook knocks it down with a ladle.

"Don't you try to jump out.
You think I'm torturing you,
I'm giving you flavor,
so you can mix with spices and rice
and be the lovely vitality of a human being.

Remember when you drank rain in the garden.
That was for this."

Grace first. Sexual pleasure,
then a boiling new life begins,
and the Friend has something good to eat.

In Canada, Alden Nowlan, whose poems are still too little known here, is a great master. In his poem, "He Sits Down on the Floor of a School for the Retarded," he talks of a young retarded woman who has sat down next to him. She says, "Hold me."

> "Hold me," she says again. What does it matter
> what anybody thinks? . . .
>
> It's what we all want, in the end,
> to be held, merely to be held,
> to be kissed (not necessarily with the lips,
> for every touching is a kind of kiss).
> Yes, it's what we all want, in the end,
> not to be worshipped, not to be admired,
> not to be famous, not to be feared,
> not even to be loved, but simply to be held.

I'd say that among the six skills I'm mentioning in this essay, this skill, talking to the heart in a way that it can hear, is in some ways the most important of them all. It carries much of the genius of contemporary American poetry.

This is the end of our little excursion into skills that poets of the past knew, skills which are not always taught in the writing workshops, or are not all visible today. Another poet might have chosen six utterly different disciplines, and that would be all right with me. Perhaps if I wrote this essay next week, I might choose six different ones myself.

Looking for Dragon Smoke

I

In ancient times, in the "time of inspiration," the poet flew from one world to another, "riding on dragons," as the Chinese said. Isaiah rode on those dragons, so did Li Po and Pindar. They dragged behind them long tails of dragon smoke. Some of the dragon smoke still boils out of *Beowulf*. The *Beowulf* poet holds tight to Danish soil, or leaps after Grendel into the sea.

This dragon smoke means that a leap has taken place in the poem. In many ancient works of art we notice a long floating leap at the center of the work. That leap can be described as a leap from the conscious to the latent intelligence and back again, a leap from the known part of the mind to the unknown part and back to the known. In the myth of Gilgamesh, which takes place in a settled society, psychic forces create Enkidu, "the hairy man," as a companion for Gilgamesh, who is becoming too successful. The reader has to leap back and forth between the golden man, "Gilgamesh," and the "hairy man." In the *Odyssey* the travelers visit a Great Mother island, dominated by the Circe-Mother and get turned into pigs. They make the leap in an instant. In all art derived from Great Mother mysteries, the leap to the unknown part of the mind lies in the very center of the world. The strength of "classic art" has much more to do with this leap than with the order that the poets developed to contain, and partially, to disguise it.

In terms of language, leaping is the ability to associate fast. In a great poem, the considerable distance between the associations, that is, the distance the spark has to leap, gives the lines their bottomless feeling, their space, and the speed (of the association) increases the excitement of the poetry.

Christian civilization took hold, and the power of the spiritual patriarchies deepened, this leap occurred less and less often in Western literature. Obviously, the ethical ideas of Christianity inhibit it. At the start most Church fathers were against the leap as too pagan. Ethics usually support campaigns against the "animal instincts." Christian thought, especially Paul's thought, builds a firm distinction between spiritual energy and animal energy, a distinction so sharp it became symbolized by black and white. White became associated with the conscious and black with the unconscious or the latent intelligence. Ethical Christianity taught its poets—we are among them—to leap *away* from the unconscious, not *toward* it.

II

Sometime in the thirteenth century, poetry in England began to show a distinct decline in the ability to associate powerfully. There are individual exceptions, but the circle of worlds pulled into the poem by association dwindles after Chaucer and Langland; their work is already a decline from the *Beowulf* poet. By the eighteenth century, freedom of association had become drastically curtailed. The word "sylvan" by some psychic coupling leads directly to "nymph," to "lawns," to "dancing," so does "reason" to "music," "spheres," "heavenly order," and so on. they are all stops on the psychic railroad. There are very few images of the Snake, or the Dragon, or the Great Mother, and if mention is made, the Great Mother leads to no other images, but rather to words suggesting paralysis or death. As Pope warned his readers: "The proper study of mankind is man."

The loss of associative freedom shows itself in form as well as in content. The poet's thought plods through the poem, line after line, like a man being escorted through a prison. The rigid "form" resembles a corridor, interrupted by opening and closing doors. The rhymed lines open at just the right moment and close again behind the visitors.

In the eighteenth century many educated people in Europe were no longer interested in imagination. They were trying to develop the "masculine" mental powers they associated with Socrates and his fellow Athenians—a demythologized intelligence, that moves in a straight line made of tiny bright links and is thereby dominated by linked facts rather than by "irrational" feelings. The Europeans succeeded in developing the practical intellect, and it was to prove useful. Industry needed it to guide a locomotive through a huge freight yard; space engineers needed it later to guide a spacecraft back from the moon through the "reentry corridor."

III

Nevertheless, this routing of psychic energy away from "darkness" and the "irrational," first done in obedience to Christian ethics, and later in obedience to industrial needs, had a crippling effect on the psychic life. The process amounted to an inhibiting of psychic flight, and as Blake saw, once the European child had finished ten years of school, he was incapable of flight. He lived the rest of his life in "Newton's sleep."

The Western mind after Descartes accepted the symbolism of black and white and far from trying to unite both in a circle, as the Chinese did, tried to create an "apartheid." In the process words sometimes took on strange meanings. If a European avoided the animal instincts and consistently leapt away from the latent intelligence, he or she was said to be living in a state of "innocence." Children were thought to be "innocent." Eighteenth-century translators like Pope and Dryden forced Greek and Roman literature to be their allies in their leap away from animality, and they translated Homer as if he too were "innocent." To Christian Europeans, impulses open to the sexual instincts or animal instincts indicated a fallen state, a state of "experience."

Blake thought the nomenclature mad, the precise opposite of the truth, and he wrote *The Songs of Innocence and Experience* to say so. Blake, discussing "experience," declared that to be afraid of a leap into the unconscious is actually to be in a state of "experience." (We are all experienced in that fear.) The state of "experience" is characterized by blocked love-energy, boredom, envy, and joylessness. Another characteristic is the pedestrian movement of the mind; possibly consistent fear makes the mind move slowly. Blake could see that after 1,800 years of no leaping, joy was disappearing, poetry was dying, "the languid strings do scarcely move! The sound is forced, the notes are few." A nurse in the state of "experience," obsessed with a fear of animal blackness (a fear that increased after the whites took Africa), and some sort of abuse in her childhood, calls the children in from play as soon as the light falls:

> When the voices of children are heard on the green,
> And whisp'rings are in the dale,
> The days of my youth rise fresh in my mind,
> My face turns green and pale.
>
> Then come home, my children, the sun is gone down
> And the dews of night arise;
> Your spring and your day are wasted in play,
> And your winter and night in disguise.

The nurse in *The Songs of Innocence* also calls the children in. But she has conquered her fear and when the children say,

> "No, no, let us play, for it is yet day
> And we cannot go to sleep:
> Besides in the sky the little birds fly,
> And the hills are all cover'd with sheep."

She replies (the children's arguments are quite convincing),

> "Well, well, go and play till the light fades away,
> And then go home to bed."
> The little ones leaped and shouted and laugh'd
> And all the hills echoèd.

She enjoys their shouts. The children leap about on the grass playing, and the hills respond.

We often feel elation when reading Homer, Neruda, Dickinson, Vallejo, and Blake because the poet is following some arc of association that corresponds to the inner life of the objects he or she speaks of, for example, the association between the lids of eyes and the bark of stones. The associative paths are not private to the poet, but are somehow inherent in the universe.

IV

An ancient work of art such as the *Odyssey* has at its center a long floating leap, around which the poem's images gather themselves like steel shavings around a magnet. Some recent works of art have many shorter leaps rather than one long one. The poet who is "leaping" makes a jump from an object soaked in conscious psychic substance to an object soaked in latent or instinctive psychic substance. One real joy of poetry—not the only one—is to experience this leaping inside a poem.

Novalis, Goethe, and Hölderlin, writing around 1800 in Germany, participated in the associative freedom I have been describing; and their thought in a parallel way carried certain pagan and heretical elements, precisely as Blake's thought did at that time in England. A century later Freud pointed out that the dream still retained the fantastic freedom of association known to most educated Europeans only from pre-Christian poetry and art. We notice that dream interpretation has never been a favorite occupation of the fundamentalists.

In psychology of the last eighty years the effort to recover the dream's freedom of association and its metaphors has been partly successful. Some of the psychic ability to go from the known to the unknown part of the psyche and back has been restored. So too the "leaping" poets: Rilke and Bobrowski, Lorca, and Vallejo, Rene Char, Yves Bonnefoy, and Paul Celan.

Yeats, riding on the dragonish associations of Irish mythology, wrote genuinely great poetry. If we, in the United States, cannot learn dragon smoke from Yeats, or from the French descenders, or from the Spanish leapers, from whom will we learn it? I think much is at stake in this question.

Let's set down some of the enemies that leaping has in this country. American fundamentalism is against the journey to dark places; capitalism is against the descent to soul; realism is against the leap to spirit; populism and social thought are against the solitary wildness; careerism in poetry doesn't allow enough time for descent; the reluctance of recent American poets to translate makes them ignorant. We notice that contemporary American poets tend to judge their poetry by comparing it to the poetry other people of their time are writing—their reviews make this clear—rather than by comparing their work to Goethe's, or Akhmatova's, or Tsvetaeva's or Blake's. Great poetry always has something of the grandiose in it. It's as if

American poets are now so distrustful of the grandiose and so afraid to be thought grandiose that they cannot even imagine great poetry.

<h1 style="text-align:center">V</h1>

Lorca wrote a beautiful and great essay called "Theory and Function of the Duende," available in English in the Penguin edition of *Lorca*. "Duende" is the sense of the presence of death, and Lorca says,

> Very often intellect is poetry's enemy because it is too much given to imitation, because it lifts the poet to a throne of sharp edges and makes him oblivious of the fact that he may suddenly be devoured by ants, or a great arsenic lobster may fall on his head.

Duende involves a kind of elation when death is present in the room. It is associated with "dark" sounds; and when a poet has duende inside him, he brushes past death with each step, and in that presence associates fast (Samuel Johnson remarked that there was nothing like a sentence of death in half an hour to wonderfully concentrate the mind). The gypsy flamenco dancer is associating fast when she dances, and so is Bach writing his cantatas. Lorca mentions an old gypsy dancer who, on hearing Brailowsky play Bach, cried out, "That has duende!"

The Protestant embarrassment in the presence of death turns us into muse poets or angel poets, associating timidly. Lorca says,

> The duende—where is the duende? Through the empty arch comes an air of the mind that blows insistently over the heads of the dead, in search of the new landscapes and unsuspected accents; an air smelling of child's saliva, of pounded grass, and medusa veil announcing the constant baptism of newly created things.

The Spanish "surrealist" or "leaping" poet often enters into his poem with a heavy body of feeling piled up behind him as if behind a dam. Some of that water is duende water. The poet enters the room excited, with the emotions alive; he is angry or ecstatic, or disgusted. There are a lot of exclamation marks, visible or invisible. Almost all the poems in Lorca's *Poet in New York* are written with the poet profoundly moved, flying. Powerful feeling makes the mind move, fast, and evidently the presence of swift motion makes the emotions still more alive, just as chanting awakens many emotions that the chanter was hardly aware of at the moment he began chanting.

What is the opposite of wild association then? Tame association? Approved association? Sluggish association? Whatever we want to call it, we know what it is—that slow plodding association that pesters us in so many poetry magazines, and in our own work when it is no good, association that takes half an hour to compare a childhood accident to a crucifixion, or a leaf to the *I Ching*. Poetry is killed for students in high school by teachers who only understand this dull kind of association.

Lorca says,

> To help us seek the duende there are neither maps nor discipline. All one knows is that it burns the blood like powdered glass, that it exhausts, that it rejects all the sweet geometry one has learned, that it breaks with all styles . . . that it dresses the delicate body of Rimbaud in an acrobat's green suit: or that it puts the eyes of a dead fish on Count Lautremont in the early morning boulevard.

The magical quality of a poem consists in its being always possessed by the duende, so that whoever beholds it is baptized with dark water.

II
The Imperfect Is Our Paradise

The Work of Jane Hirshfield

There is something subtle and new in Jane Hirshfield's poems. It's clear she has been grazing in the fields of possibility (especially those fields cultivated by old Buddhist farmers). She brings in the harvest from that mountain farm, many bales of grief, many bushels of smooth-flowing grain, and some watermelons of wonder.

It is surprising to find a mind that has trained itself not to be wholly willful. She accepts what comes, and what goes. She sees a hope come into the room, pass by the stove and leave. Why should she waste effort crying out?

> I woke and remembered
> nothing of what I was dreaming.
>
> The day grew light, then dark again—
> In all its rich hours, what happened?
>
> A few weeds pulled, a few cold flowers
> carried inside for the vase.
> A little reading. A little tidying and sweeping.

I had vowed to do nothing I did not wish
to do that day, and kept my promise.

Once, a certain hope came close
and then departed. Passed by me in its familiar
shawl, scented with iodine woodsmoke.

I did not speak to it, nor it to me.
Yet still the habit of warmth traveled
between us, like an apple shared by old friends—

One takes a bite, then the other.
They do this until it is gone.

("Apple")

If there isn't any real "you," nor any secure, pronounced "I," why should one
expect a hope or a thought to stay?

Once, a certain hope came close
and then departed. Passed by me in its familiar
shawl, scented with iodine woodsmoke.

I did not speak to it, nor it to me.

Well, a despair or a hope is an independent being, an entity going somewhere; we don't always speak to strangers in train stations. Yet we are not
desolate. We are not abandoned; here is nothing to beat the chest, nothing
to weep.

Yet still the habit of warmth traveled
between us, like an apple shared by old friends—

The experience is not necessarily going to increase us, give us some huge gift,
increase our estate—no, no, it's as it is with an apple:

One takes a bite, then the other.
They do this until it is gone.

We recover in this poem of distance, of separation, the joy of companionship.

I know from hearing her tell stories at a reading that she takes deep delight in the imaginary exchanges so familiar to Zen Buddhists, in which a student is not allowed to fly up into transcendence.

> Who is Buddha?
> Answer: Have you eaten breakfast yet?
> Is Buddha a transcendent being?
> Answer: Don't forget to wash your bowl.

These examples do not deconstruct the transcendent, nor break the world of light into small bits. The reponses of the teacher want the transcender to come home and rest in the butter dish, or just understand it. In any case, it is best not to wait impatiently for meeting or grieve departures. Here is "Muslin":

> "I never knew when he would come,"
> my friend said of her lover,
> "though often it was late in the afternoon."
>
> Behind her back the first plum blossoms
> had started to open,
> few as the stars that salt the earliest dusk.
>
> "Finally weeks would go by; then months,"
> she added, "but always I let him in.
> It made me strong, you see,
>
> "the gradual going without him.
> I think it taught me a kind of surrender,
> though of course I hated it too."
>
> Why he would appear or stay away
> she never fathomed—
> "I couldn't ask. And that also seemed only good."

A small bird fluttered silent behind her left shoulder,
then settled on some hidden branch.
"Do you ask the weather why it comes or goes?"

She was lovely, my friend, even the gray
of her hair was lovely. A listening rope-twist
half pity, half envy tightened its length in my chest.

"When he came, you see, I could trust
that was what he wanted.
What I wanted never mattered at all."
The hands on her lap seemed quiet,
even contented.
I noticed something unspoken begin to

billow and shimmer between us,
weightless as muslin,
but neither of us moved to lift it away.

We understand that the speaker is visiting a friend—we don't learn her
age until later—who puts up with a lover who comes to stay occasionally.
The woman who speaks is not classifying the man's unexpected arrival and
impulsive departure as a sign of male power. The unpredictability was irri-
tating, but it was somehow true to some permanent quality of life.

". . .I think it taught me a kind of surrender,
though of course I hated it too."

We mustn't take this literally as a tale of man and woman, though it is; but
it is also a tale of patience when our dearest hope or our most grievous
despair comes and goes at will.

"Do you ask the weather why it comes or goes?"

Now the poem becomes even better, more powerful, more subtle, more fierce.

She was lovely, my friend, even the gray

of her hair was lovely. A listening rope-twist
half pity, half envy tightened its length in my chest.

"When he came, you see, I could trust
that was what he wanted.
What I wanted never mattered at all."

The woman who speaks is faithful to the absence of surety, perhaps more subtle in her knowing than the woman friend who has just come. They are touching on something, shall we say, deeper than transcendence?

The hands on her lap seemed quiet,
even contented.
I noticed something unspoken begin to

billow and shimmer between us,
weightless as muslin,
but neither of us moved to lift it away.

We recognize that Jane Hirshfield, by her years under a Zen teacher, has entered a discipline so old and towering that it could have silenced her, or crushed her, or at least hampered her ability to follow that weedy, peculiar, home-grown path called American poetry, which wanders out of meadows of Dickinson and Whitman, and continues along the city streets where Rexroth and Crane placed their feet, curbsides where even Eliot and Moore's skirts have passed by. She has gone through the discipline of those bare wooden rooms where one is married only to sitting, and come out with deeply American poems, typically quirky and homespun. American life is now overwhelmingly horizontal and I suppose that's all right, but our current poetry often lacks the vertical line than most national poetries—such as Persian or Russian—have as a birthright. She absorbed the vertical line through her discipline, and it gives her poems an intensity that doesn't kill ordinary life, nor subdue the body as some vertical studies do.

The poem that best evokes those wooden rooms where the sitter spends so many years is the opening poem in *Given Sugar, Given Salt*, called "The Envoy." It goes this way:

One day in that room, a small rat.
Two days later, a snake.

Who, seeing me enter,
whipped the long stripe of his
body under the bed,
then curled like a docile house-pet.

I don't know how either came or left.
Later, the flashlight found nothing.

For a year I watched
as something—terror? happiness? grief?—
entered and then left my body.

Not knowing how it came in,
Not knowing how it came out.

It hung where words could not reach it.
It slept where light could not go.
Its scent was neither snake nor rat,
neither sensualist nor ascetic.

There are openings in our lives
of which we know nothing.

Through them
the belled herds travel at will,
long-legged and thirsty, covered with foreign dust.

So a rat and a snake come in. We are far here from optimistic spiritual
writing:

I don't know how either came or left.
Later, the flashlight found nothing.

I love that flashlight which seems to be the flashlight of Western psychology,

66

looking for the steady-state character of individuated substance that we call our personality, but it finds nothing. It is also the ordinary flashlight with two D batteries that lights up nothing under the bed.

> For a year I watched
> as something—terror? happiness? grief?—
> entered and then left my body.

It's interesting that she doesn't describe the emotion—terror, happiness, grief—as a living being, but as "something"; and she doesn't say it entered her mind, but rather her body.

Now the tough part of the poem comes:

> It hung where words could not reach it.

So apparently therapy would not have reached it, nor conversation, nor even prayer.

> It slept where light could not go.

That line is rather frightening.

> Its scent was neither snake nor rat,
> neither sensualist nor ascetic.

I like those lines very much. She is refusing to live, or let it live—in the dualistic world we love so well—where the snake is reptile, and the rat is mammal, where the prosaic person is a sensualist, the spiritual person is an ascetic. Hafez remarked eight hundred years ago:

> The fire of ascetic renunciation and hypocrisy
> Will eventually consume the harvest of religion.

So whatever the something is, it's not ascetic.

> There are openings in our lives
> of which we know nothing.

Through them
the belled herds travel at will,
long-legged and thirsty, covered with foreign dust.

I always feel like shouting when I read these lines. Once more, she notes that the animals coming and going in our bodies, or souls, "travel at will." Moreover, they are not wild animals belonging to prehistoric times: they are belled. They belong to some human community, and seem to be a community themselves, coming from somewhere else, "long-legged and thirsty, covered with foreign dust."

That is superb. The poem itself is one of the greatest poems of the last fifty years.

Perhaps we can leave this matter of coming and going now. She offers "The Button" later in her book for those who want to go over this ground of leaving and entering more playfully.

We have praised Hirshfield's soft and sharp poems. Her language in general walks like an acrobat on a slim rope; the language carries a long bamboo stick to balance itself. The elephant trainers watch her with amazement.

To stay in touch with her language, we'll look at two more poems, poems that stay closer to earth. "In Praise of Coldness" belongs to the poetry of advice.

It begins:

"If you wish to move your reader,"
Chekhov wrote, "you must write more coldly."

Herakleitos recommended, "A dry soul is best."

And so at the center of many great works
is found a preserving dispassion. . . .

"Dispassion?" Nothing could be farther from the Sixties enthusiasm and flamboyance, nor from Ginsberg's "Howl" or Kinnell's "Bear", than this "preserving dispassion" which she says resembles

the tiny packets of dessicant enclosed
in a box of new shoes or seeds

We see once more differing flavors in carefully chosen words, for example in the phrase "packets of dessicant " She is not recommending Michaux's visions of disarranged reality, but she wants a language that is interesting in its own stubborn way:

> Chekhov, dying, read the timetables of trains.
> To what more earthly thing could he have been faithful?

A moment later she says:

> Neither a person entirely broken
> nor one entirely whole can speak.

She's telling you she doesn't admire the works of addicts, nor the calm of the genuinely saved. Neither work is quite cold enough. In this attitude of hers, we hear a trace of Ecclesiastes, a little whisper of Lao Tzu, and maybe a remark or two from a good book of contemporary psychology. She ends this particular poem:

> In sorrow, pretend to be fearless. In happiness, tremble.

She says it's all right to fake the walk of a warrior at times; it's all right to fear that a hurricane is coming even if you see no evidence. Yeats said:

> Cast a cold eye on life, on death.
> Horseman, pass by.

In her poem, "Habit," she warns the reader that those habits which we learn from others, and even from ourselves, may turn into our destiny.

> The shoes put on each time
> left first, then right
>
> The morning potion's teaspoon
> of sweetness stirred always
> for seven circlings—no fewer, no more—
> into the cracked blue cup.

Touching the pocket for wallet,
for keys,
before closing the door.

How did we come
to believe these small rituals' promise,
that we are today the selves we yesterday knew,
tomorrow will be?

How intimate and unthinking,
the way the toothbrush is shaken dry after use,
the part we wash first in the bath.

Which habits we learned from others
and which are ours alone we may never know.
Unbearable to acknowledge
how much they are themselves our fated life.

Open the traveling suitcase—

There the beloved red sweater,
bright tangle of necklace, earrings of amber.
Each confirming: I chose these, I.

But habit is different: It chooses.
And we, its good horse,
opening our mouths at even the sight of the bit.

So the technologically advanced human being which we have today, a product
of the best schools, the receiver of masterful metaphors from immensely old
and cultured civilizations, which a living teacher has passed straight to us . . .
Well, she says this huge, vital, high-spirited horse will open its mouth even
if it glimpses in a fraction of a second the bit of habit.

   She is not overly confident about the results even of any discipline. The
Zen people say,

   All the teachings are yellow leaves given to children to keep them
   from crying.

The poems I've discussed here come from her new book, *Given Sugar, Given Salt*. She has published four earlier books, *Aliyah, Of Gravity and Angels, The October Palace*, and *The Lives of the Heart*.

So we have here in our culture a delicate writer who is a bit like Elizabeth Bishop, a delicate watcher, sometimes looking not over your shoulder but over her own, and noticing—what? The slight disarrangement of a room (perhaps she scans too many rooms and too few wildernesses). We have someone who holds her own life in solution, the way a science student holds manganese in solution for days.

She is wary, she observes. She accompanies her own body through the world, and doesn't expect too much from shoulders or waists. She is like someone in a royal family who decides that she needn't take a job. And yet she has—she watches invisible beings. The huge sloshing about of the Campbell gods—the mythological gods—she quiets by ignoring them. She doesn't watch Ganesha—carried down the street by the kind of people who throw themselves off waterfalls—no, no, no. Nor the Lithuanian gods who show up a thousand miles away in hot lava, smiling and faintly warmed. She doesn't watch them. She watches the gods who appear in a fraction of a second after an artist has drawn a face well. Her gods are more like the gods who move a shawl a few inches just after the funeral. The job she has accepted is to watch these gods. She reminds us a bit of E. M. Forster and some 18th century watercolorists who work in brown washes. She makes subtle offerings to the temple as married women do in Bali. She experiences the divine by never talking of it or her. She describes shadows of the divine that move across the sunlit floor and do disturb the dust.

Wallace Stevens and Dr. Jekyll

The literature of the American earth is many thousands of years old, and its rhythms are still rising from the serpents buried in Ohio, from the shells the Yakuts ate of and threw to the side. The literature of the American nation is only two hundred years old. How much of the darkness from under the earth has risen into poems and stories in that time?

All literature, both of the primitive and the modern peoples, can be thought of as creations by the "dark side" to enable it to rise up from earth and join the sunlit consciousness again. Many ancient religions, especially those of the matriarchies, evidently moved so as to bring the dark side up into the personality slowly and steadily. The movement started early in the person's life and, in the Mysteries at least, lasted for twenty to thirty years. Christianity, as many observers have noticed, has acted historically to polarize the "dark personality" and the "light personality." Christian ethics usually involves the suppression of the dark one. As the consequences of this suppression become more severe, century after century, we reach at last the state in which the psyche is split, and the two sides cannot find each other. We have "The Strange Story of Dr. Jekyll and Mr. Hyde." The dominant personality in the West tends to be idealistic, compassionate, civilized, orderly, as Dr. Jekyll's, who is so caring with his patients; the shadow side is deformed, it move fast, "like a monkey," is younger than the major personality, has vast sources of energy near it, and no morality at all. It "feels" rage from centuries of suppression.

How did the two persons get separated? Evidently we spent the first twenty or twenty-five years of life deciding what should be pushed down into the shadow self, and the next forty years trying to get in touch with that material again. Cultures vary a lot in what they urge their members to exile. In general we can say that "the shadow" represents all that is instinctive in us. Whatever has a tail and lots of hair is in the shadow. People in secular and Puritanical cultures tend to push sexual desire into the shape under our *shadow* feet, and also fear of death; usually much ecstasy goes with them. Old cave impulses go there, longings to eat the whole world—if we put enough down there, the part left on top of the earth looks quite respectable.

Conrad is a great master of shadow literature; *The Secret Sharer* describes the healing of the same split that Stevenson could not heal. Conrad suspects that at times the shadow will not rejoin the consciousness unless the person has a serious task, which he accepts, such as captaining a ship. *Heart of Darkness* describes a failure in the same effort. Conrad noticed that the European solved his shadow problem less often after the invasion of Africa. The European now has a financial interest in the suppression of the shadow. Kurtz's history suggests that for a white man to recover his shadow at the same time he is exploiting blacks is a task beyond the power of the human being.

This speculations sends reverberations through American fiction also, both North and South. Mark Twain makes a similar point in *Huckleberry Finn*, brilliantly, joyously. Sometimes in the United States the "decent man" is hidden in the shadow, along with a lot of other stuff, and, as Huckleberry Finn finds out, the "decent man" will rejoin you only if you refuse to sell Jim.

Most of our literature describes efforts the shadow makes to rise, and efforts that fail. Ahab fails; it isn't clear why; he has a strong connection with the "old ethic" through the rhetoric of the Hebrew prophets. Dimmesdale's shadow fails. Apparently his fear of women blocks his own shadow from rising. I prefer to use the term "shadow," rather than "evil," in talking of literature, because "evil" permanently places the energy out there, as a part of some powerful being other than ourselves. "Shadow" is clumsy, but it makes it clear that these energies are inside of us.

Alexandra David-Neel tells a disturbing story. When she was studying with some Tibetan teachers early in this century, they suggested she try to get a clearer experience of her life-energy or libido. They suggested that she put it outside herself, where she could see it more clearly, and not in objects, but into a thought-form, a figure she herself would visualize and which would not exist outside of her head. She decided not to choose a typical Tibetan visualization—some energetic dancing figure with necklaces of skulls, and flames coming out of the hairs on his chest—on the grounds that she herself might consider it to be a simple transfer from a Tibetan unconscious. She decided instead to visualize an English monk of the Middle Ages. After a few weeks of visualization, which she did among some other duties, she noticed one day, while walking outside the monastery on the road, an English monk dressed in gray who approached and passed her. After several such meetings, he began to greet her when they met, and she could see his eyes. He would disappear if she "unthought" him. Soon, however, she noticed that he was growing bolder; he appeared to be drawing energy from her without her will, and to be taking on a life of his own. She became frightened then. Eventually she went to her Tibetan teacher, who taught her how to perform a rather long ritual to get ride of the monk. A man or woman who talks of evil in *Moby Dick* is the kind of person who would believe that monk was real.

The group of American poets born form 1875 to 1890, namely Wallace Stevens, Frost, Eliot, Williams, Marianne Moore, Pound, and Jeffers, are all shadow poets. They are not only shadow poets, but they did much shadow work. Most shadow work appeared in novel form in the last century; in this century it has tended to appear in poetry. Wallace Stevens is usually not thought of as a shadow writer, so we can take him; and his work will have to stand for the others in that marvelous group.

It is interesting to compare Wallace Stevens's background with Kenneth Rexroth's, as it appears in Rexroth's autobiography. The Rexroths tended to live out their shadow. Stevens's family, upper middle-class German Americans, appear to be successful repressors of the dark side. How the shadow returns in a complicated man like Wallace Stevens I don't know; I don't understand the return of the shadow at all well, and everything I say here is speculation. But it seems the shadow energies need special channels in order to return. Eliot's sharp griefs, coming first in his marriage, and followed then by his wife's insanity, are linked with the rising of much shadow energy in him, but none of that violent anguish appears in Stevens. In Stevens shadow material rises in perfect serenity, associated with the awakening of the senses, especially of hearing and smell. Our senses do form a natural bridge to our animal past, and so to the shadow. The senses of smell, shades of light and dark, the awareness of color and sound, so alive in the primitive man, for whom they can mean life or death, are still alive in us, but numbed. They are numbed by safety, and by years inside schoolrooms. Wallace Stevens, it seems, when he was working in insurance early on, would try to end the day at some New England town that had a museum. He would then spend a couple of hours looking at pictures. This is a practical way of reawakening the senses, as walks are. Both reawaken more of the senses than reading does.

> Among twenty snowy mountains,
> The only moving thing
> Was the eye of the blackbird.

It is said that eyes in the West receive a disproportionate amount of psychic energy; all the other senses have become weakened to the degree that reading has laid emphasis on sight. The old harmony between the five senses has been destroyed. Stevens is careful of hearing:

> I do not know which to prefer,
> The beauty of inflections
> Or the beauty of innuendoes,
> The blackbird whistling
> Or just after.

> ✳   ✳   ✳

> It was evening all afternoon.
> It was snowing
> And it was going to snow.
> The blackbird sat
> In the cedar-limbs.

The last poem has the most marvelous and alert sense for changes of light, the deepening darkness, sensed with the body, as snow is about to fall. He pays more attention than most men to uniting the senses of color and smell:

> The night is of the color
> Of a woman's arm:

Night, the female,
Obscure,
Fragrant and supple,
Conceals herself.
A pool shines,
Like a bracelet
Shaken in a dance.

He works to join the eyes to the sense of touch:

The light is like a spider. . . .
The webs of your eyes
Are fastened
To the flesh and bones of you
As to rafters or grass.
There are the filaments of your eyes
On the surface of the water
And in the edges of the snow.

He works to become aware of weather, and its mergings with emotion:

Passions of rain, or moods in falling snow;
Grievings in loneliness, or unsubdued
Elations when the forest blooms; gusty
Emotions on wet roads on autumn nights.

He begins to see how, if the senses are sharpened by labor, you begin to merge with the creatures and objects around you:

I am what is around me.

Women understand this.
One is not duchess
A hundred yards from a carriage.

Curious and mysterious substances rise in the poems when he starts to glide out on the rays of his senses:

He rode over Connecticut
In a glass coach.
Once, a fear pierced him,
In that he mistook
The shadow of his equipage
For blackbirds.

That describes a pure shadow instant, in which shadow material shoots up into the conscious mind. Often, when the shadow shoots up into consciousness for a split second, it brings with it the knowledge that we will die. Oddly, concentration on ants sometimes carries that information to the consciousness:

I measure myself
Against a tall tree.
I find that I am much taller,
For I reach right up to the sun,
With my eye;
And I reach to the shore of the sea
With my ear.
Nevertheless, I dislike
The way the ants crawl
In and out of my shadow.

I would guess it would be difficult for readers who read Stevens in translation to understand the shadow energy moving so elegantly through the senses, because the extraordinary richness of his sensual intelligence appears as delicate auras surrounding the words in English, as a perfume surrounds each sort of metal and each tree. Readers brought up in English whose sense of language has been coarsened by too much newspaper reading probably don't feel the complicated aura around Stevens's words either.

By this light the salty fishes
Arch in the sea like tree-branches,
Going in many directions
Up and down.

Senses intersect in those phrases. It is the opposite of academic poetry or philosophic diction. Stevens notices that:

> It is better that, as scholars,
> They should think hard in the dark cuffs
> Of voluminous cloaks . . .

Bashō said, listening in his garden to a temple bell:

> The temple bell stops—
> but the sound keeps coming
> out of the flowers.

Bashō worked both as a Buddhist meditator and as a haiku poet in awakening the senses:

> The sea grows dark.
> The voices of the wild ducks
> turn white.

American haiku poets don't grasp the idea that the shadow has to have risen up and invaded the haiku poem, otherwise it is not a haiku. The least important thing about it is its seventeen syllables or the nature scene.

The "Harmonium" that Stevens talks of, and wanted, in vain, to use as a title for his *Collected Poems*, refers to this union of all the five senses, and perhaps of eight or nine more that only Australian hunters or Bashō could identify. The serenity that gives music to Stevens's lines is a mark of the presence of that ancient union of the senses.

It was amazing to me recently to find out that one of his main helpers in this effort was William James. We ordinarily think of the senses and thought as opposites, so we assume that if one wants to reawaken the senses, one must stop thinking. When I first read *Harmonium,* I was surprised to see that the thinking is expressed through odor and sound images, and the sense images become more intense through the thinking going on. What I didn't know is that the thinking is of the sort recommended by William James. Margaret Peterson set all that out in a spirited essay printed in *Southern Review*'s Stevens issue, Summer 1971. It turns out that some of the most enigmatic and vivid poems in *Harmonium* are rephrasings of paragraphs by James. How unpredictable it all is!

William James warned his students that a certain kind of mind-set was approaching the West—it could hardly be called a way of thought—in which no physical details are noticed. Fingernails are not noticed, trees in the plural are mentioned, but no particular tree is ever loved, nor where it stands; the hair in the ear is not noticed. We now see this mind-set spread all over fresh-man English papers, which American students can now write quickly, on ut-terly generalized subjects; the nouns are usually plurals, and the feelings are all ones it would be nice to have. The same mind-set turns up on the Water-gate tapes, and working now with more elaborate generalizations, in graduate seminars in English, in which all the details in Yeats's poems turn out to be archetypes or Irish Renaissance themes. It is the *lingua franca*, replacing Latin. The mind-set could be described as the ability to talk of Africa without vi-sualizing the hair in a baboon's ear, or even a baboon. Instead the mind-set reports "wild animals." Since the immense range of color belongs to physical detail—the thatness—of the universe, it is the inability to see color. People with this mind-set have minds that resemble white nightgowns. For people with this mind-set, there's not much difference between 3 and 742; the count of something is a detail. In fact the number they are most interested in, as James noted, is one. That's a number without physical detail. As I read Pe-terson's essay, I was amazed to see "Metaphors of a Magnifico," which I have always loved as a zany poem of high spirits, become a serious process poem. The poem describes how to begin to free yourself from this mind-set; how to avoid being murdered by it. (So Ph.D.'s on *Harmonium* are especially funny.) He begins:

> Twenty men crossing a bridge,
> Into a village,
> Are twenty men crossing twenty bridges,
> Into twenty villages,
> Or one man
> Crossing a single bridge into a village.

He knows he is beginning by singing the sad little song hummed by Ph.D. candidates and politicians and experts in government planning: "One thing equals another thing."

> This is old song
> That will not declare itself . . .

Then he says what to do. Stop juggling ideas. Go to this place with your body, bring the senses forward, sound first, then sight, then smell if possible. Ask your imagination to bring you the sound:

> The boots of the men clump
> On the boards of the bridge.
> The first white wall of the village
> Rises through fruit-trees.
> Of what was it I was thinking?
> So the meaning escapes.

> The first white wall of the village . . .
> The fruit trees . . .

How strange! It is a Purgatory poem, laying out a road, a sort of guru poem. How beautiful!

William James observed the approaching mind-set and associated out from it sideways. He noticed the mind-set resembled the upper class of Boston. They too disliked the sordid details—the hair in the ear of religion, the smells of the Irish entryway—and preferred the religion of the One. Naturally, they became Unitarians. If the "cultured people" move into this mind-set, a curious thing happens the upper (spiritual) half of life and the lower (sensual) half of life begin to part company. One part ascends; the other part, no longer connected to the high, sinks. The gaps between grow wider and wider. The educated class has the Pure One, the working class people are left with nothing but the crude physical details of their lives— the husband's old pipe and the spit knocked out of it, the washing tub, the water and slush from the children's boots on the entry floor, the corns on the feet, the mess of dishes in the sink, the secular love-making in the cold room. These physical details are now, in the twentieth century, not only un- penetrated by religion, but they somehow prove to the unconscious that "re- ligion is a nullity." James emphasized that perception, and Stevens grieved over the insight all his life. For the working class there's nothing left but the Emperor of Ice Cream. The middle class is now the working class, and so the majority of people in the West are worse off than they were in the Mid- dle Ages.

James also noticed that the presence of this mind-set in India explains why certain Vedanta philosophies are so boring. An Indian meditation teacher, working with Ananda Marga, told me recently that before he did any meditation at all himself, and while he was working as an engineer in a compressor factory in India, he would at night visit the meeting of whatever holy man was in town. After the talk, he would ask the man, from the audience: What is the relation of your path to the poor in India? Usually—I think he said invariably—ten or twelve times in a row—two husky-looking men would come back and escort him out of the hall. Stevens would have understood that. For most holy men in India, the poor are the hair in the ear of India. They prefer the One, who has no hair.

James made sure his students understood a third sideways association, namely, the link of the mind-set to the German idealists. They were represented in England by Bradley and in the United States by Josiah Royce and the Anglo-Hegelians—horrible types, specialists in the One, builders of middle-class castles, and upper-class Usher houses, writers of boring Commencement speeches, creepy otherworldly types, worse than Pope Paul, academics who resembled gray jars, and who would ruin a whole state like Tennessee if put into it; people totally unable to merge into the place where they live—they could live in a valley for years and never become the valley. Antonio Machado, who did all his academic work in philosophy, describes them also:

> Everywhere I've gone I've seen
> excursions of sadness,
> angry and melancholy
> drunkards with black shadows,
>
> and academics in offstage clothes
> who watch, say nothing, and think
> they know, because they do not drink wine
> in the ordinary bars.
>
> Evil men who walk around
> polluting the earth . . .

Machado also remarked:

Mankind owns four things
that are no good at sea:
rudder, anchor, oars,
and the fear of going down.

If we think of the idealists in terms of Jung's speculations about the shadow,
it's clear the idealist is a man or woman who does not want to go down. They
plan to go to the grave with the shadow still repressed. The idealists are
shadow-haters. They all end as Dr. Jekyll, with a monkey-like Mr. Hyde
scurrying among back buildings elsewhere in the city.

By exclusive interest in "the truth," they exile the shadow, or keep it ex-
iled. . . . When Stevens takes his stand against all that, he takes a stand against
perfect Paradises, against abstract churches, against the statistical mentality,
against too easy transcendentalizing, too easy ignoring of the tragic:

The imperfect is our paradise.
Note that, in this bitterness, delight,
Since the imperfect is so hot in us,
Lies in flawed words and stubborn sounds.

Stevens did not make Dimmesdale's mistake. He invited the feminine in;
Florida, the moon, convolvulus and coral, glade-boats, sombreros, the soles
of feet and grape leaves, cabins in Carolina, and so much sound!

Only the shadow understands the ecstasy of sound. You know the
shadow has found a way for part of it to return when you hear the joyful
and primitive music of Vincentine, as energetic as Mozart, as insistent as
Australian drums:

Yes: you came walking,
Vincentine.
Yes: you came talking.

And what I knew you felt
Came then.
Monotonous earth I saw become
Illimitable spheres of you,
And that white animal, so lean,

Turned Vincentine,
Turned heavenly Vincentine,
And that white animal, so lean,
Turned heavenly, heavenly Vincentine.

So Stevens learned how to go home. He learned that the idealist-Christian-Hebraic insistence that there is one truth is all that is needed to block the shadow from rising forever, for a human being, with his frail psychic processes, so easily altered or ground to a stop. He wrote the clear and sweet poem, "On the Way Home":

It was when I said,
"There is no such thing as the truth,"
That the grapes seemed fatter.
The fox ran out of his hole.

You . . . You said,
"There are many truths,
But they are not parts of a truth."
Then the tree, at night, began to change,

Smoking through green and smoking blue.
We were two figures in a wood.
We said we stood alone.

It was when I said,
"Words are not forms of a single word.
In the sum of the parts, there are only the parts.
The world must be measured by eye";

It was when you said,
"The idols have seen lots of poverty,
Snakes and gold and lice,
But not the truth";

It was at that time, that the silence was largest
And longest, the night was roundest,

The fragrance of the autumn warmest,
Closest and strongest.

After writing such a masterpiece as *Harmonium*, guided by the secret knowledge James offered him in his books, and walking the path—he knew he
was walking it—why then is there no more to the story?

Sometimes we look to the end of the tale
where there should be marriage feasts,
and find only, as it were,
black marigolds and a silence.

Critics usually accept the world the poet creates. If he says east is north, they
say: Why didn't I think of that before! So Stevens's critics on the whole see
constant development in his work, in a chosen direction. But it's not so. The
late poems are as weak as is possible for a genius to write; what is worse,
most of them have the white nightgown mentality.

There are some good poems, but somehow there are no further marriages in his work. Yeats's work picked up more and more detail as it went
on, the sensual shadow began to rise, the instinctual energy throws off its
own clown clothes and fills more and more of the consciousness.

Why that did not happen to Stevens I don't know for sure, but I think
we have to look to his life for an explanation. Boehme has a note before one
of his books, in which he asks the reader not to go farther and read the book
unless he is willing to make practical changes as a result of the reading. Otherwise, Boehme says, reading the book will be bad for him, dangerous. We
have the sense that Wallace Stevens's relation to the shadow followed a pattern that has since become familiar among American artists: he brings the
shadow into his art, but makes no changes in the way he lives. The European
artists—at least Yeats, Tolstoy, Gauguin, Van Gogh, Rilke—seem to understand better that the shadow has to be lived too, as well as accepted in the
work of art. The implication of all their art is that each time a man or
woman succeeds in making a line so rich and alive with the senses, as full of
darkness as:

quail
Whistle about us their spontaneous cries
he must from then on live differently. A change in his life has to come as a
response to the change in his language. Rilke's work moves on, shifting to

84

deeper and deeper marriages, over wider and wider arcs, and we notice that he was always ready to change his way of living at a moment's notice if the art told him to. He looked one day at a statue for a long time, an old statue centered around ecstatic Apollonianism, and saw that the shape was alive not only in the head parts, but in every square inch of the body, throughout the chest and stomach, all of which dived down toward the genitals: every inch is looking at you, he said. Out of that he drew the conclusion that by tomorrow morning he would have to make some changes in the way he lived. I recall teachers in college laughing at Yeats for a remark he made in his journal during his twenties, something like: It seems to me my rhythms are becoming slack; I think I had better sleep on a board for a while. But that says the same thing as Rilke's poem.

Wallace Stevens was not willing to change his way of life, despite all the gifts he received, and all the advice he read in his own poems. He kept the house fanatically neat, evidently slept in a separate bedroom for thirty or forty years, made his living through the statistical mentality, and kept his business life and poetry life separate—all of which amounted to keeping his dominant personality and his shadow personality separate in his daily life. That was so much true that when he took a literary visitor to his club to eat, it seems Stevens entered and conversed there as a businessman, and warned visitors against eccentric behavior. In 1935, during Mussolini's attack on Ethiopia, when Stevens was 56, he wrote in a letter to Ronald Latimer:

> The Italians have as much right to take Ethiopia from the coons
> as the coons had to take it from the boa-constrictors.

This sentence was intended to be playful, in part at least, and it does not represent a crime that has to be laid to him. And yet it is a sentence that everyone who loves Stevens's poems has to face sooner or later. It seems to indicate that he was not living his shadow very intensely. He had urged the shadow energies to enter *Harmonium*, but at the point where they might have disturbed the even tenor of his life, or the opinions appropriate to it, he shut the door.

I realize that making serious comments on a group of poems by mentioning the author's life violates every canon of New Criticism, canons still very much alive. But surely we must see now that this critical insistence on examining only the work is another example of shadow-hatred and shadow-

85

ignoring. It is an idealist position. Williams James's and Stevens's warning on the mind-set were rejected, and by the 1940s the idealist position in literature was established, and all of us who began to write in the '40s and the '50s felt that fact keenly. The critic's assumption was that the author's life had no bearing whatever on the poem. Eliot helped to bring that attitude about, yet I heard him complain in a hockey stadium in St. Paul around 1957 that one of his poems had recently appeared in an anthology holding eight long poems, and that nothing whatever was said about the author of the poems—their nationality was not given, nor the century in which they had lived. "They were all dead except me, and opening the book made me feel dead too." The mentality of the anthologist was exactly what Stevens called the mentality of the white nightgown. In any case, by 1950 the idealist position had found a good home in literary criticism, and none of us writing then got much help from it on how to bring our own shadows—or the national shadow—into our poems.]

Wallace Stevens's statement at the club—don't talk too much about poetry, or too wildly—is somehow the opposite of Tolstoy, who, when he got ready in his old age to free his serfs, found to his amazement that his wife and two of his daughters were ready for no such thing, but considered them a part of the property and dowry, and that was an end of it. He left the house in a blizzard with his youngest daughter, Alexandra, and died in a railway station shortly after. He was willing to change his way of life that late!

That story is probably a bad example, because it implies that changing your way of life involves sensational events, catastrophes, turmoil, leaving wife and children, leaving husband and children, slamming the door in the Ibsen manner. The contrary seems to be true. Enormous changes—divorce, throwing away children, abandoning responsibilities, look to be clear ways to join your shadow again, but oddly that doesn't happen most of the time. When a person divorces, he or she usually sets up a similar life with a different person. All the verbal storms of confessional poetry that the poets and readers have gone through in the last years did not achieve anything for the poet—the poet's shadow is still miles away after the confessional book is written. As Plath's and Sexton's and Berryman's lives made clear, nothing has happened at all, and the death energy is still waiting to pounce on the unintegrated soul.

What is meant by Rilke's "You must change your life" is evidently something more subtle. I don't understand it at all myself, so I can only speculate.

Conrad evidently made use of the information the shadow gave him by ceasing to be a ship's captain on the Congo, and so a low-level exploiter of Africa. Rilke, when he realized what his work was telling him, interrupted his writing of poetry, and spent months watching animals in the zoo, and blind men on the streets, and years alone. He began to ask less from the world, not more. The Taoists would probably say that changing your way of life means giving up having an effect upon the world. It involves "wu-wei," not playing any role. Wu-wei is also translated as doing nothing. Wang Wei said once:

> In the old days the serious man was not an important person.
> He thought making decisions was too complicated for him.
> He took whatever small job came along.
> Essentially, he did nothing, like these walnut trees.

His friend P'ei Ti answered this way:

> I soon found doing nothing was a great joy to me.
> You see, here I am, keeping my ancient promise!
> Let's spend today just strolling around these walnut trees.
> The two of us will nourish the ecstasies Chuang Tzu loved.

A man has an effect on "the world" mainly through institutions. So we could say that in the second half of life a man should sever his link with institutions. I think the problem is more complicated for women, but I don't understand it. Conceivably for women the change might involve accepting more responsibility for affecting the world.

In any case severing ties with institutions is not a habit in the United States, where a man ordinarily becomes more deeply embedded in the institution, whether it be an insurance company or a university, during his forties and fifties than he ever was earlier. John Barth is a contemporary example of the American artist who tries to bring the shadow into his work, but refuses to live it. His work cannot help but follow the same path as Stevens's— it is an ascent into vacuity, intellectualist complexity, a criticism of dry reason from inside the palace of dry reason.

If the shadow's gifts are not acted upon, it evidently retreats and returns to the earth. It gives the writer or person ten or fifteen years to change his life, in response to the amazing visions the shadow has brought him—that change may involve only a deepening of the interior marriage of male and female within the man or woman—but if that does not happen, the shadow goes back down, abandoning him, and the last state of that man is evidently worse than the first. Rilke talks of the shadow retreating in this poem:

Already the ripening barberries are red,
and the old asters hardly breathe in their beds.
The man who is not rich now as summer goes
will wait and wait and never be himself.

The man who cannot quietly close his eyes
certain that there is vision after vision
inside, simply waiting until nighttime
to rise all around him in the darkness—
he is an old man, it's all over for him.

Nothing else will come; no more days will open;
and everything that does happen will cheat him—
even you, my God. And you are like a stone
that draws him daily deeper into the depths.

My Doubts About Whitman

Whitman and Dickinson are the two perky progenitors of American poetry. Whitman bases his lines on the big-roomed, overconfident, tower-shouting poems of the Hebrew prophets; and Dickinson bases her lines on the cramped, doubt-filled, agonized poems of the early Puritans. Whitman brings the Mediterranean in by swelling up his voice to the level of Italian opera, and Dickinson brings North Europe in by holding to the narrow-celled, four-sided box of the hymn stanza, sometimes cutting off legs and arms to make her thought fit.

Whitman gives many blessings, as if he were a rakish, rich parent. I'll name a few. He created a clear speaking voice, not encumbered by the class system—a way of sound-walking which does not pause every few seconds to make a gesture that identifies him as a familiar of the court:

> A child said, What is the grass? Fetching it to me with full hands.
> How could I answer the child? I do not know what it is any more
>   than he.
> I guess it must be the flag of my disposition, out of hopeful green
>   stuff woven.

A second blessing is an exquisite attention to the wild ascending lisp of the carpenter's plane as it dresses a plank, a way of honoring those instants of life that have no political significance:

The pure contralto sings in the organ loft,
The carpenter dresses his plank—the tongue of his foreplane
    whistles its wild ascending lisp,
The married and unmarried children ride home to their
    thanksgiving dinner,
The pilot seizes the king-pin, he heaves down with a strong arm,
The mate stands braced in the whale-boat, lance and harpoon are
    ready,
The duck-shooter walks by silent and cautious stretches,
The deacons are ordained with crossed hands at the altar,
The spinning-girl retreats and advances to the hum of the big wheel,
The farmer stops by the bars of a Sunday and looks at the oats and
    rye,
The lunatic is carried at last to the asylum a confirmed case,
He will never sleep any more as he did in the cot in his mother's
    bedroom. . . .

Third, an honoring of our physical ancestors, healthy, full-hipped mothers
and wide-browed fathers, all of whom seem to have some ideal freshness
and vigor:

She too is not only herself—she is the teeming mother of mothers,
She is the bearer of them that shall grow and be mates to the
    mothers.

Her daughters, or their daughters' daughters—who knows who shall
    mate with them?
Who knows through the centuries what heroes may come from
    them?

In them, and of them, natal love—in them that divine mystery, the
    same old beautiful mystery.

A fourth blessing is the music of vowels, the delicate ornamentation, brilliant, in which vowels deliciously mingle with consonants, in which the *or*'s
mingle their cries to God with the intricate whispers of lovers at night. In
this poem the *or* sound in *organ* and *quartet* and *mourn* modulates toward the

ur in church, *murmur, heard, perfect*; and all this ornamentation ends finally in the delicate sound *ear*.

> I heard you solemn-sweet pipes of the organ as last Sunday morn I
> pass'd the church,
> Winds of autumn, as I walk'd the woods at dusk I heard your long-
> stretch'd sighs up above so mournful,
> I heard the perfect Italian tenor singing at the opera, I heard the
> soprano in the midst of the quartet singing;
> Heart of my love! you too I heard murmuring low through one of
> the wrists around my head,
> Heard the pulse of you when all was still ringing little bells last
> night under my ear.

His fifth blessing is the beauty of the healthy ego, the ego after it has reached adulthood, and—praised by either mother or father—does not lie or evade or curry favor or eat sand to die or curl back to inhabit the tiny baby's body long left behind.

> I see the workings of battle, pestilence, tyranny—I see martyrs and
> prisoners,
> I observe a famine at sea—I observe the sailors casting lots who
> shall be killed, to preserve the lives of the rest,
> I observe the slights and degradations cast by arrogant persons upon
> laborers, the poor, and upon negroes, and the like;
> All these—All the meanness and agony without end, I sitting, look
> out upon,
> See, hear, and am silent.

So I have much praise to offer this rakish parent. "Walt Whitman," Neruda said, "has taught me more than Spain's Cervantes." He was "the first man in history to speak with a truly continental American voice, to bear a truly American name . . . He had no fear of either moralizing or immoralizing, nor did he seek to separate the fields of pure and impure poetry."

Now keeping all these blessings in mind, I want to edge toward my doubts about his legacy, what he did not say or did not represent. I'll touch on five areas of that doubt.

He doesn't identify his immediate poetic and intellectual ancestors. When he was nearly 70, Whitman finally wrote a short piece on Elias Hicks, from whom he had received so much. Many earlier men said in prose what he managed to say, in his own way, in poems later, but about them he is mostly silent. He pretends that his ideas have come to him spontaneously. "Take no illustrations whatever from ancients and classics," Whitman said in his journal. In differing ways, Thoreau and Whitman each wanted a clean slate. Thoreau, in the opening pages of *Walden,* said, "I have lived some thirty years on this planet, and I have yet to hear the first syllable of valuable or even earnest advice from my seniors. They have told me nothing, and probably cannot tell me anything to the purpose." Thoreau, fourteen years younger than Emerson, had read his mentor's essay "On Nature" many times. Thoreau in fact wrote the above sentence in 1847, and had by that time already lived several months in Emerson's house, and written love poems to his wife. The refusal of Whitman and Thoreau to identify their intellectual ancestors has, I think, thrown many descendants off in their relationship to the past or to the writers they have loved. Many Irish writers—Seamus Heaney is an example—keep Yeats, Synge, Joyce, A.E., and Kavanagh in their hearts and write essays about them.

Secondly, Whitman was not frank about his limitations or about what one might call the amount of "lead," the unregenerate elements in a person, within his family and inside him. Our unregenerate element might be the way we habitually isolate ourselves or steal from others or enjoy guilt. It might be our way of looking down on other people. Certain parents gave birth to us, and certain parents bore them, and so certain dark energies are built into our natures, and part of the poet's work is owning up to the origins of this darkness.

The brave self-portraits that Rembrandt did showed his heaviness and his limitations so clearly. In his poems, Baudelaire keeps his lead well to the front, very much in view. He imagines, for example, a prince or a king seated on a throne; everyone is serving him and bustling about, all trying to figure out what could possibly make this man so sad. He titled one of his prose poems "Let's Beat Up the Poor." In another poem, he describes coming home after being dishonest with people whom he met on the street. He ends the poem: "Oh Lord God, grant me the grace to produce a few good verses, which shall prove to myself that I am not the lowest of men, that I am not inferior to those whom I despise." George Trakl said,

Over the white fishpond
The wild birds have blown away.
An icy wind drifts from our stars at evening. . . .

The white walls of the city are always giving off sound.
Under arching thorns
Oh my brother blind minute-hands we are climbing toward
            midnight.

Whitman doesn't admit the darker energies; he is generally optimistic:

I am of old and young, of the foolish as much as the wise,
Regardless of others, ever regardful of others,
Maternal as well as paternal, a child as well as a man,
Stuffed with the stuff that is coarse, and stuffed with the stuff that
            is fine,
One of the great nation, the nation of many nations, the smallest
            the same, and the largest the same,
A southerner soon as a northerner, a planter nonchalant and
            hospitable,
A Yankee, bound my own way, ready for trade, my joints the
            limberest joints on earth and the sternest joints on earth,
A Kentuckian, walking the vale of the Elkhorn in my deer-skin
            leggings. . . .

I won't quote all of it, but it ends:

Of every hue, trade, rank, caste, and religion,
Not merely of the New World, but of Africa, Europe, Asia—a
            wandering savage,
A farmer, mechanic, artist, gentleman, sailor, lover, Quaker,
A prisoner, fancy-man, rowdy, lawyer, physician, priest.

This really is quite mad. It is a drastic solution to the problem of family
pain, too drastic. He wasn't all those people, but rather a grandson of Dutch
and English farmers from Long Island; and two of his sisters ended up in
mental wards; his brother was retarded. He must have been terrified by his

family situation, and yet somehow we expect more from him in the way of frankness. He transmutes to gold too easily. How could he be of every hue, trade, rank, caste, and religion? Of course we understand him to say that he doesn't mean that he is all of these beings, a planter, a savage, a lawyer, a mechanic, a rowdy, a priest, but rather that he is Being itself. But that is the most dangerous solution of all.

In the *New York Quarterly*, John Ashbery remarked, "I find it very easy to move from one person in the sense of a pronoun to another and this again helps to produce a kind of polyphony in my poetry which I again feel is a means toward greater naturalism." Helen Vendler went further: "A crowd of voices, as Stevens called it, is spoken by the single poet; as we feel ourselves farther and farther from uniqueness and more and more part of a human collective, living, as Lowell said, a generic life, the pressure of reality exerts a pressure on style—a pressure to speak in the voice of the many. . . ."

It's interesting to hear Wallace Stevens's name appear in this passage. Wallace Stevens allows very little of his lead to come into his poems either. We know that at a party he was a kind of emotional redneck, telling appallingly bad jokes and making racist remarks. The morning after some embarrassing event, he would write an elegant letter, in a sense papering it over. Stevens actually referred to the life which he wanted others to see as "a paper life." On paper everything was fine. This strange doubleness reminds us curiously of Whitman's cheerfulness.

Whitman allows, even encourages his suffering and his particular nature to disappear in the mush of Being. D. H. Lawrence objects to Whitman's repeated moves into "the State of Allness":

> Walt wasn't an Eskimo. A little, yellow, sly, cunning, greasy little Eskimo. And when Walt blandly assumed Allness, including Eskimoness, unto himself, he was just sucking the wind out of a blown egg-shell, no more. Eskimos are not minor little Walts. They are something that I am not, I know that. Outside the egg of my Allness chuckles the greasy little Eskimo. Outside the egg of Whitman's Allness too.

My third doubt is that Whitman walks under the banner of a large audience. Whitman said, "To have great poets we must have great audiences." During the Fifties and Sixties, those of us who wrote poetry read this sentence hundreds of times, since *Poetry* magazine printed it on their cover for many years. Whitman said many other things too, and yet to single out this sentence is not wholly unjust; something of him is in it. I think the American poets' current concern with numbers, with how many people attend poetry readings, how many people buy or don't buy poetry books, how the NEA could widen the audience for poetry, all of these resonate somehow to Whitman's concern with audience. Of course European poets are concerned with audiences too, but many are content with and loyal to small audiences. The old editor of *Poetry*, Henry Rago, once told a story about meeting T. S. Eliot on the streets of London and asking him about the subscriber list for his magazine *Criterion*, which had such an enormous influence. Eliot said, "I think the subscriber list was 341." The next day Eliot corrected himself and said, "I was wrong. There were 343 at the peak." Gerard Manley Hopkins wrote magnificently with an audience of one, Robert Bridges. In this matter of audiences, Thoreau was more relaxed. When *Walden* sold only a few copies, he mentioned to Emerson, "I have a library of 800 books, over 700 of which I have written myself." Emily Dickinson wrote a lot of great poetry without brooding about audiences. Great poetry is more likely to be written by a man or woman who has a few friends who love poetry and are willing to talk about it for hours.

My fourth doubt is that there seems to be no possibility of conversation or exchange with Whitman. Poetry is best imagined as a conversation between two beings, even if it's a conversation between body and soul. If two beings talk inside a poem, the reader usually has a chance to get a thought in edgewise and participate, so to speak, in the poem. A reader may then feel noticed rather than feeling one of the mob watching and listening. Frost could not have achieved his conversational poems if he had not rebelled against Whitman's monologues. Frost was a great talker in daily life, an endless talker in fact; and yet in his poems a second speaker is often given full permission. That helps the reader not to feel sermonized and so fall silent. Frost creates a major argument between husband and wife in the great poem "Hill Burial." We remember the power that Herbert achieves with two speakers. Yeats wrote many conversations:

> I met the Bishop on the road
> And much said he and I.
> "Those breasts are flat and fallen now,

Those veins must soon be dry;
Live in a heavenly mansion,
Not in some foul sty."

"Fair and foul are near of kin,
And fair needs foul," I cried.
"My friends are gone, but that's a truth
Nor grave nor bed denied,
Learned in bodily lowness
And in the heart's pride.

"A woman can be proud and stiff
When on love intent;
But Love has pitched his mansion in
The place of excrement;
For nothing can be sole or whole
That has not been rent."

It may be an odd thing to say, but it seems to me that poets who allow another speaker to come in often have more respect for pauses. The so-called Anglo-Saxon meter, as in *Beowulf*, insists on a pause after three or four syllables. That makes a great contrast to Whitman. I suspect that pauses are more likely to call in the reader and allow him or her to agree or object. Robert Creeley:

Love comes quietly,
finally, drops
about me, on me,
in the old ways.

What did I know
thinking myself
able to go
alone all the way.

This kind of pause is something I'm trying to learn myself. Many of my earlier poems have been affected by the forward rush, so characteristic of

Whitman and the Neruda of *Residencia.* We can take an example of that forward rush from "Chants Democratic, Part III":

> Iron-works, forge-fires in the mountains, or by riverbanks, men
> around feeling the melt with huge crowbars—lumps of ore, the
> due combining of ore, limestone, coal—the blast-furnace and
> the puddling-furnace, the loup-lump at the bottom of the melt
> at last—the rolling-mill, the stumpy bars of pig-iron, the strong
> clean-shaped T-rail for railroads. . . .

The final doubt I'll mention is related to the absence of complicated syntax in his work; his repetitive syntax seems to be a part of the sermonizing and endless flow of supporting pictures. I am contrasting this to the complicated sentence structures so prevalent in 17th, 18th and 19th century English, which do the job of balancing various competing perceptions and ranking them. Such sentence structure allows for or even forces the writer to decide which of the various perceptions or opinions are his or her main one—that goes into the main clause—and then the perceptions that are not quite to the point appear in subordinate clauses, arranged in a way that is not democratic, so to speak. It is understood that ideas cannot be humiliated by being ranked, so this ranking is not cruel to thought. However, it is evidence of discrimination and an attempt to be honest about what seems true or truest at this very second. Much contemporary poetry, particularly that which identifies itself as progressive, is made of nothing but lists of emotions or instances of bad luck or scenes from a marriage or simple details noticed on the street. Much contemporary poetry is a matter of observing more than thinking and of listing rather than discriminating.

But even when I've spoken all my doubts, it doesn't mean that I won't continue to love and admire Whitman. I will. I notice that his chief admirer in my generation, Galway Kinnell, has found a way on his own to bring in the dark energies of the bear and the porcupine, and to bring in his own loneliness. "When one has lived a long time alone." I can open his work and Whitman's at any page, and pull in my breath at what I see. My copies of Whitman are all worn and raggedy.

Upward Into the Depths

Tomas Tranströmer has a strange genius for the image; images rise seemingly without effort on his part. The wide space we feel in his poems perhaps occurs because the four or five main images in each poem come from widely separated sources in the psyche. His poems are a sort of railway station where trains that have come enormous distances stand briefly in the same building. One train may have some Russian snow on the undercarriage, and another may have Mediterranean flowers fresh in the compartments, and Ruhr soot on the roofs.

The poems are mysterious because the images have traveled a long way to get there. Mallarmé believed there should be mystery in poetry, and urged poets to get it, if necessary, by removing the links that tie the poem to its occasion in the real world. In Tranströmer's poems, the link to the worldly occasion is stubbornly kept, and yet the mystery and surprise never fade, even on many readings.

2.

There is a layer in our consciousness or memory, it seems, that runs alongside our life experience, but is not drawn from our life. It is perhaps older. "With his work, as with a glove, a man feels the universe," Tranströmer says. "Schubertiana" begins:

> Outside New York, dusk coming, a place where with one glance
>   you take in the houses where eight million human beings live.

The enormous city at night, he says, looks "like a spiral galaxy from the side." And he evokes scenes of coffee cups being pushed across desks, air-moved doors, fire escapes, people slumped over in the subway. Then he says:

> I know also—statistics to the side—that at this moment in some
>   room down there Schubert is being played, and for some
>   person the notes are more real than all the rest.

Tranströmer often edges toward ways of containing in words the before-birth intensities, the intensities not entirely *ours*. After all, what are notes? Sounds shaped by, say, a string quartet, contain almost no life stuff. They are pure sound vibrations, yet connected apparently to feelings that resonate somewhere inside us. Tomas Transtömer ends a prose poem, "Funchal," saying,

> The innermost contradiction, parking ramp flowers, the ventila-
> tor toward the good dark. A drink that bubbles in an empty glass.
> A loudspeaker that amplifies silence. A path that grows up again
> after every step. A book that can only be read in the dark.

Some works of art do cross the line that separates worlds. A poem of that sort might include a loudspeaker and silence, a parking ramp and flowers, the banal outer world and a mysterious underworld. In this double world it is difficult to keep one's balance, and it's best to leave all rhetoric out.

> It's been a hard winter, but summer is here and the fields want
> us to walk upright. Every man unimpeded, but careful, as when
> you stand up in a small boat. I remember a day in Africa: on the
> banks of the Chari, there were many boats, an atmosphere posi-
> tively friendly, the men almost blue-black in color with three par-
> allel scars on each cheek (meaning the Sara tribe). I am welcomed

on a boat—it's a canoe hollowed from a dark tree. The canoe is incredibly wobbly, even when you sit on your heels. A balancing act. If you have the heart on the left side you have to lean a bit to the right, nothing in the pockets, no big arm movements, please, all rhetoric has to be left behind. Precisely: rhetoric is impossible here. The canoe glides out over the water.

(from "Standing Up")

It was Rilke who created the metaphor that poets are "bees of the invisible." Making honey of the invisible suggests that the artist remains close to his own earthly history, but moves as well toward the spiritual and the invisible. As an artist, Transtromer seems to be steadied by such efforts, and by the example of other European poets who have done so.

Tomas's love of Schubert carries him to the boundary between worlds; and at such a boundary, he sees landscapes ordinarily hidden:

> The five instruments play. I go home through warm woods where
>   the earth is springy under my feet,
> curl up like someone still unborn, sleep, roll on so weightlessly into
>   the future, suddenly understand that plants are thinking.

Art helps us, he says, as a banister helps the climber on a dark stairwell. The banister finds its own way in the dark. In Schubert, "happiness and suffering weigh exactly the same." The depths are above us and below us at the same instant. The melody line is a stubborn

> humming sound that this instant is with us
> upward into
> the depths.

Transtromer suspects that as an artist he is merely a way for "the Memory" to get out into the world. Even at 17 he was aware that the dead "want to have their portraits painted." He says we are "lowered" into the past. In "About History," he says we are like a microphone that has been lowered under the ice of a spring lake.

His poem, "December Evening '72," begins:

Here I come the invisible man, perhaps in the employ
of some huge Memory that wants to live at this moment.
            And I drive by

      the white church that's locked up. A saint made of wood is inside,
      smiling helplessly, as if someone had taken his glasses.

Tranströmer is an elegant and humorous servant of the "Memory." In "Sentry Duty" he says:

      Task: to be where I am.
      Even when I'm in this solemn and absurd
      role: I am still the place
      where creation works on itself.

      Dawn comes, the sparse tree trunks
      take on color now, the frostbitten
      forest flowers form a silent search party
      after something that has disappeared in the dark.

      But to be where I am . . . and to wait.
      I am full of anxiety, obstinate, confused.
      Things not yet happened are already here!
      I feel that. They're just out there:

      a murmuring mass outside the barrier.
      They can only slip in one by one.
      They want to slip in. Why? They do
      one by one. I am the turnstile.

Even after hard work during the day, he has high spirits:

      After a black day, I play Haydn,
      and feel a little warmth in my hands.

      The keys are ready. Kind hammers fall.
      The sound is spirited, green, and full of silence.

The sounds says that freedom exists
and someone pays no taxes to Caesar.

I shove my hands in my haydnpockets
and act like a man who is calm about it all.

I raise my haydnflag. The signal is:
"We do not surrender. But want peace."

The music is a house of glass standing on a slope;
rocks are flying, rocks are rolling.

The rocks roll straight through the house
but every pane of glass is still whole.

3.

Tomas Tranströmer was an only child, born in Stockholm in 1931, on April 15th. His father and mother divorced when he was three; he and his mother lived after that in an apartment in the working class district of Stockholm. As a student, he pursued music and psychology.

The early Fifties were a rather formal time, both here and in Sweden, and Tranströmer began by writing highly formal poems, some in iambic and Alcaic meter. His first book, *17 Poems,* published in 1954, which glowed with several baroque elements, contained only seventeen poems, but people noticed the power of it immediately. Tranströmer decided to make his living as a psychologist. For some years he worked at a boys' prison in Linköping. The boys he counseled in that prison evidently took in a lively impression of him. Someone sent me a clipping from Sweden during that time, which recounted the adventures of a youth who had escaped a short time before from the Linköping reformatory. It transpired that he registered in various Swedish hotels and motels as "T. Tranströmer, psychologist."

In 1965 he moved with his wife Monica and his two daughters Paula and Emma to Västerås, a town about forty miles west of Stockholm. He continued to work as a psychologist, this time for a labor organization funded by the State. He helped juvenile delinquents reenter society, persons with physical disabilities choose a career, and he counseled parole offenders and those in drug rehabilitation. Once, during a reading in New York, a member of the audience asked him if his work had affected his poetry. He did reply, but mentioned how odd it seemed that so few people asked him: "How has your poetry affected your work?" In a printed interview later, he remarked that he had early learned to admire active syntax when composing a poem. When counseling juveniles, he urged them to do likewise. If they were liable to say "I found myself in this apartment . . ." or "As it happened, I . . ." He urged them to say, "I broke the window and crawled in."

His wife Monica, who was trained as a nurse, has accepted various jobs during their marriage, sometimes with new-born children and their mothers; for a time she was in charge of Vietnamese refugees who were resettling in Sweden. When one sees Monica and Tomas together, one can still glimpse in the room the freshness of their first meetings.

Tranströmer's poems have been translated into many languages, something like thirty-eight so far. During the Seventies and Eighties, a number of American poets translated his work, including May Swenson, Samuel Charters, Joanna Bankier, Eric Sellin, and in Great Britain we might mention Robin Fulton and John F. Deane. Robert Hass edited a selected poems for Ecco Press in 1987.

In Europe the praise for his poems has steadily grown. He has received almost every important poetry prize in Europe, including the Petrarch Prize in Germany, the Bonnier Award for Poetry, the Pilot Prize in 1988, the Nordic Council Prize in 1990, the Swedish Academy's Nordic Prize in 1991, and the Horst Bieneck Prize in 1992.

4.

Tomas Tranströmer's poems are a luminous example of the ability of good poetry in one culture to travel to another culture and arrive. As Tranströmer said in a letter to the Hungarian poets, published in the magazine *Uj Iras* in 1977, "Poetry has an advantage from the start. . . . Poetry requires no heavy, vulnerable apparatus that has to be lugged around. . . ."

Tomas writes playfully about technology. He has remarked that when he first began to write, in the early Fifties, it still seemed possible to write a nature poem into which nothing technological entered. Now, he says, many

objects created by technology have become almost parts of nature; and the
fact that Sweden has a highly developed technology is always visible in his
recent poems. He doesn't exile technology, nor does technology dominate
the poem:

> and every year the factory buildings go down another
> eighth of an inch—the earth is gulping them slowly.

> Paws no one can identify leave a print
> on the glossiest artifacts dreamed up here . . .

> And no one knows what will happen, we only know
> the chain breaks and grows back together all the time.
> (from "Traffic")

Even in the countryside of Sweden there are hints:

> All at once I notice the hills on the other side of the lake: their
> pine has been clear-cut. They resemble the shaved skull-sections
> of a patient about to have a brain operation.

Swedish society is most famously a welfare society, the welfare society;
it is perhaps the first society in history that has had the will and the wealth
to insist on the abolition of poverty. But it is also a technological society
like ours, and one given to secular solutions. Tranströmer reports how difficult it is in Sweden to keep in touch with certain kinds of tenderness. In
"Below Freezing," he writes:

> We are at a party that doesn't love us. Finally the party lets
> the mask fall and shows what it is: a shunting station for freight
> cars. In the fog cold giants stand on their tracks. A scribble of
> chalk on the car doors.
> One can't say it aloud, but there is a lot of repressed violence
> here. That is why the furnishings seem so heavy. And why it is so
> difficult to see the other thing present: a spot of sun that moves
> over the house walls and slips over the unaware forest of flickering
> faces, a biblical saying never set down: "Come unto me, for I am
> as full of contradictions as you."

He returns again and again to a childhood home in Runmarö, an island in the archipelago off the east coast of Sweden; and he is as deeply attached to it as Jean Giono to the Vaucluse, or Hardy to "Wessex." The long poem "Baltics," which Samuel Charters translated, draws its images from the landscape and history of that island, out of which his grandfather worked as a ship pilot. On his father's side, he comes from pilots who guided ships among the islands in the Stockholm Archipelago.

5.

In his work, Tranströmer is always aware of something approaching over the border. The title of his fourth book, *Sanningsbarriären*, literally "The Truth Barrier," suggests a customs house, or the customs table at an airport. *Sanningsbarriären* also contains a slight pun on the English phrase, "sound barrier."

As "Start of a Late Autumn Novel" begins, he is lying half asleep on the island, and hears a thumping sound outside. It seems to vanish and return. Or perhaps there is some being inside the wall who is knocking:

> someone who belongs to the other world, but got left here anyway, he thumps, wants to get back. Too late. Wasn't on time down here, wasn't on time up there, didn't make it on board in time.

Dreams surely come from over the border. "Citoyens" rose from a dream Tranströmer had the night following an automobile accident (the one he describes in "Solitude"). Danton with his pock-marked face appeared, but the dreamer could only see half his face, as we only see one side of the moon. Danton seemed to be standing on stilts:

> I saw his face from underneath:
> like the pitted moon, half lit, half in mourning.
> I wanted to say something.
> A weight in the chest: the lead weight
> that makes the clocks go,
> makes the hands go around: Year I, Year II . . .
> A pungent odor as from sawdust in tiger cages.

And—as always in dreams—no sun.
But the alley walls
shone as they curved away
down towards the waiting-room, the curved space,
the waiting room where we all . . .

The alley walls curve away toward a "waiting room," which reminded Tranströmer of the hospital lobby where he waited so often to see his mother while she was dying of cancer. "The waiting room where we all..."

During the Eighties Tranströmer wrote a masterpiece centered on the Dutch painter Vermeer and his painting "Woman in Blue Reading a Letter." The poem evokes the terror lying behind that calm canvas.

It's not a sheltered world. The noise begins over there, on the other
    side of the wall
where the alehouse is
with its laughter and quarrels, its rows of teeth, its chiming of
    clocks,
and the psychotic brother-in-law, the murderer, in whose presence
    everyone feels fear. . . .

She is eight months pregnant, two hearts beating inside her.
The wall behind her holds a crinkly map of Terra Incognita.

We see a chair covered with a blue fabric:

Just breathe. An unidentifiable blue fabric has been tacked to the
    chairs.
Gold-headed tacks flew in with astronomical speed
and stopped smack there
as if they had always been stillness and nothing else.

The ears experience a buzz, perhaps it's depth or perhaps height.
It's the pressure from the other side of the wall. . . .
And what is empty turns its face to us
and whispers:
"I am not empty, I am open."

A second masterpiece, from the Nineties, is "Grief Gondola #2" (the title is from a piano piece by Franz Liszt). We feel again Tranströmer's devotion to music. Richard Wagner was married to Cosima, the daughter of Franz Liszt, and the two of them were living in Venice in 1882. The father-in-law, Liszt, came to visit them. There was something heavy in the visit, and Wagner in fact died soon after. In the opening lines, Tranströmer playfully calls Wagner King Midas:

> . . . King Midas—
> I mean the one who turns everything he touches into Wagner.

He goes on:

> Wagner has received the Mark . . .
> The heavily loaded gondola carries their lives, two return tickets and
> a one-way.

Tranströmer finds an amazing way to allow those moments in Venice to reach forward into the European future:

> Liszt has composed a few chords so heavy one should send them
> off to the Institute for Mineralogical Studies in Padua.
> Meteorites!
> Far too heavy to stay where they are, they start sinking and sinking
> down through the coming years until they reach
> the year of the Brownshirts.

Tranströmer doesn't leave out his own life; he talks of himself:

> I dreamt that I had sketched piano keys out
> on the kitchen table. I played on them, without a sound.
> Neighbors came by to listen.

Back to Liszt:

> When Liszt plays tonight he holds down the C pedal so that the
> ocean's green force

rises through the floor and penetrates every stone of the building. Good evening to you, beautiful deep!

6.

Tranströmer's life was interrupted, tragically, in 1990 when he suffered a stroke. His blood pressure had always been high; he had been traveling a lot and was tired. He survived the stroke, but the right side of his body has remained partially paralyzed. The stroke impaired his ability to find and speak words as well. Nevertheless his spirits remain high; he continues to compose poems, and has recently completed a group of new haikus.

Tomas and Monica moved, during the last year, from Västerås to an apartment in Stockholm, near the old neighborhood where Tomas once lived as a boy. The town of Västerås gave an elaborate farewell ceremony for Monica and Tomas, complete with medieval music and a choir and formal readings of his poems at the old castle. He brought his piano along, and in the Stockholm apartment, he plays that piano brilliantly with his left hand. Composers in Sweden have begun to send him piano works which they have newly written for his left hand. That detail suggests how much affection there is in Sweden for Tomas and his poetry.

> Tourists have crowded into the half-dark of the enormous
> Romanesque church.
> Vault opening behind vault and no perspective.
> A few candle flames flickered.
> An angel whose face I couldn't see embraced me
> and his whisper went all through my body:
> "Don't be ashamed to be a human being, be proud!
> Inside you one vault after another opens endlessly.
> You'll never be complete, and that's as it should be."
> Tears blinded me
> as we were herded out into the fiercely sun-lit piazza,
> together with Mr. and Mrs. Jones, Herr Tanaka and Signora
> Sabatini;
> within each of them vault after vault opened endlessly.

So here we are. We have a funny, brave, affectionate poet of great depth. He fought for his way—essentially a religious way—against enormous opposition during the Sixties and Seventies from the doctrinaire critics and Maoist skinflints who dominated Swedish intellectual life at that time. He didn't waver. In "Fire Script" he says to his wife,

> The night heavens gave off moos.
> We stole milk from the cosmos and survived.

Rilke and the Holy

I.

Rilke's first large book, and the first he had confidence in, was *Das Stun-denbuch*, which I have translated as *A Book for the Hours of Prayer*. The German title suggests a medieval monk's or nun's handbook of prayers. *Innigkeit* is the German word associated with such poetry, which becomes "inwardness" in English; but the syllables of the German word have so much more drive and finality than the English sounds. *Innigkeit* has the depth of a well where one finds water. And water is the element of this book, a water whose source Rilke found inside himself.

The first group of poems in the book, called "The book of Monkish Life," came in a wonderful rush, shortly after Rilke returned home from a trip to Russia with Lou Andreas-Salomé and her husband in 1899. He was twenty-three years old. Until then he had felt his life to be constricted and restrained: the narrow streets of his native Prague seemed stiflingly provincial, and his mother's love and her piety left little space for him. He later said of her:

> In some heart-attic she is tucked away
> and Christ comes there to wash her every day.

The power of Lou Andreas-Salomé's personality and the open spaces of the Russian plains astounded him. He understood Russia's outer space as inner space. It lay east of "Europe":

Sometimes a man stands up during supper
and walks outdoors, and keeps on walking
because of a church that stands somewhere in the East.

And his children say blessings on him as if he were dead.

And another man, who remains inside his own house,
stays there, inside the dishes and in the glasses,
so that his children have to go far out into the world
toward that same church, which he forgot.

He doesn't mean any orthodox church, but says that if a man walks toward
that inner space, he will free his children. It is not too late.

Because One Man wanted so much to have you,
I know that we can all want you.

He is astonished to realize that this wanting and having are perfectly possible
right now, even for twentieth-century man. Growth is growth into space, as
a tree grows through its rings, as the snail grows in spirals and the solar system moves in circles:

I live my life in growing orbits
which move out over the things of the world.
Perhaps I can never achieve the last,
but that will be my attempt.

I am circling toward God, around the ancient tower,
and I have been circling for a thousand years,
and I still don't know if I am a falcon, or a storm,
or a great song.

In his surprise he doesn't even identify himself as a man; he could be a falcon
or a storm.

Before his Russian trip, Rilke had spent a few months in Italy, and he
loved the religious paintings of the early Renaissance, the heavy gold frames,
the gold flake: he noticed that the Mediterranean psyche associated gold

with religious feeling. But he saw something different when he looked within himself—what we could call a North European unconscious.

> I have many brothers in the South.
> Laurels stand there in monastery gardens.
> I know in what a human way they imagine the Madonna,
> and I think often of young Titians
> through whom God walks burning.

> Yet no matter how deeply I go down into myself
> my God is dark, and like a webbing made
> of a hundred roots, that drink in silence.

He then realizes that he may have claimed too much for himself, and he delicately suggests how unformed he is:

> I know that my trunk rose from his warmth, but that's all,
> because my branches hardly move at all
> near the ground, and only wave a little in the wind.

The language broods; it stays in the moist mood of the North European unconscious. The holy is below us, not above; and a line moves to descend, to dip down, to touch water that lies so near we are astonished our hands haven't dipped into it before. The lines suggest holy depth, always distant, always close.

> I love the dark hours of my being
> in which my senses drop into the deep.

He becomes aware that he has two separate lives.

> My life is not this steeply sloping hour,
> in which you see me hurrying. . . .
> I am only one of my many mouths,
> and at that the one that will be still the soonest.

He loves the tension between the poles, hurry and quiet, life and death. Even though death's note wants to dominate, he is the rest between two notes:

> . . . in the dark interval, reconciled,
> —they stay there trembling.
>> And the song goes on, beautiful.

The problem is not whether the song will continue, but whether a dark space can be found where the notes can resonate. This dark space resembles the hub of a wheel, a pitcher, the hold of a ship that carries us "through the wildest storm of all," the grave earth under the tree, the lower branches of a pine, the darkness at the edge of a bonfire. The dark space is the water in the well. This hub, or hold, or dark space, is not a Pre-Raphaelite preciosity, nor the light of narcissism; the dark space can be rough and dangerous. It is something out there, with the energy of an animal, and at the same instant it is far inside. Once a man or a woman inhabits that space, he or she finds it hidden inside objects, in walnuts or tree roots, in places where people don't ordinarily look for it.

> I find you in all these things of the world
> that I love calmly, like a brother;
> in things no one cares for you brood like a seed;
> and to powerful things you give an immense power.
>
> Strength plays such a marvelous game—
> it moves through the things of the world like a servant,
> groping out in roots, tapering in trunks,
> and in the treetops like a rising from the dead.

How magnificent the last line is! In German: "*und in den Wipfeln wie ein Aufer-stehn.*" This "darkness" or "hub" or "circling power" is a strength best discovered in objects. The word Rilke loves, *Ding*, literally "thing," is difficult. Of course, he means "things" and "objects" by it, but also animals, and even thunder and rocks. "Things of the world" is an attempt to include what he includes in it. He notices that the energy takes the shape and mood of the creature it is in—when it roots, it gropes; when it trunks, it tapers.

A Book for the Hours of Prayer circles, then, with an athletic power inside inner space, among secret things.

> and in the silent, sometimes hardly moving times
> when something is coming near,
> I want to be with those who know secret things
> or else alone.

It can be a shock for readers used to public literature. Most American writers begin proudly, even aggressively, in the outer world: Thoreau, Mark Twain, Howells, Robinson Jeffers, Marianne Moore, Robert Frost, the Eliot who listened to conversations in bars, the William Carlos Williams who paid attention to back sheds and wheelbarrows. Their start in the outer world is marvelous, but Rilke begins elsewhere. When I first read Rilke in my twenties, I felt a deep shock upon realizing the amount of introversion he had achieved, and the adult attention he paid to inner states. From the pragmatist or objectivist point of view, Rilke goes too far in this attention; he goes over the line. The American, in Latin America or North America, is willing to accept some introversion, but when it goes this far, he may dismiss the whole thing as solipsism, or as an evasion of political responsibility. Neruda attacked Rilke on precisely this point, in "Poetes Celestes," though late in his life he took back the criticism.

Rilke knows what Tolstoy knows in *The Death of Ivan Ilyich*: that our day-by-day life, with its patterns and familiar objects, can become a husk that blocks anything fresh from coming in. Before the industrial revolution brought its various creature comforts, it is conceivable that the shocks of winter cold, sudden poverties, plague, brutal invasions, abrupt unexplainable deaths regularly broke the husk. In our time the husk is strong, and Rilke turns to look at it. A man or woman inside the husk, Rilke says, resembles a medieval city that has succeeded—so far—in withstanding or ignoring a siege.

> All of you undisturbed cities,
> haven't you ever longed for the Enemy?

The fairy tale called "Sleeping Beauty" describes this situation of invisible siege, where the woman—and perhaps the soul—sleeps undisturbed inside a wall of thorns. No one can get through. In the fairy tale, the "man" or the "suitor" is the awakening force, who fails again and again; the Sufis interpret the last suitor as the spiritual teacher or master. In Rilke's poem the awakening force is a massive energy *out there*, symbolized by an encamped army and the countryside itself:

> He lies outside the walls like a countryside. . . .
> Climb up on your roofs and look out:
> his camp is there, and his morale doesn't falter,
> his numbers do not decrease, he will not grow weaker,
> and he sends no one into the city to threaten
> or promise, and no one to negotiate.

When I translated the last few lines, I felt frightened; the lines imply that the awakening force will not make the first move; perhaps no one will come to help, no parents, no gurus, no Christ. When the walls break, Rilke says, they break "in silence."

When the walls are broken, the energy approaches.

> and in the silent, sometimes hardly moving times
> when something is coming near,
> I want to be with those who know secret things
> or else alone.

Realizing that the energy that tapers in trunks and gropes in roots can be met or touched, Rilke begins to speak of that energy as "you." Sometimes the "you" is the dark space I've mentioned, inhabiting the hold or the pitcher:

> You darkness, that I come from,
> I love you more than all the fires
> that fence in the world. . . .

Sometimes the "you" is a primitive initiatory force, female in tone:

> you are the early dawn, from whom the whole morning rose . . .

At other times it is the inner guide, a Khadir or "Faithful John"; at yet other times it is the collective "God" in his more conventional role.

> And if that is arrogance, then I will stay arrogant
> for the sake of my prayer
> that is so sincere and solitary
> standing before your cloudy forehead.

When he speaks of it as "deltas," or when he says

> . . . your primitive wind is blowing
> the fragrance of your marvelous power
> to every being and every creature in need

We sense it is related to the primitive uprushing of non-ego waters that Freud called "the unconscious." Freud published *The Interpretation of Dreams* in 1899, the same year Rilke wrote the first group of these poems. Rilke does not insist on any one identification of the "you," nor does he insist that he is always active. In one energetic and sweet poem, he describes himself as no more active than a watchman in the wine fields, who stays in a shed at night to keep robbers away.

> odor pours out from your heavy boughs,
> and you never ask if I am keeping watch or not;
> confident, dissolved by the juices, your depths
> keep climbing past me silently.

In *A Book for the Hours of Prayer*, Rilke included three separate groups of poems, written in different places at different times. The second group, which he called "The Book of Pilgrimage," was written two years after his return from Russia. A selection from that group begins here with poem number 18. He had moved to an artists' colony called Worpswede, near Bremen, in a moorlike country, and was living among landscape painters. We notice in Rilke's creative life, as in Yeats's and Mallarmé's, the cross-fertilization between poetry and painting; in Rilke's case, between poetry and sculpture as well. The two painters Heinrich Vogeler and Otto Modersohn became close friends of Rilke's at Worpswede; Rilke was probably in love with both Paula Becker and Clara Westhoff. He loved Paula Becker deeply but she married Otto

Modersohn, and it was Clara, a sculptor of great ability, whom Rilke married.

The sense of "the road" continues in "The Book of Pilgrimage"; the sense of danger also increases. Rilke sees that it is possible to "die on the road" if you leave the conventional warmth of collectivized feeling.

> The tiny town is only a passing-over place,
> worried and afraid, between two huge spaces. . . .
>
> And those who leave the town wander a long way off
> and many perhaps die on the road.

During this time he wrote "Already the ripening barberries are red," his marvelous poem on fall. In fall Rilke always tried to give himself time alone to look within; in the fall, he found, one can look down long avenues of trees inside, when the vision is not blocked by leaves.

> Already the ripening barberries are red,
> and the old asters hardly breathe in their beds.
> The man who is not rich now as summer goes
> will wait and wait and never be himself.

The test of whether you owned yourself was this: to close the eyes, and wait to see what sort of images rose up around you in the dark.

> The man who cannot quietly close his eyes,
> certain that there is vision after vision
> inside, simply waiting until nighttime
> to rise all around him in the darkness—
> it's all over for him, he's like an old man.

The danger is greatest for those who have started on the road. If the psychic power is then dissipated by sociability or dishonesty or triviality, the man or woman is in danger.

> Nothing else will come up; no more days will open,
> and everything that does happen will cheat him.

Even you, my God. And you are like a stone
that draws him daily deeper into the depths.

God himself is dangerous. These lines mark the first appearance of this idea,
which will later dominate the Second Elegy.

Rilke named the last group of poems "The Book of Poverty and
Death," and a selection from that group begins here with poem number 22.
By that time two more years had passed; Clara and he had married, and their
daughter Ruth had been born. Supporting a family at Worpswede was impossible, and he and Clara decided he should accept a commission on a prose
piece and move to Paris. He wrote the third set of poems in a rush, at Viareg-
gio, but they came after his first experience of a great modern city, of Paris.

And the great cities, Lord, what are they?
Places disintegrating and abandoned.
The city I know resembles animals fleeing from a fire.
The shelter it gave me has no shelter now,
and the age of the cities is nearly over.

Neither writing nor living was easy.

It's possible I am pushing through solid rock
in flintlike layers, as the ore lies, alone;
I am such a long way in I see no way through,
and no space: everything is close to my face,
and everything close to my face is stone.

Saint Francis, whom he loved, had praised poverty; but the idea didn't seem
useful to the poor in Paris.

And where is he, the clear one, whose tone rings to us?
Why don't the poor feel him, the rejoicing one,
mastering us, the young one, even though far off?

Why doesn't he climb then in their dusk—
the great evening star of poverty.

Rilke in Paris, then, began to experience a poverty that does not necessarily lead to spirit; and his tremendous energy turned to face that dark.

2.

Clara Westhoff had been a student of Rodin. Through her, Rilke received a commission to write a monograph on the sculptor. He was twenty-six when he arrived in Paris. With that move, he became a European, and a city poet as well, living on the edge of poverty. *The Notebooks of Malte Laurids Brigge* contains some of this Paris life. Rilke's superb gift for the image helped him to grasp what he saw there and to understand why it frightened him. He discovered that faces wear out. In the old days, faces were made to last a whole lifetime, but now sometimes the face grows thin, and the "no-face" begins to show through. He found himself thinking that after the industrial revolution the ready-made death dominates—the stroke death, the heart-attack death, the accident death, the cancer death. . . . They were all ready-made, and one simply stepped into one or the other as into ready-made clothes. "O Lord, give each person his own personal death."

Rilke had begun a way of living that later—except for visits to castles or the apartments of the rich—became typical for him: a city, not much money, one respectable suit, a small room, often on a noisy street because it takes money to purchase silence, meals eaten alone in a dairy restaurant, a sense of being hunted, living as an outsider, the richness all hidden in his chest, none visible on the outside. He would rent a room, and next door a man would play the violin till late at night. This had happened in so many cities.

> Strange violin, are you following me?
> In how many distant cities already
> has your lonely night spoken to mine?
> Are a hundred playing you? Or only one? . . .
>
> Why am I always the neighbor to those men
> who force you in fear to sing
> and to say: The heaviness of life
> is heavier even than the weight of things.

Rilke now began to notice the heaviness inside things—how much angry, even malevolent, energy there is in a blind man's cane, how much contagious despair in the chair inherited with a furnished room, especially in the shiny spot on the chair back where so many failed introverts have leaned their heads. He feels utterly out of place in a middle-class living room. Sofas are so packed with gross energy they terrify the unconscious.

His poem "The Solitary Person" helped me so much in my twenties. Like many others of my generation, I was trying to live for my talent or maybe for "the infinite," with almost no money, in a rented room with one chair and a table, not talking. What a shock it was to go home for Thanksgiving. The sofas and the self-confident turkey said that the life I was leading was wrong; they were right. But Rilke's poem says to the young man or woman that the "objectless" life they are leading is not wrong. The not fitting in they experience comes from the best part of themselves, not the weakest part, and the pain is the cracking of the walls as the room grows. Writing these poems, Rilke is not an aesthete, but a wise grandfather.

During his first four years in Paris he worked on an intense book called *Das Buch der Bilder,* the mood very different from the mood of his first book. The title translates as a book of images or paintings. I've called it *The Book of Pictures* to emphasize that he is not writing a literary book about images but rather a painterly book in which he adopts some of the disciplines of painting.

"From Childhood" is an example. This poem, which describes how caught up he was in his mother as a boy, he composed the way a painter like Rembrandt composed a canvas. Rilke paints both background and foreground, the shadows and the light. Two figures only are painted in, the boy and his mother.

> The darkness in the room was like enormous riches:
> there the child was sitting, wonderfully alone.
> And when the mother entered, as if in a dream,
> a glass quaked in the silent china closet.
> She felt it, how the room was betraying her,
> and kissed her child, saying, "Are you here?"
> Then both looked toward the piano in fear,
> for often at evening she would have a song
> in which the child found himself strangely caught.

Among the furniture, a single glass is lit up and the large dark piano. As a painter must, he chooses one instant to stand for the whole flowing relationship: the moment the mother plays the song. The mother's hand with its big ring moves eternally over the keys, and the boy eternally watches.

> He sat alone still. His great gaze hung
> upon her hand, which, totally bowed down by the ring,
> walked over the white keys
> as if plowing through deep drifts of snow.

I once heard a story of Rilke's early life with his mother. It seems she wanted a girl, not a boy; and she gave him seven or eight middle names, including Maria. When he was two or three years old, Rilke would knock on the living room door from the hall. "Who is there . . . is it Rainer?" "No, that naughty Rainer is dead." "Is it Margaret?" "Yes." "Well, then you can come in." Rilke would then enter, wearing a small dress, and he and his mother would have tea. I tell this story because so often his critics omit, in the interest of aesthetics, the root details of his life. American critics tend to write of Rilke's using an elaborate and attenuated language, praising so justly his powers of discrimination, that we don't realize what a fierce and sordid struggle he fought with his mother—like Kafka did with his father. He fought through and won. Without cunning, courage, and discipline, Rilke would have been wiped out.

The mood of *The Book of Pictures* is psychic change, the mood when the soul ground is shaken. There are times for all of us when the poles of life become inexplicably reversed, the feelings go naked, one is exposed; and yet one is pleased that some old dependencies, especially a shameful dependence on comfort, are ending. Robert Lowell mentions it at the end of "The Exile's Return": "and your life is in your hands." Rilke opens his picture book with the poem "Entrance" or "The Way In," in which the young, doubtful, world-shy, room-loving writer is urged to leave what he knows so well.

> Whoever you are: some evening take a step
> out of your house, which you know so well.
> Enormous space is near, your house lies wherever it begins,
> whoever you are.
> Your eyes find it hard to tear themselves

from the sloping threshold, but with your eyes
slowly, slowly, lift one black tree
up, so it stands against the sky: skinny, alone.
With that you have made the World. The world is immense
and like a word that is still growing in the silence.
In the same moment that your will grasps it,
your eyes, feeling its subtlety, will leave it. . . .

In the masterpiece "The Man Watching," Rilke pours out his substance in generous rivers.

I can tell by the way the trees beat, after
so many dull days, on my worried windowpanes
that a storm is coming,
and I hear the far-off fields say things
I can't bear without a friend,
I can't love without a sister.

The storm, the shifter of shapes, drives on
across the woods and across time,
and the world looks as if it had no age:
the landscape, like a line in the psalm book,
is seriousness and weight and eternity.

What we choose to fight is so tiny!
What fights with us is so great!

Rilke then moves to shape and contain the picture of fighting by means better known to painters than to poets. A poet might list many examples of struggle—with a dragon, with a teacher, with a woman, because language can move through time. Rilke chooses one pair of fighters, Jacob and the Angel, and says everything through them. He has chosen as if he were a sculptor, and he treats the two figures as if he were sculpting bodies.

I mean the Angel who appeared
to the wrestlers of the Old Testament:
when the wrestler's sinews

grew long like metal strings,
he felt them under his fingers
like chords of deep music.

So the discipline of concentration here is a gift from painters and sculptors. The waters that flowed through his first book have become stronger. Leaving behind the triumphant joy of longing, Rilke stands alone with his own life, not triumphant, not defeated, watching a sunset.

Slowly the west reaches for clothes of new colors
which it passes to a row of ancient trees.
You look, and soon these two worlds both leave you,
one part climbs towards heaven, one sinks to earth . . .

leaving you (it is impossible to untangle the threads)
your own life, timid and standing high and growing,
so that, sometimes blocked in, sometimes reaching out,
one moment your life is a stone in you, and the next, a star.

By now he has learned to write not only out of the assurance that his underground water is inexhaustible, but also out of the quivering of growth, so close to defeat, when the whole life seems in doubt; perhaps it is a life lived by a fool. He values that sensation of failure. He eats the shock for the sake of the seed. And he writes more fall poems. He feels a truth in fall expressed by the sound of dry leaves scraping along a street.

Whoever has no house by now will not build.
Whoever is alone now will remain alone,
will wait up, read, write long letters,
and walk along sidewalks under large trees,
not going home, as the leaves fall and blow away.

He holds the reader to a sense of how alone the soul is.

We're all falling. This hand here is falling.
And look at the other one. . . . It's in them all.

Rilke wants to provide readers with a book that would be like a big room full of paintings. Here the man or woman who resists the collective can enter and walk around; no one will bother him or demand conversation. The stroller can go up to one of the poems in the book and look at it closely, for its detail, and then back away and look from a distance. Rilke avoids the old moral poem with its closing couplet; when his poem ends it is still moving. He simply passes the poem to the reader, and goes back to his solitude. Vermeer often paints an open window, perhaps to suggest outer space; a room's interior to suggest inner space; a map on the wall to suggest roads; and, finally, a mysterious shape seen from the back. Rilke's poems are surprisingly intimate, and yet he has a reserve like Akhmatova's: he tells and he doesn't tell. In a poem like "Moving Forward," there is no evasive persona as in Eliot's work; we see Rilke looking at a painting. When he is growing, he says, he feels that dogs and trees are relatives, and that he can see farther into a painting, see into it more deeply.

> The deep parts of my life pour onward,
> as if the river shores were opening out.
> It seems that things are more like me now,
> that I can see farther into paintings.
> I feel closer to what language can't reach.
> With my senses, as with birds, I climb
> into the windy heaven, out of the oak,
> and in the ponds broken off from the sky
> my feeling sinks, as if standing on fishes.

The last two lines in German are:

> und in den abgebrochnen Tag der Teiche
> sinkt, wie auf Fischen stehend, men Gefühl.

I have always loved these lines, the fish image is a triumph, an amazing union of senses. It embodies exultation, humility, and danger in a single image. And we feel that the image doesn't say less than the truth, nor more than the truth. A translator can sometimes carry over such an image if it is vivid; but Rilke's elaborate and thoroughgoing labor on sound cannot be conveyed. In English his poems sound colorless. I've tried for ten years to get the last three lines of "October Day" right, with their lonely sound of blowing leaves and their pride in solitude, but I can't do it. So the reader shouldn't believe he has the power here of the poems in German.

The first edition of *Das Buch der Bilder* was published in 1902. Rilke added a few poems for the second edition, among them the ten called The Voices, which I've included in this collection. Rilke sent them to his publisher with a note, in which he remarks that perhaps this group will "keep the book from being purely aesthetic." I think he means that his sensibility is not the point of these poems. Translating them, one has to try to catch the voice tones of suicides, and the thought rhythms of mad people. The poems are a leap across the gap between people. To play his part, the reader should read them aloud.

3.

In September of 1905, Rodin offered Rilke a job as his secretary. Rilke accepted, moved to Meudon, and by doing so, brought himself into a strong friendship with Rodin. Rodin taught him a great deal. For an artist, Rodin said, the thing is not dreaming, or talking, but work. "Travailler, travailler, travailler!" he shouted once, trying to explain how new works came to him. When Rilke confided one day that he hadn't been writing lately, Rodin did not advise him to change diet or find a new relationship; he suggested that Rilke go to the zoo. What shall I do there? Look at an animal until you see it. Two or three weeks might not be too long. Rilke chose a panther; and wrote the first of his "seeing" poems, the famous poem which imitates in its sound the panther's walk. Rilke's letters mention a small and ancient sculpture of a panther which Rodin owned, on which he also practiced his seeing. Rilke sensed something new in this panther poem, and though he finished it before *The Book of Pictures* was published, he saved it, to see what other poems might come to join it.

Rilke's early poetry did not satisfy him; he felt many of the poems were vague, poetic, and talky. His dissatisfaction led to a massive effort, which I've mentioned, to make the poems in *The Book of Pictures* blocky and weighty, with human shapes in them. His poems by 1906 had a marvelous solidity, but with Rodin's help he as about to enter a new area. He was about to ask an object a question and then listen. As Antonio Machado said:

To talk with someone,
ask a question first . . .
then, listen.

In *The Book of Pictures* Rilke still wrote from personal memory—the poem
about his mother and himself is an example—or from historical memory:
the poems about Karl the Twelfth or the Last Supper are examples. Memory
offered its mysterious substance, unseen by the physical eye, and then the
poet made sure by vivid images that we could see it.

Through Rodin's example and words, Rilke began to think that seeing
may be something quite different from what he had been doing. Other poets
have practiced seeing. Goethe observed plants meticulously with scientific
method, and this labor seemed to feed his oceanic, passionate poems, to fill
them with inward intensity. Goethe respected the discipline of seeing. Novalis, slightly younger than Goethe, wrote an aphorism in 1800 and declared
that there are two natural stages in an artist's life. During the first stage the
artist goes inward, to *Innigkeit*, exclusive contemplation of the self, a stage that
may last years. But if an artist stays there, he or she has gone only halfway,
because the second stage, according to Novalis, involves a "sober and spontaneous" observation of the outer world. Putting "sober" and "spontaneous"
next to each other is wonderful. Both adjectives are apt for Dürer's crab or
his clump of marsh grass or his rabbit; both apply to the meticulous detail
Chinese artists influenced by Buddhism brought into their paintings. It's as
if there was some spiritual force that leaves our body through the eyes, spontaneously pulled out, and this force or being gets stronger precisely by being
out there, seeing what is not us. It gets stronger because there is something
that responds. Walter Spink has called attention to the old Chinese statement, "When a question is posed ceremoniously, the universe responds."

The living master of the "seeing" poem is Francis Ponge. His poems on
"The Orange," "The Oyster," "The End of Autumn," "The Pleasures of
the Door," are masterpieces. Ponge declares that the seeing poem represents
a new kind of literature, which goes beyond the categories "Romantic" and
"Classical." It does this by "the primacy accorded to matter, to the object,
to the unbelievable qualities that emerge from it." "Nothing can prevent the
meanings which have been locked into the simplest object or person from
always striking the hour. . . . In these terms, one will surely understand what
I consider to be the function of poetry. It is to nourish the spirit of man by

giving him the cosmos to suckle."

Rilke now gave himself to the discipline of Novalis's "second stage." He worked fiercely, intensely on the object, even listing objects not yet written about, and checking them off when he had finished his poem about them. The list still exists. All this work he saw as new, and he gave the title *Neue Gedichte* to his next collection. He wrote over two hundred of these poems working many hours a day from 1903 to 1908. Not all the poems in *New Poems* center on objects, but all involve concentrated seeing. "The Panther" and "The Swan" are strong examples of the seeing power. We are at a disadvantage reading the poems in translation, because Rilke's raft movement into the object is carried by the sound as it flows from one vowel to another. He uses sound in an ingenious, humorous, and sober way. Even those who do not know German can hear, if they read over the four opening lines of "The Panther" the *ä* sound repeating, returning monotonously, incessantly, like the bars before the panther's eyes.

> Sein Blick ist vom Vorübergehn der Stäbe
> so müd geworden, dass er nichts mehr hält.
> Ihm ist, als ob es tausend Stäbe gäbe
> und hinter tausend Stäben keine Welt.

In "The Swan," Rilke says that our lives are clumsy because we have to move constantly through what we haven't yet accomplished.

> This clumsy living that moves lumbering
> as if in ropes through what is not done
> reminds us of the awkward way the swan walks.

The German line waddles:

> Diese Mühsal, durch noch Ungetanes
> schwer und wie gebunden hinzugehn,
> gleicht dem ungeschaffnen Gang des Schwanes.

In the third stanza, the swan slips into the water. Rilke brings the swan's sailing into an eerie association with death; now the German changes and begins to sail. The motion itself becomes a thing. "Another way of approaching the thing is to consider it unnamed, unnameable," Ponge said.

Rilke wrote a poem on an old Roman road he knew well, lined with gravestones and tombs; the sound in German becomes nervous, tight, even hysterical. The road possesses some sort of nonhuman intelligence, which gives and receives "emptiness."

> . . . he lifts in a pitiful
> way his empty places up to the sky,
> looking around quickly, if any window
> is peeking. And while he waves
>
> the broad aqueducts to come on,
> the sky takes up his offer and gives him
> its empty places, which are longer lived.

His sound is once more crucial in the poem on the swan's lovemaking with Leda. I consider this poem a masterpiece several times over. Many poets have written on Leda and the Swan. With his work on seeing guiding him, Rilke writes not as a man interested in myth but as a person interested in the sensual experience of the swan during the lovemaking. A surprising union takes place at the end, not of a human being and myth, as in Yeats's brilliant poem, nor of woman and lover, but of the god and his feathers.

I've mentioned Rilke's love of sculpture; it was a force throughout his life. One is not surprised that he would write several of his seeing poems on statues, and I've included two of them. The Apollo statue, a headless torso, he saw again and again in the Louvre, where it has the title "Torso of a Youth from Miletus." There's a good photograph of it in the booklet called "The Visual Arts and Rilke's Poetry," published by the German Department at the University of Kansas (1978). Rilke's view of Apollo is startling, particularly in 1906, for its emphasis on Apollo's sexuality. Europe in general always took Apollo to be the god of rationality; recent speculation by Lopez-Pedraza and others sees Apollo as an energy linked to Dionysus and Hermes, much wilder and darker than "reason." Rilke's power of seeing pulled Apollo's dark side right out of the stone, before this side was know to Western students. Rilke emphasizes the animal nature of Apollo's body, and its sexual center. He draws from that concentrated study, that sensual experience of the eyes, one sentence: "You must change your life."

Apparently Rodin kept the Buddha statue in his garden at Meudon, a seated Buddha, with a golden oval shape around the head, suggesting developed spiritual light. Through looking at the oval, Rilke arrived at the almond.

> The core of every core, the kernel of every kernel,
> an almond! held in itself, deepening in sweetness:
> all of this, everything, right up to the stars,
> is the meat around your stone. Accept my bow.
>
> Oh, yes, you feel it, how the weights on you are gone!
> Your husk has reached into what has no end,
> and that is where the great saps are brewing now.
> On the outside a warmth is helping
>
> for, high, high above, your own suns are growing
> immense and they glow as they wheel around.
> Yet something has already started to live
> in you that will live longer than the suns.

4.

A new book by Rilke, as the reader will realize by now, did not mean merely a new collection but a new stage. A new stage was slow in coming after the publication of the "seeing" poems in 1908, perhaps because of the war tension in 1914-1918. (The German army drafted Rilke, and he served as an archivist in Vienna during 1916.) There were other reasons. From 1908, when he published the enlarged second edition of *Neue Gedichte,* until 1923, when he published the *Duino Elegies* and the *Sonnets to Orpheus,* no important collection appeared. Rilke waited with patience for fifteen years. He published a cycle on the Virgin Mary in 1913, but considered this to be an occasional poem.

It wasn't that he wrote no poetry during those years. He continued to write, and many of the poems were magnificent. But he had his heart set on a new departure, something deep and amazing that would justify his life, and it didn't happen. He didn't want occasional poems; he wanted something intense, fierce: a single work, a unified creation. As it turned out, he received two such works, at almost the same time. But in the meantime he wrote the group of poems I'm giving a sample of here. The poems are not well known because Rilke did not honor them by putting them in a book, and also because some have not been available in English, and finally because the official English translator chosen by the Rilke estate was J. B. Leishman, whose translations are so bad one sometimes can't figure out what the subject of the poem is. Leishman's translations have been a great frustration to everyone, and only now that Rilke's work is in the public domain can other translations come out.

Between the "seeing poems," then, and the waterfalls of feeling called the *Duino Elegies* and the *Sonnets,* there are the scattered or uncollected poems. Rilke wrote over two hundred ungathered poems during the last twenty years of his life. Also, many occasional poems have been found, in flyleafs or guestbooks, or composed spontaneously in letters. Some of the occasional poems are very fine, especially those he and Erika Mitterer exchanged in lieu of letters. Many treasures are waiting there for good translators.

After 1908, some of Rilke's certainties disappeared; his life lost some forward drive. He felt exhausted after *Neue Gedichte* and *Malte Laurids Brigge.* Europe itself seemed to falter. The European psyche had created with astounding intensity through the whole nineteenth century, throwing out indefatigable empire soldiers, fierce industrialists, energetic inventors, ingenious linguistic students, serious archeologists, exciting philosophical speculators, and psychological geniuses such as Janet, Bleuler, and Fechner. The peak was around 1888-89. About 1908, Europe began to falter, and in 1914 it committed suicide. Eliot, Pound, and Graves did not inherit the abundant high-spirited thought energy of Europe, as did Rilke, born only a few years earlier, but rather the flat death energy hidden inside the abundance. So we can expect despair in Rilke's poems after 1914, as he watched his inheritance, that tremendous human energy, collapse.

> Heart, whom will you cry out to? More and more alone,
> you make your way through the ununderstandable
> human beings. All the more hopeless perhaps
> since it holds to its old course,
> the course toward the future,
> that's lost.

Happened before. Did you mourn? What was it? A fallen
berry of joy, still green.
But now my oak of joy is breaking,
what is breaking in storm is my slowly
grown oak of joy.

Rilke wrote in August of 1914 a small group of poems welcoming the "war
god." He was later ashamed of them. His regret for that contagion slowed
his work. When he did write, he looked at what was missing in his first book:
his losses.

In 1914 he also decided he had done enough visualization work. What
he had not done was heart work. He wrote a poem that year called "Wen-
dung," which can be "Crisis" or "Turning." Michael Hamburger has a good
translation of it in his *Modern German Poetry 1910-1950*.

Work of seeing is done,
now practice heart-work
upon those images captive within you . . .

In his letters he blames himself for coldness, for being unable to give himself
as others do, especially as the great women lovers he had read of, Gaspara
Stampa and Marianne Alcoforado, had done. Why couldn't he do that? He
thought some of his coldness came from his mother's conventionality, and
he blamed her.

But also he and Clara throughout their lives had put their obligation to
art above their human obligations. They saw their road as heroic, the intense,
the noble one. The clarity with which they saw it was Europe's great gift to
them. Their daughter, Ruth, came second. They gave up trying to live together after 1902 or so. Ruth sometimes stayed with her mother in the studio,
sometimes with her grandmother. The dedication to art finally took the
form of a vivid, unforgettable detail. Rilke did not go to his daughter's wedding for fear of losing his concentration. This seems too heroic to me, but
the whole tradition has been virtually lost in the United States, so it is difficult to judge.

The life without heart no longer satisfied him. He wrote astonishing
letters, pledging eternal love to women he had never met. His poems, he said,
contained secret mating calls; one woman who heard that call was the superb

pianist Magda von Hattingberg, whom he called "Benvenuta." After corresponding passionately for several months, they decided to meet; but the meeting didn't seem to bear out the feeling in the correspondence. Her intelligence and feeling were immense, and the two became deep friends; but the fall from the earlier height made it clear to him that something was wrong, either his ideas of relationship ("each person protecting the solitude of the other") or his ability to love a human being.

A few of the ungathered poems show him struggling against his old Romantic idealization of women. One of them is "We Must Die Because We Have Known Them," from 1914, in which he adopts a saying from ancient Egypt to throw some dark light on his fear of women. The poem is well balanced, and brilliant in its images. The enthusiastic "anima" moods of adolescence, as Jung would call them, are compared to the adult male's more calm awareness of danger. He faces this fear clearly, and doesn't try to explain it, or give cultural reasons for it.

The ungathered poems in general leave the highly disciplined, chiseled technique of the seeing poems, and take on the mood of water. The lines are often uneven in length, the associations swift. Rilke moves more and more like Hermes each year, flying swiftly into the invisible and back. The poem "Left Out to Die" is not written for a reader who needs to be led by the hand through a poem. Rilke follows intuitive paths, doesn't look back, and strides surely along.

> Left out to die on the mountains of the heart. Look, how tiny it is,
> do you see: the final barn of language, and, above it,
> still tiny, one final
> granary of feeling. You've seen it before?
> Left out to die on the mountains of the heart.

Because the poem is so powerfully intuitive, it is difficult to comment on the lines without diminishing their mystery. We know the machine civilization shrivels Eros, and that diminishing surely lies under this poem. But is this fear in the heart an experience peculiar to writers and intellectuals? They leave the unconsciousness of popular culture, its unconscious sociability, and spend their lives trying to increase their store of consciousness. The poem moves through material similar to what Edmund Wilson explored in *The Wound and the Bow* and Thomas Mann in *Death in Venice*. Why is it that a person of sensibility in Western culture so often does not conclude in a joyful old age?

> Many goats and deer go here, their knowing whole,
> many surefooted mountain animals
> change grass or stay. And the big cared-for bird
> circles around the pure refusal of the peaks. But
> not cared for, here on the mountains of the heart . . .

The large protected bird retains his mystery, circling around the *Verweigerung* of the peaks. That *Verweigerung*—literally "denial"—could be an eternal nay-saying, or self-denial, or even asceticism.

I suppose the most astonishing of these late poems are about music and about the hand. In both, the concentration learned in the seeing poems reappears, now concentrated on feelings shared with others. He doesn't say, "I like music"; in fact, the word "I" never appears in "On Music" at all. But he hears, and hears what others hear. Astonishing transformations take place in the poem: ears turn to eyes, music turns into a "countryside we can hear." He suggests that in Bach's music, for example, the deepest, most interior thing in us suddenly appears out there, as amazing space, as "the other side of the air."

His hand poem I find astonishing too. His longing to take the hands of others deepened, I think, as he grew older, and two years before he died, he wrote "Palm." The roads in the palm walk themselves, he says; that is, the lines in our palm alter according to our experiences. A beautiful detail appears: we notice the hills of our own palm only when it meets another person's. Entering another person's hand resembles traveling through a countryside; when we arrive at the other palm, we fill it, as a train station is filled with a train, with the joy of having arrived.

As he gets older, Rilke urges poets again and again to train their imagination like a body, to aim and struggle for something intense. Being carried along, drifting, is not enough. He wants them to reach far out, not to be so lazy, to labor.

> To work with things is not hubris
> when building the association beyond words;
> denser and denser the pattern becomes—
> being carried along is not enough.

He imagines vast associations, the intricate harmony the Renaissance thinkers guessed at, the dream that each particle knows of every other particle, and even knows that we are observing it. To do nothing in such a world implies, as Rumi says, that "no gifts have been given."

> Take your well-disciplined strengths
> and stretch them between two
> opposing poles. Because inside human beings
> is where God learns.

5.

I decided not to include the *Elegies* in this collection. There were two reasons. The *Elegies* are the most accessible part in English of Rilke's work; they have been rendered by a surprising number of translators. Stephen Spender worked over the Leishman translation years ago, improving it vastly; MacIntyre did the *Elegies* for the University of California Press; Stephen Garney and Jay Wilson published a new version in 1972; both Al Poulin and David Young have published new versions since then. It is true that the sound of the *Elegies* has not yet been brought over into English. I'm not sure what that would require. Moreover, I'm not convinced that the *Elegies* are Rilke's great work. There's something about them that is admirable but not likable. When Rilke's friend Magda von Hattingberg heard Rilke read some of the early passages, she told him that she felt a hostility to life in them. She had always disliked his essay attacking dolls; and she concluded there was a force in him that wanted to destroy certain simple joys. Western culture often instills in its artists an anxious craving to create the monumental work. The *Elegies* are magnificent in theme and sound, but they feel almost too cultured, as if they belonged to the memory banks of Europe, and not to an uncertain person called Rilke. I sense that certain weaknesses Rilke grieved over in private have become triumphs in the massive music of the *Elegies*. *Sonnets to Orpheus* is the masterpiece of his late life, I think. I glimpse his swiftly appearing, swiftly disappearing Hermes personality more clearly in these poems than anywhere else.

Rilke always felt that there was something sinister in him, a hankering that stories would turn out badly, that bodies in the Resurrection would stand up with worms; he felt a constant anger at Christian piety, which turns into a cold hostility toward Christ, a rage against Christ's "interference." He felt in his own personality a blackness, the weight that appears in *Malte Laurids Brigge,* so heavy that Rilke wasn't sure that he could get out from under that book and walk again.

Yet he had always believed that the greatest art includes praise, amounts to praise. "To praise is the whole thing!" That instinct to praise, so apparent and persistent in primitive poetry, in Pindar, in ancient China, in Persia, in Provence, became weakened in later Europe; poetry of praise became unfashionable, especially among twentieth-century poets. For years Rilke had wanted to praise, but he couldn't find the door to the mine. One day, in February of 1922, while strolling about Valais, he saw in a shopwindow an old sketch of Orpheus, which Cima de Conegliano had sketched in 1518. It showed Orpheus playing a flute, surrounded by animals, listening. Our complaints about life do not intrigue animals, so perhaps Orpheus was praising. Furthermore, Orpheus's ability to play so that animals could hear it was surely connected to his descent into the dark. The ancient world loved that scene: Orpheus is playing, surrounded by listening animals. A third element might be the listening.

Rilke had adopted the discipline of seeing: he spent years on that road. It occurred to him now that listening might be a road in itself. It might be a great road. Perhaps one of the strengths of the twentieth century is our ability to listen. And he opened the sonnets with speculation on what is happening to the ear.

> Orpheus is singing! A tree inside the ear! . . .
>
> Animals created by silence came forward from the clear
> and relaxed forest where their lairs were,
> and it turned out the reason they were so full of silence
> was not cunning, and not terror,
>
> it was listening. Growling, yelping, grunting now
> seemed all nonsense to them.

We didn't always know how to listen. Learning to listen is a cultural gift.

                              And where before
             there was hardly a shed where this listening could go,

             a rough shelter put up out of brushy longings,
             with an entrance gate whose poles were wobbly,
             you created a temple for them deep inside their ears.

Certain artists do open a new space in the ear, so that we hear something we've never heard before; I suppose Bach belongs to that group, Rameau, Cervantes, Chaucer, Rumi, Vallejo.

The *Elegies* and *Sonnets* came, as Rilke's great work had always come, in rushes, in a flood. The first group of sonnets arrived fully formed, images and rhythm and rhymes in place. In fact, sitting at a window seat, writing, he would occasionally miss a rhyme, even though he was writing as fast as he could. He regarded the *Sonnets* and *Elegies* as a gift from outside himself.

This experience of inflooding becomes a part of the content of the sonnets. To return to the theme: if listening is a road, a road on which one can travel, and if one learns at last how to listen, then following the road downward should be easy. "A god can do it." But it isn't. When a fork appears, we're lost. The ancient Greeks sometimes built a small temple for Apollo at a crossroads, and Rilke mentions that; if a man or woman came to the crossroads, and didn't know which road to take, he or she could go inside the temple, meditate in silence, and find out which way to go.

             A man is split. And where two roads intersect
             inside us, no one has built the Singer's Temple.

Then we arrive at the problem of desire, desiring ecstasy, desiring salvation.

             Writing poetry as we learn from you is not desiring,
             not wanting something that can ever be achieved.

When a man or a woman is singing, or writing poems—in the ancient world they were identical—what is going on? True singing, Rilke says, does not involve the attempt to accomplish something, to become a better person, to achieve salvation, or to publish a book. Using the heavy syllable "ah," which can't be reproduced in translation, he says: *"Gesang ist Dasein."* The sounds are rooted and strong. If we translate the phrase literally as "Singing is being," the result is pitiful. The whole meaning is gone, because the vowels are too light. I compromised, saying, "To write poetry is to be alive." "For a god that's easy." Rilke, then, surprisingly to me, declares that the love poems one writes in one's twenties are not true "singing." There's something a bit mechanical in them, unearned, and maybe also they lack terror.

> Yes, you are young, and you love, and the voice
> forces your mouth open—that is lovely, but learn
>
> to forget that breaking into song. It doesn't last.
> Real singing is a different movement of air.
> Air moving around nothing. A breathing in a god. A wind.

Rilke not only announces a theme, he thinks about it. Into this one sonnet he pours enough ideas to keep the normal poet working for five years. Oversimplifying, one could say that each poet feels inside his or her poem, that is, contributes feeling; other poets contribute perceptions as well, or perceive. Still others feel and perceive and think also. Wallace Stevens is surely one of those. It is wonderful to watch Goethe think in a poem, or Rumi. Rilke's thinking, when it arrives, does not appear as an ironic conceit, which is an offshoot of logic. Rilke in fact warned young poets against irony; when they feel irony is "becoming too intimate," they should avoid it. "Try to get at the depth of things—that is one place irony never goes down to." Rilke wants the energy of thought, and doesn't find that it pushes out joy. Thinking brings new force into a poem, then, but it is risky, because if the reader finds an idea untrue, he rejects the whole poem. But in the eighth sonnet Rilke declares that grief doesn't belong in a poem unless praise has already been there. That idea, if adopted, would alter our poetry considerably. So Rilke takes the risk of thinking, and produces one of the most magnificent sequences of poems done in a Western language.

For the second sonnet especially, it might be helpful to mention Wera Ouckama Knoop. She was the daughter of old friends in Munich. Around seventeen, she became ill; it was an incurable glandular disease. She stopped dancing then, and as her body became more heavy and massive, she began to play music, and when her body became still heavier, she began to draw. The sequence touched Rilke. He wants the reader to understand that her figure is not an "anima figure"; she is a real girl.

> It was a girl, really—there is a double joy
> of poetry and music that she came from—
> and I could see her glowing through her spring clothes:
> she made a place to sleep inside my ear.

Because she continued to "dance," she overcame greediness. "See, she got up sleeping." Because of her listening as she neared death, a space opened inside him where she could enter his being. "And she slept in me." He didn't feel an obligation to instruct her, or she him. Her calm helped Rilke feel again many twentieth-century experiences: pastures seen from trains, and "every miracle I found in myself." Rilke responds to the flood of perceptions by writing apparent contradictions, as if the Awakener had preserved her from awakening, as if she had awakened still sleeping, as if the instant Eurydice faded back into Hades was exactly the instant she became solid . . . as if true being is not something that can ever be achieved. . . .

The simple facts of Orpheus's story became more and more nourishing to Rilke. Orpheus descended to the underworld and to the dark side of the psyche. Poetry doesn't mean much unless the writer has experienced the dark side. If you arrive at the Grail Castle, you may not ask the question. The dark sexual areas need to be entered. A man's praise of a woman, or hers of a man, become real after the descent to the other world. And the dead are also in that world. The world of the dead—which human beings enter with the help of a medium, or through imagining their own deaths, or through descending into Hades—also underlies true praise.

> He can bend down the branches of the willow best
> who has experienced the roots of the willow.

Do not entice the dead, Rilke says; simply be confident that they are under your eyelids. He remarks then that those who descend to the dead praise all those inventions that bring the living together: the ring, the water jar, and the bodice clasp.

Rilke suggests that ecstasy, constant good feeling, bliss, hopeful philosophical systems, enlightenment, mean nothing unless the shadow energies have been invited to take part. If people look straight ahead, or look up, and fail to see the Dark Ones standing near, the food will not be nourishing. With that statement he joins Freud's thoughts for the second time, and joins the thought of Wilhelm Reich, and the whole pre-Christian trust in animals, in sexual life, and dark roots. Rilke early on had written: "My God is dark, and like a webbing made of a hundred roots."

> Is he from our world? No, his deep nature
> grows out of both of the kingdoms.

James Hillman in *The Dream and the Underworld* reminds us that the soul's ground is below us, in Hades. He says that to the Greeks Hades is moist and nourishing. "Each soul longs to go down." His concern parallels Rilke's concern. Rilke asks: "How do people learn now?" He imagines the three sisters Rejoicing, Longing, and Grief, as if they were sisters in a fairy tale. Rilke thinks that we have exhausted for now the possibility of learning through rejoicing. Longing doesn't pick up much now either, because it is constantly confessing error. "Only Grief still learns."

Rilke doesn't say that we must all praise, or we must all grieve; rather he tries to understand when it is time to do either. Perhaps praising when too young is wrong; perhaps one should be seeing then. After seeing, after listening, after going down, a man or woman could begin to praise. I sometimes think of Emily Dickinson when I read these lines:

> To praise is the whole thing! A woman who can praise
> comes toward us like ore out of the silences
> of rock. Her heart, that dies, presses out
> for others a wine that is fresh forever.

One other details might be helpful for the seventh sonnet. Archeologists were at work opening tombs. In one untouched tomb the King, the Queen, their family, the servants, the horses, all were lying in the dust. Just over one threshold wrist bones and finger bones were found, and nearby a silver platter, on which one could still see what had been apples and oranges. Rilke found this the most marvelous image conceivable for the poet who gives true praise.

> The mold in the catacomb of the king
> does not suggest that his praising is lies, nor

the fact that the gods cast shadows.

> He is one of the servants who does not go away,
> who still holds through the doors
> of the tomb trays of shining fruit.

One or two notes about the remaining sonnets: the old Roman coffins of stone, which had the lively name "body-eaters" (sarcophagi), survived the fall of Rome. During the Middle Ages, Italian farmers found a use for them. They would knock the ends out and line them up, so they became irrigation canals, carrying water from field to field. Rilke saw that, and it delighted him: water and mourning together.

> You stone coffins of the ancient world, I think of you
> with joy, you who have never left my feelings,
> through which the joyful waters of the days
> of Rome flow like some walker's singing.

At Arles he saw a large ancient earth grave; as he watched, butterflies flew out of it.

> Or those other graves so open, like the eyes
> of a shepherd who wakes up glad,
> inside full of silence and pale nettles—
> excited butterflies came flying out of them—

The tenth sonnet ends soberly. Even though, helped by our listening, we pass back and forth between the two worlds, traveling swiftly, we still may not know what silence is.

> Do we know what silence is, my friends, or not?
> This life that faces both ways
> has marked the human face from within.

In this selection you will find only the first ten sonnets. There are forty-five more of them, many of them just as magnificent as the first ten.

When at last the *Sonnets to Orpheus* and the *Duino Elegies* had arrived, Rilke understood that his life's work was over. Despite his neuroticism, his rootlessness, his uncertainty about which class he belonged to, his constant poverty, his confused human obligations, the war, he had done his work. He felt that life had given him a blessing, and in his turn, he laid the *Sonnets* "in the hands of Lou" (Lou Andreas-Salomé).

To me, Rilke stands for toughness, freedom from self-pity, ability to work, whatever one's life situation. He loves spades and hoes and uses images to dig down deeper. His attitude toward the past is to breathe in great art until it fills the lungs. His mode is sacrifice for the sake of that art. His spiritual friend, Rudolf Kassner, told him a sentence he brooded over for years: *"Der Weg von der Innigkeit zur Grösse geht durch das Opfer."* "Going from inwardness to greatness, the road passes through sacrifice." Having arrived at this sentence, we must leave him because we don't know what he sacrificed or what he gained.

In 1922 the *Sonnets* and *Elegies* were done. When not traveling, Rilke lived alone in his last home, the small tower at Muzot, in French-speaking Switzerland. His workroom is there as he left it. In the fall of 1923, he understood that something was wrong with his body, and spent the month of December in the sanatorium of Valmont. He had a rare form of leukemia, but the leukemia was not diagnosed until the late fall of 1926, and there was no cure. He lived in considerable pain throughout December, accompanied only by Nanny Wunderly-Volkart, and died in the very early morning of December 29, 1926. He had already written his epitaph. People all over Europe were reading his poems. The question is, how can a poet whom so many people read keep his privacy? It goes:

> *Rose, oh reiner Widerspruch, Lust,*
> *Niemandes Schlaf zu sein unter soviel*
> *Lidern.*

The difficult word is *Lidern.* This is the word for "eyelids" as well as for the petals of a rose. *Lidern* also makes a pun on *Lieder,* the German word for "songs" or "poems." No single English word forms a resonating box for these three realities. So we could make three versions.

> Rose, O pure contradiction, the desire
> to be no one's sleep under so many
> petals.

Rose, what a contradiction, desire
to be no one's sleep under so many
eyelids.

O rose, you say two things at once, the desire
to be no one's sleep under so many
poems.

Rilke died at fifty-one, and lies buried in the small Swiss churchyard in
Raron, with this epitaph above him.

James Wright's Clarity and Extravagance

In great poets we often find a calmness and undisturbed beauty, a serenity and a clarity. Li Po said:

> If you ask me why I dwell among green mountains,
> I would laugh silently. My soul is serene.
> The peach blossom follows the moving water.
> There is another heaven and earth beyond the world of men.
> <p align="right">(<i>translation by Robert Payne</i>)</p>

The poem becomes transparent. The Latin word associated with this quality is claritas. It's good to taste of this clear heaven, to bring it close to your chest, to experience it in youth before trouble, illness, poverty fall on you, and the dark times come

In James Wright's early poems, we meet a master of *claritas*. To some extent, he learned it from his teacher, John Crowe Ransom, whose prose and poetry shine with a consistent serenity that never faded. Wright learned claritas as well from the poems of Po Chu-I and Li Po, which Robert Payne gathered in *The White Pony*, published in the late Fifties.

Wright wrote a poem called "Three Steps to the Graveyard," which was published in his first book.

> When I went there first,
> In the spring, it was evening,

It was long hollow thorn
Laid under the locust,
And near to my feet
The crowfoot, the mayapple
Trod their limbs down
Till the stalk blew over.
It grew summer, O riches
Of girls on the lawn,
And boys' locks lying
Tousled on knees,
The picnickers leaving,
The day gone down.

When I went there again,
I walked with my father
Who held in his hand
The crowfoot, the mayapple,
And under my hands,
To hold off the sunlight,
I saw him going,
Between two trees;
When the lawn lay empty
It was the year's end,
It was the darkness,
It was long hollow thorn
To wound the bare shade,
The sheaf and the blade.

O now as I go there
The crowfoot, the mayapple
Blear the gray pond;
Beside the still waters
The field mouse tiptoes,
To hear the air sounding
The long hollow thorn.
I lean to the hollow,
But nothing blows there,

The day goes down.
The field mice flutter
Like grass and are gone,
And a skinny old woman
Scrubs at a stone,
Between two trees.

Transparency and lightheartedness can be intensified by a careful (if apparently careless) repeating of musical notes; we can feel these notes often in Whitman's poems.

Wright deepens the *claritas* by carefully singling out and repeating certain vowels. In the final stanza, *oh* occurs ten times, *ee* is repeated four times, and *ay* three times. The phoneme *er* repeats eight times, and so on. When we take in the poem, it is as if we see into a meadow through brilliant windows of sound.

Claritas brings some sort of inner shining. The language is transparent as water in a pool, dignified, shining from inside, clairvoyant, undisturbed, ecstatic. Jiménez says:

My beloved is only water,
that always passes away and does not deceive,
that always passes away and does not change,
that always passes away and does not end.

(translation by James Wright)

Juan Ramón Jiménez stayed in this shining all his life. Po Chu-I did the same; Wallace Stevens and Wislawa Szymborska are faithful to it. When poets remain in *claritas* all their life, Lorca delightedly calls them "angels."

In "Grandmother's Ghost," published in 1957, Wright imagines her ghost slipping over a shallow river and fluttering up a path:

Even before she reached the empty house,
She beat her wings ever so lightly, rose,
Followed a bee where apples blew like snow;
And then, forgetting what she wanted there,
Too full of blossom and green light to care,
She hurried to the ground, and slipped below.

James Wright didn't remain an "angel" all his life, so what was his route? He took a deep breath and went down.

> My name is James A. Wright, and I was born
> Twenty-five miles from this infected grave,
> In Martins Ferry, Ohio, where one slave
> To Hazel-Atlas Glass became my father.

The infected grave he mentions refers to the spot where a murderer named George Doty was buried by the State. Wright's poem "At the Executed Murderer's Grave," published in *Saint Judas* in 1959, is confusing, and confused: the author insists that he himself is a liar, and partly mad ("I run like the bewildered mad at St. Clair Sanitorium"). We could say that this poem opens the second stage of his work. He agrees to his own shame and guilt. Perhaps his guilt will heal "when every man stands still / By the last sea." He gives us for the first time the curious mix of honesty, hostility and bravado that will be his mood in many new poems.

> Order be damned, I do not want to die,
> Even to keep Belaire, Ohio, safe.

The revelation of fear and sorrow continues in dozens of poems, including those in *The Branch Will Not Break*, a title that, of course, implies it may break. On the flyleaf of my copy of *The Branch*, he wrote, "Let us hope the precious herbs will really be found."

The Branch Will Not Break begins with a poem that is set not in Ohio but in ancient China. It is called "As I Step Over a Puddle at the End of Winter, I Think of an Ancient Chinese Governor." There is a change here from his early poems, not only in mood, but in language habits; he no longer fills out the line with reassuring literary language. The second line ends abruptly after three words:

> Po Chu-i, balding old politician,
> What's the use?
> I think of you,
> Uneasily entering the gorges of the Yang-Tze,
> When you were being towed up the rapids

Toward some political job or other
In the city of Chungshou.
You made it, I guess,
By dark.

But it is 1960, it is almost spring again,
And the tall rocks of Minneapolis
Build me my own black twilight
Of bamboo ropes and waters.
Where is Yuan Chen, the friend you loved?
Where is the sea, that once solved the whole loneliness
Of the Midwest? Where is Minneapolis? I can see nothing
But the great terrible oak tree darkening with winter.
Did you find the city of isolated men beyond mountains?
Or have you been holding the end of a frayed rope
For a thousand years?

The poem is just as subtle and intimate as the light-hearted early poems, but we can feel the adult fatigue— "being towed up the rapids toward some political job or other" —and room is left in the poem for depression, exasperation, and sorrow. Perhaps the most important presence is a failure that can't be blamed on anyone else. The last image—of a man holding the end of a frayed rope for a thousand years—does express this failure, even if there were no other images in the poem.

If Wright were a painter, we would say that dark brown, purple and black have entered the palette. One impatient critic calculated that the words "dark," "darkness," and "darkening" appear over forty times in the 26 pages *The Branch Will Not Break* occupies in the *Collected Poems*. A fellow poet, Robert Hass, who greatly admires Wright's work, was exasperated by Wright's constant emphasis on shadowy material. Hass points to these lines from *Saint Judas:*

From prudes and muddying fools,
Kind Aphrodite, spare
All hunted criminals,
Hoboes, and whip-poor-wills,
And girls with rumpled hair.

None of these shadowy beings is Apollonian; they all share in some metaphorical dark. Hass worries that Wright is suffering from some sort of cultural disease, perhaps typical of the Sixties, in which everything dark is good. He expresses the fear that if Wright—or any poet—begins to celebrate the dark, the unlucky poet will stray into the confused and undifferentiated, and pull literature in after him. He will lose his ability to distinguish between light and dark. On the other side, we notice that the alchemists honored the "massa confusa" and they began their search there for the glory of the universe.

This turn toward the darkness in Wright's poetry does become persistent. In the *Branch Will Not Break* poems, it is clear that the shadow has become as nourishing as the light once was in his crowfoot and mayapple poems.

> My face is turned away from the sun.
> A horse grazes in my long shadow.

The doubts that many critics expressed about Wright's direction doubled and redoubled when he published "Lying in a Hammock at William Duffy's Farm in Pine Island, Minnesota." The title is a playful acknowledgment of the elaborate titles that old Chinese poets gave to their poems. We could say the poem moves in a way well-known in classic Chinese poems, but the last line is definitely American.

> Over my head, I see the bronze butterfly,
> Asleep on the black trunk,
> Blowing like a leaf in green shadow.
> Down the ravine behind the empty house,
> The cowbells follow one another
> Into the distances of the afternoon.
> To my right,
> In a field of sunlight between two pines,
> The droppings of last year's horses
> Blaze up into golden stones.
> I lean back, as the evening darkens and comes on.
> A chicken hawk floats over, looking for home.
> I have wasted my life.

Many people love the marvels of this poem, right up to the chicken hawk. But it is the last line that drove critics mad, and still does. When he has written such beautiful poems, how could he even say he has wasted his life! What can one say? The abruptness of the last line efficiently pulls the poem from the angel category. He says, "I'll fix this poem so you can't put it in an anthology of angel poems." One might add that he knows that the images in the poems are marvelous and are testimonies to the glory of the universe, but it's also true that he has lost much of his life precisely by devoting himself to such marvelous images. The miracle takes place even if no poet notices it; the universe itself arranges for horse droppings to blaze up in the afternoon sun, and for trees to show a black trunk with a bronze butterfly on it. What seems easy for the universe is often hard for us. Many readers wanted the poem to remain conventionally positive to the very last syllable. It didn't. Ed Ochester has also mentioned that Wright's longing for home was so intense at this moment in his life, that as soon as he set down the chicken hawk line ending with the word "home," his own life looked desolate to him.

Wright spent a lot of time in *Saint Judas* describing the ruined landscape around the Ohio River. In "Stages of a Journey Westward," published in 1963, he checks to see how the rest of the country is doing. In western Minnesota he notices:

> The only human beings between me and the Pacific Ocean
> Were old Indians, who wanted to kill me.

This is a reasonable paranoia. These are the words of a grandson of immigrants noticing that his ancestors had not won the continent fairly. In part four, James finally arrives at the Pacific:

> Defeated for re-election,
> The half-educated sheriff of Mukilteo, Washington,
> Has been drinking again.
> He leads me up the cliff, tottering.
> Both drunk, we stand among the graves.
> Miners paused here on the way up to Alaska.
> Angry, they spaded their broken women's bodies
> Into ditches of crab grass.

I lie down between the tombstones.
At the bottom of the cliff
America is over and done with.
America,
Plunged into the dark furrows
Of the sea again.

We've been reading Wright's poems of darkness, which amount to a new stage. The "dark" poems lack some of the elegance of the poems in the stage of clarity, but they bring in depth and fierceness. In any case, Wright was himself living the dark. About the time he was writing these poems, Allen Tate refused to give him tenure at the University of Minnesota, which had the effect of driving him deeper into the darkness. He had been teaching at the University of Minnesota for three years, but as a specialist in Dickens and a general lecturer in literature. Wright got a temporary job teaching at Macalester in St. Paul for two years, but hostile letters Tate placed in his dossier prevented his getting a real job elsewhere. When lead after lead dried up, James said to me, "Robert, I am never going to get a job again. I'm never going to be loved by a woman again either." He suffered several serious breakdowns during that time. His marriage broke up; subsequently he lost any close association with his two sons. His drinking got worse. He was assigned an English doctor, Dr. Lamb, who liked shock treatments. He gave Jim a number of them. When Jim's wife came to see him, he gave her a shock treatment as well. Jim had no job, and in addition had lost all his teeth. It was a hard time.

America is over and done with.
America,
Plunged into the dark furrows
Of the sea again.

This travel from transparency to darkness is like traveling from one island to another. The cost is high for a writer who travels from the first island to the second. There is a big difference between *All's Well That Ends Well* and *Macbeth*. Sometimes the second stage means breakdowns, but on the other hand, as Pound remarked, one doesn't get through hell in a hurry. T. S. Eliot, who had to give up a lot of self-esteem, remarked, when asked if a life of hell was worth it for the sake of the poem, said, "No." Pablo Neruda, at that stage in his life, said:

It so happens I am sick of being a man.
And it happens that I walk into tailorshops and movie houses
dried up, waterproof, like a swan made of felt
steering my way in a water of wombs and ashes. . . .

It so happens I am sick of my feet and my nails
and my hair and my shadow.
It so happens I am sick of being a man.

Still it would be marvelous
to terrify a law clerk with a cut lily,
or kill a nun with a blow on the ear. . . .

(translated by R.B.)

César Vallejo said:

Well, on the day I was born,
God was sick.

They all know that I'm alive,
that I'm vicious; and they don't know
the December that follows from that January.
Well, on the day I was born,
God was sick. . . .

(translated by James Wright)

Years earlier Wright had found Trakl, who wrote, in Wright's translation:

The white walls of the city are always giving off sound.
Under arching thorns
O my brother blind minute-hands we are climbing toward midnight.

Wright published in *1977* a remarkable poem called "Hook," which I'll set
down here:

I was only a young man
In those days. On that evening

The cold was so God damned
Bitter there was nothing.
Nothing. I was in trouble
With a woman, and there was nothing
There but me and dead snow.

I stood on the street corner
In Minneapolis, lashed
This way and that.
Wind rose from some pit,
Hunting me.
Another bus to Saint Paul
Would arrive in three hours,
If I was lucky.

Then the young Sioux
Loomed beside me, his scars
Were just my age.

Ain't got no bus here
A long time, he said.
You got enough money
To get home on?

What did they do
To your hand? I answered.
He raised up his hook into the terrible starlight
And slashed the wind.

Oh, that? he said.
I had a bad time with a woman. Here,
You take this.

Did you ever feel a man hold
Sixty-five cents
In a hook,
And place it

Gently
In your freezing hand?

I took it.
It wasn't the money I needed.
But I took it.

Here the emotion is carried not by clear, open vowels, but by short, awkward language particles, *k*'s and *t*'s. Wright could have said to the Sioux man, "I'm all right. You keep it." But in the phrase "I took it," we can feel both desperation and compassion; he accepts his position as one of the low ones of earth; all of the elevation he had gained through language is gone.

A poem is only a poem; "scar" and "hook" are only words; but before or under them are years of difficult living. We've talked about the first and second acts in the life of a poet. It's possible Wright's late poems from Italy represent a third act.

These poems are set mostly in Tuscany, especially in its hill cities, Verona and Sienna, where he felt the culture of St. Francis, Giotto, Catullus, Cimabue, Ausonias. . . . He experienced the presence of beauty more deeply in these cities than in the towns around Martins Ferry, and since it has always been for beauty that Wright lived, it seems right that his poems would settle finally in Tuscany.

Wright's mode of writing changes now from restless moments of beauty interspersed with brutal truth-telling, to a complicated poetry of gratitude. Remembering that Virgil had said, "*Optima dies prima fugit*"—"The best days go first"—Wright said, speaking of a bee caught in a ripe pear which he had released with a knife:

The bee shuddered, and returned.
Maybe I should have left him alone there,
Drowning in his own delight.
The best days are the first
To flee, sings the lovely
Musician born in this town.

At the end of "Butterfly Fish," he remarks that this little fish

. . . grazes up his tall corals,

153

Slim as a stallion, serene on his far-off hillside,
His other world where I cannot see
His secret face.

By this time he has quit drinking, and he is stronger than before. Speaking of sumac, he said:

The skin will turn aside hatchets and knife-blades...

In "The Secret of Light," he said:

I am startled to discover that I am not afraid. I am free to give a blessing out of my silence into that woman's black hair. I trust her to go on living. I believe in her black hair, her diamond that is still asleep. I would close my eyes to daydream about her. But those silent companions who watch over me from the insides of my eyelids are too brilliant for me to meet face to face.

We have the feeling that he is doing more seeing than he has for a long time:

... and all I could see behind me were the diminishing cicadas, lindens, and slim cedars rising, one feather folding upwards into another, into the spaces of evergreen and gold beyond the Roman arena.

In the town of Sirmione, he sees:

An easy thousand of silver, almost transparent piccolini are skimming the surface of the long slab of volcanic stone.

He praises a musician he has seen in Verona:

He just waved me as gently as he could on the way out ... and he did his best I suppose. He owns that heavenly city no more than I do. He may be fallen, as I am, but from a greater height unless I miss my guess.

The language tends to be sweet, airy, and extravagant. Wright says in "The

Gift of Change":

> But the lizard lying beside me now has gone too far. Wholly
> abandoning himself to his gift of change, he lifts his head above
> the edge of a linden blossom freshly fallen and alone. His exqui-
> site hands have given up clinging to anything. They lie open. The
> leaf on the flower is so smooth, a light wind could blow him
> away. I wonder if he knows. If he knows, I wonder that my breath
> doesn't blow him away. I am that close to him, and he that close
> to me. He has gone too far into the world to turn back now.

It's interesting that as Wright adapts his language to the prose poem, he
asks it to convey this new mood of praise. Stephen Yenser, who has written
a marvelous essay on Wright's late poems, remarks, speaking of *Moments of
the Italian Summer:* "Its fourteen prose poems. . .are as transparent as anything
he has written, though they are shot through by whimsy. In fact, in the best
of them, extravagance provides coherence and sophistication alike."

If we compare the prose poems I've cited to "Grandmother's Ghost"
lines and the mayapple poem, we now see beings that need forgiveness. In
the third act we see an intelligence like that of Prospero's looking back on a
life of many mistakes but admiring the mysterious wholeness of it all. Moreover, we could say—even though the comparison is a bit presumptuous—
that we don't get to *The Tempest* without going through *King Lear* and *Macbeth.*

Yenser says, "Wright's version of the prose poem, with its evident tol-
erance for loose ends, its appetite for digression, its fugitive unity, seems exactly the form to contain [the journal passages] without warping them."
Yenser continues, "What happens in such pieces is that the bud of the actual
blossoms into the extravagant flower of vision."

Wright says of a turtle:

> . . . It was as near as I've ever come to seeing a turtle take a pleasant
> bath in his natural altogether. All the legendary faces of broken old
> age disappeared from my mind, the thickened muscles under the
> chins, the nostrils brutal with hatred, the murdering eyes. He filled
> my mind with a sweet-tasting mountain rain, his youthfulness, his
> modesty as he washed himself all alone, his religious face.

Wright, in a poem set in Fiesole, said:

> And me there a long way from the cold dream of Hell.
> Me, there, alone at last,
> At last with the dust of my dust,
> As far away as I will ever get from dying,
> And the two great poets of God in the silence
> Meeting together.

He meant Bach and Dante. Late in his life, a mathematician said, "When thinking as a mathematician, human bodies, emotions, and interpersonal relationships take on less and less importance, whereas the universe as an expression of number relationships takes on more and more. There are ecstatic moments." I think the important word is *universe*. The honor is not given to human beings, but to the universe.

Wright says in "To the Creature of the Creation":

> Lonely as my desire is,
> I have no daughter.
> I will not die by fire, I
> Will die by water.

By this time he had worked for years as a highly valued teacher at Hunter. He had met and married Annie. He had taken part in a sweet concord. They had become a pair. With her, he could praise the sweetness of a deep culture still somehow existent. In this passage, he mentions the pleasure of a visit from a fellow poet, Galway Kinnell, and his wife:

> . . . The moon and the stars
> Suddenly flicker out, and the whole mountain
> Appears, pale as a shell.
>
> Look, the sea has not fallen and broken
> Our heads. How can I feel so warm
> Here in the dead center of January? I can
> Scarcely believe it, and yet I have to, this is
> The only life I have. I get up from the stone.
> My body mumbles something unseemly

And follows me. Now we are all sitting here strangely
On top of the sunlight.

* * * *

James Wright had an immense love of literature, and he memorized vast quantities of it. I happened to be with him when he was challenged one night early in his reading and teaching career by an exasperated English department critic who implied he was a barbarian. Wright responded by reciting the entire last chapter of *Tristram Shandy* by heart. He had good teachers at Kenyon and in Seattle. He enlisted in the army in the fall of 1945, after the war was over; he had made an education possible through the G.I. Bill. He was born into a generation that had seen many men their age die in battle, and he was determined to sacrifice something himself for those dead. He loved being with bike riders and drinkers in Minneapolis bars, and he was capable of feeling the suffering "of the bewildered mad." All of those enthusiasms add to his intensity, but in the end it is his power as a verbal alchemist and his truth-telling that holds his readers close to him.

Wright rails at the United States as a way of gaining its attention, to see if the United States can defend itself and phrase what it stands for. He doesn't lie to himself about the enormous defects in American culture or the banality of its cities.

And nobody would commit suicide, only
To find beyond death
Bridgeport, Ohio.

He never gave up his fellowship with the condemned. He wouldn't have been surprised that the governor of Illinois recently released to the ordinary prison a number of men on Death Row because the judicial system has so many flaws in it. The longing for justice is at the very center of his poems.

What else did Wright want? He wanted clear language; he wanted to get rid of the clutter of language in American poetry of his time. Speaking about the year he spent in occupied Japan just after World War II, he wrote that he was able in Japan "to conceive of a poem as something which, with the greatest modesty, is brought up close to its subject so that it can be suggestive and evocative. Japan was a revelation to me." He achieved that closeness in a number of poems, among them "A Blessing."

He wanted less attention to deathless abstractions such as democracy, freedom, and Christianity, and more honoring of actual creatures that live and die. In "From a Bus Window in Central Ohio, Just Before a Thunder Shower," he says:

> Cribs loaded with roughage huddle together
> Before the north clouds.
> The wind tiptoes between poplars.
> The silver maple leaves squint
> Toward the ground.
> An old farmer, his scarlet face
> Apologetic with whiskey, swings back a barn door
> And calls a hundred black-and-white Holsteins
> From the clover field.

The trees and farm buildings are all given some human sympathy. The wooden corncribs, holding roughage, "huddle together / Before the north clouds," the silver maples are a little like a cross-eyed person. Suddenly the farmer appears, "his scarlet face / Apologetic with whiskey." Even when drunk, he does what needs to be done. He

> swings back a barn door
> And calls a hundred black-and-white Holsteins
> From the clover field.

When Amiri Baraka, then known as LeRoi Jones, wrote Jim a blistering letter about this poem, ending with a sarcastic question, "How did you know there were a hundred Holsteins?", Jim was not rattled. He understood that he was being attacked as a foolish praiser of nature. He wrote a postcard back which said, "I counted the tits and divided by four. Yours sincerely, James Wright."

What more did Jim Wright want from poetry? He wanted truth-telling and passion. It was rather cruel of him to ask for that from America in the late Fifties, almost as cruel as asking for it now.

As for passion, it implies staking a lot on one throw, all or nothing. He often referred to a woman who had drowned herself in the river. In "To the Muse," published in 1968, he says:

Come up to me, love,
Out of the river, or I will
Come down to you.

Wright doesn't suggest that it's easy to live your life in poetry.

It is all right. All they do
Is go in by dividing
One rib from another. I wouldn't
Lie to you. It hurts
Like nothing I know. All they do
Is burn their way in with a wire.

Three lady doctors in Wheeling open
Their offices at night.
I don't have to call them, they are always there.
But they only have to put the knife once
Under your breast.
Then they hang their contraption
And you bear it.

Why are James Wright's poems so good? Besides his truth-telling, his grief, his affections, he has genius in language. His gift has something to do with the interstices between words, the mysterious events that happen when simple words are placed next to each other.

. . . At a touch of my hand,
The air fills with delicate creatures
From the other world.

I'll end with his poem, "In Memory of Leopardi." We see an amazing variety of nouns—barbs, oblivions, lame prayers, smoke marrow, hunchbacks, even invented adjectives such as "jubilating Isaiah." His genius shows in the touches of surprise, in the drawing upon an immense vocabulary, in the drawing down of words by some part of the brain far from daylight consciousness, far from reason.

I have gone past all those times when the poets
Were beautiful as only
The rich can be. The cold bangles
Of the moon grazed one of my shoulders,
And so to this day,
And beyond, I carry
The sliver of a white city, the barb of a jewel
In my left clavicle that hunches.
Tonight I sling
A scrambling sack of oblivions and lame prayers
On my right good arm. The Ohio River
Has flown by me twice, the dark jubilating
Isaiah of mill and smoke marrow. Blind son
Of a meadow of huge horses, lover of drowned islands
Above Steubenville, blind father
Of my halt gray wing:
Now I limp on, knowing
The moon strides behind me, swinging
The scimitar of the divinity that struck down
The hunchback in agony
When he saw her, naked, carrying away his last sheep
Through the Asian rocks.

A Few Notes on Antonio Machado

I.

Antonio Machado is the most thoughtful, modest, and lovable poet of the twentieth century. His quiet labor on sound and rhythm over many years, his emphasis on the sufferings of others rather than his own, the passageways that he creates inside his poems that lead back to the ancient Mediterranean past, his inner calm, even joyfulness—all of these gifts nourish people wherever he is read.

*   *   *

His poetry secretes in itself the rhythm of the walker. When John Dos Passos, just out of college, traveled to see Machado in Segovia, he found an awkward man with a deep voice, "an old-fashioned teacher," dressed in a black double-breasted suit, who walked for hours in Segovia and the countryside. When a person walks, he experiences objects one by one at a pace agreeable to the body. And every walk ends; sooner or later the walk is over and we are back home.

*   *   *

Yeats connected true poetry with trance. And when Lorca says:

161

> one day . . . the enraged ants
> will thrown themselves on the yellow skies that have taken refuge in
> the eyes of cows

we fall into a trance immediately. But Machado has vowed not to soar too much; he wants to "go down to the hells" or stick to the low and ordinary: flies, blind mules working the water wheels, stony earth, dogs, old men who stare straight ahead for hours astonished by nothing, boring schoolrooms, unsolvable philosophical problems. How does he help the reader to fall into a trance then? By his vowel sounds, exquisite, astonishing, magical, and by his care in measuring time inside the line. Sometimes a hypnotist swings a watch; Machado does that: the beats return regularly, the vowels come again, time passes so slowly it can be measured; we listen. The trance of ordinary life, chaotic, gives way to an ordered trance, and water goes on flowing while we are asleep. Perhaps water flows best in the river while we are asleep. Water through the fountain lifts itself in the air. But we are asleep.

* * *

Machado had an answer to what poetry is: "la palabra en el tiempo." We could translate this cryptic phrase as: "the word in time," "human language in which we feel time passing," or "words that pick up the energy of time," or "words that take their place, like drumbeats, in time already counted." He loved to get a phrase like "la palabra en el tiempo" and repeat it until no one could understand what it meant. Of course he adored narrative in poems, which contains time as a jar of water contains water.

And doesn't form move through time? "A Chinese jar still moves perpetually in its stillness." Doesn't a snail develop its gorgeous logorhythmic shell-curve by moving through time? We could say that only when the snail agrees not to be eternal, when it accepts the descent into earth time that unfolds slowly, only then does the snail achieve that form which we foolishly associate with eternity. Machado adored the well-made thing:

> Form your letters slowly and well:
> making things well
> is more important than making them.

* * *

One of the first poems of Machado's that attracted me was his poem on the bean fields, which I saw in 1959 in Willis Barnstone's translation:

> The blue mountain, the river, the erect
> coppery staffs of slender aspens,
> and the white of the almond tree on the hill.
> O flowering snow and butterfly on the tree!
> With the aroma of the bean plants, the wind
> runs in the joyful solitude of the fields!

We feel that Machado is laying a relatively light hand on nature here. I was more accustomed to poems in which the author uses nature to make philosophical points: What a certain ape did is brought in to bolster an argument, the swan sailing becomes a symbol of pride, the snake is either evil or wisdom, but seldom a real snake. John Donne writes well, but his fleas always seem to fit into some elaborate human system, alchemical, Christian, or occult. There is nothing the matter with that, except that we may not have asked the snake or the flea how he feels about it.

It seems that in the West, in general, when we write about a field, we bring the field into our study and close the door. Not all poets do, of course. But one feels that Machado doesn't ask the field to come to his poem, but he brings his poem to the bean field . . . and even more amazing, he leaves it there!

> With the aroma of the bean plants, the wind
> runs in the joyful solitude of the fields!

That doesn't mean that Machado is a nature Romantic (he is in fact suspicious of the Romantics), nor that he undervalues the intellect (he took in fact his advanced degree in philosophy). I think it means that he wishes to give to the fields a respect similar to the respect he gives to an idea.

* * *

His favorite philosopher was Pythagoras. Pythagoras appears in his poetry from beginning to end. Pythagoras' doctrine of the "music of the spheres" is probably present, along with God, in the early poem:

> It's possible that while sleeping the hand
> that sows the seeds of stars
> started the ancient music going again
>
> —like a note from a great harp—
> and the frail wave came to our lips
> as one or two honest words.

Pythagoras gave him confidence to write brief poems, for Pythagoras left only sayings. And yet his sayings suggest a secret bond between the "sower of the stars," and the lyre-player on earth. We see a gesture of someone sowing grain, whose hand sweeps the strings of a lyre, and from it comes a wave of music that reaches even to Spain. When Spain lost the remains of her empire in 1898, the writers of that generation realized that the old rhetorical bluff was over, and they had to live now with reduced expectations, a diminished thing, sadness, grief, limited resources, a few words that were honest.

* * *

Reading Machado, one is moved by his firm and persistent efforts to see and to listen. He does not want to be caught as the narcissist is, in an interior world, alone with his consciousness, but he wants to cross to other people, to the stars, to the world:

> To talk with someone,
> ask a question first,
> then—listen.

Daydreaming is not useful for crossing, but eyes are. "Today, just as yesterday, the job of the eyes, the eyes in the head and in the mind, is to see." The landscape around Soria he studies with fierce attention. How to study the outer world without losing inward richness—that is the issue Rilke and Ponge lived. If we look only at our problems, Machado said, the inner world dissolves; if we look only at the world, it begins to dissolve. If we want to create art, we have to stitch together the inner world and the outer world. How to do that? Machado concludes, well, we could always use our eyes.

One of his earliest memories, which he included in Juan de Mairena's notebooks, is this: "I'd like to tell you the most important thing that ever happened to me. One day when I was still quite young, my mother and I were out walking. I had a piece of sugar cane in my hand, I remember—it was in Seville, in some vanished Christmas season. Just ahead of us were another mother and child—he had a stick of sugar cane too. I was sure mine was bigger—I knew it was! Even so, I asked my mother—because children always ask questions they already know the answer to: 'Mine's bigger, isn't it?' And she said, 'No, my boy, it's not. What have you done with your eyes?' I've been asking myself that question ever since."

The Ch'an teachers tell a story about a man of the world who one day confronts a master, and asks him to sum up what he has learned in his life as a Buddhist monk. The master hands him a piece of paper with one word written on it: "Attention!" The worldly man now insists that he is a serious student, and implies that the master is holding back. He takes the paper back and writes "Attention. Attention." He worldly man now appeals to the master's humanity, points out that he too has a soul, and they will both die soon; it is the master's duty to tell him what he needs to know. Taking the paper he writes three words: "Attention! Attention! Attention!" Much of Machado's life he spent in this effort of attention.

* * *

Machado in his work makes clear that we in the West have our own tradition of attention. Pythagoras, for example, listened to vibrations. He usually began a lecture with the monochord, which he plucked so that his listeners could hear the note clearly; then, breaking the string at its nodes, he let them hear the overtones. He then pointed out that the relationships between the vibrations they had just heard corresponded to the relationships between the speeds of the planets. Paying attention, in the tough sense of the phrase, means paying attention to nonhuman vibrations, the life of catgut and planets. Pythagoras said, "When you get up in the morning, smooth out the shape of your body from the bed."

When Machado pays attention, he pays attention to time, which surely existed before human beings; to landscape, whose rhythm Machado said is slower than human rhythm; to the past of each city he lived in, for each city's life extends beyond our individual life; to the way colors unfold (Goethe studied color also); to synchronicity, that is occasional identity of human and natural events; and to the curious world of dreams. "Pythagoras' lyre goes on resonating in dreams," he said.

Yet he did not want to lose "we." He knew that a secret "you" was present in the feelings evoked by a landscape. In poetry every feeling, he said, "needs for its creation the distress of other frightened hearts among a nature not understood. . . . In short, my feeling is not only mine, but ours."

* * *

Antonio Machado was born on July 26, 1875, in Seville. Until he was eight, he lived in the enormous Palacio de las Dueñas, where his father, a teacher and early collector of folk poetry and folk music in Spain, lived as a kind of caretaker for the Duke of Alba. It had long passageways. When Antonio was eight, the family moved to Madrid; there Antonio and his brothers attended the Free Institution of Learning, whose founder, Francisco Giner de los Ríos, had a profound effect on two or three generations of Spanish intellectuals and writers. Antonio tended to be torpid and slow; he took ten extra years to get his B.A. He published his first book when he was twenty-eight. Eventually he chose a career as secondary-school teacher of French, passed the examination, and when he was thirty-two got his first job at Soria, a poor and exhausted town in the grazed-out mountainous area of Castile. He stayed there five years. During the second year he married the daughter of the family in whose pension he lived, Leonor, then fifteen. He watched her sicken of tuberculosis and die after two more years, in the fall of 1911. "She is always with me," he said; he addressed her often in later poems, and never remarried. He abandoned the idea of suicide, with arguments rather like Frost's: He wrote to Jiménez that he did not want to annihilate whatever in him was helpful and constructive. He resigned his position at Soria, and transferred to Baeza, in the south, nearer his first home, and stayed there seven years. During 1912, his last year in Soria, his second book, *The Countryside of Castile,* came out; and he continued to add poems to it during his years in Baeza. In 1919, he transferred again, this time to Segovia, which is only an hour from Madrid. He was able now on weekends to escape from provincial life, which he complained was boring and deadening; and he began writing plays and taking part in the intellectual life of Madrid. He lived in Segovia from 1919 to 1932, thirteen years, during which he fell in love with a married woman he called "Guiomar," invented two poet-philosophers named Abel Martín and Juan de Mairena, and published his third book, *Nuevas canciones (New Poems)*. He became more and more active in public life, writing in the papers on political and moral issues during the exciting period that led in 1931 to the proclamation of the Second Spanish Republic. He lived in Madrid after 1932 with his brother José and wrote, disguised playfully as Juan de Mairena, many articles in the newspapers defending the Republic and its plans. After the civil war began in 1936, he continued to write prose, but little poetry, and finally, January 28, 1939, moving ahead of Franco's army, crossed the Pyrenees as a passenger in an old car, holding his mother on his lap. He died at Collioure, just over the border, on February 22, and as the gravestones make clear, his mother survived him by only a few days. His attitude toward his own life resembled James Wright's toward his: that it was a bookish life, and the events were not too important.

* * *

What about liveliness? Everything is to be lively. When he was living at Segovia, he began to feed his made-up philosopher Juan de Mairena bits of prose that he had written earlier. Here is a little scene:

> "Mr. Pérez, please go to the board and write:
> The daily occurrences unfolding on the avenue."
> The student did as he was told.
> "Now go ahead and put that into poetic language."
> The student, after some thought, wrote:
> What is going on in the streets.
> "Not bad!"

So Machado, though he wanted poetry to have nobility and beauty, refused to achieve that through poetic or archaic language, which he knew involved a misuse of time.

> "Mr. Martínez, go to the board and write:
> Those olden swords of the glorious times . . ."
> The student obeyed.

"To which time do you think the poet was alluding here?"
"To the time when the swords were not old."

"Every day, gentlemen, literature is more 'written' and less spoken. The result is that every day we write worse, in a chilly prose, without grace, however correct it may be: our eloquence is merely the written word fried again, in which the spoken word has already been encased. Inside every orator of our time there is always a clumsy journalist. The important thing is to speak well: with liveliness, thought, and grace. The rest will be given us as a gift."

He distrusts ancient eloquence:

"The truth is the truth,"—perhaps Agamemnon said it or his
    swineherd.
Agamemnon: "Absolutely clear."
Swineherd: "I'm not sure about that. . . ."

2.

Antonio Machado wrote some of his dream poems in his first book, *Soledades,* in 1899; Freud published his *Interpretation of Dreams* the same year. Machado independently makes dreams a primary subject of his poems, descends into them, looks to them for guidance, goes downward, farther and farther until he finds water. The water he has found makes *Soledades* refreshing. One could say that "the world" exerts tremendous pressure on the psyche, collective opinion terrorizes the soul; the demands of the world obsess the psyche, and the world and its attractions offer to use up all the time available. Each person needs then, early on, to go inside, far enough inside to water the plants, awaken the animals, become friends with the desires, and sense what Machado calls "the living pulse of the spirit," start the fire in the hearth, and close the door so that what is inside us has sufficient power to hold its own against the forces longing to invade. Machado has achieved this inner strengthening by the time he finishes his first book, and his praise of dreams is clear:

Memory is valuable for one thing,
    astonishing: it brings dreams back.

His deep-lying confidence he perhaps received as a reward for his labor,
or perhaps it was given as a gift; we can't tell. But the confidence is unmis-
takable:

                         There the good and silent spirits
        of life are waiting for you,
        and one day they will carry you
        to a garden of eternal spring.

                    *   *   *

But She will not fail to come.

                    *   *   *

                            In the golden poplars
        far off, the shadow of love is waiting for you.

It's clear that his confidence rises from some source far below the intellect, far below even the security provided by the healthy mind in the healthy
body. This sort of confidence seems to spring from earliest infancy. The
positive, energetic mother holds the child near her heart, and he looks out
on the world: it seems all blossoming, all good, and he carries that confidence
with him all his life. Machado suggests that if he were a Provençal love poet,
and wrote a poem to a woman's eyes, it would probably go this way:

        your clear eyes, your eyes have
        the calm and good light,
        the good light of the blossoming world, that I saw
        one day from the arms of my mother.

Even though *Soledades* is the book of a young man, he asks questions in
it usually not asked until old age. One poem begins:

        Faints sound of robes brushing
        the exhausted earth!

This is not a romantic poem about village life, as I first thought: he says that if one really wants to be depressed, one can listen to this sound—the Spanish priest's robe brushing worn-out soil. It reminds us of Blake's despair in London. Machado warns us that we are not alone:

> Snowy Roman ghosts
> go about lighting the stars.

And he warns that in such situations, it is very easy for "a phantasm" to come, and throw off our sense of reality.

And he asks hard questions about what is going on inside. What if we, out of fear or recklessness or carelessness have stopped the soul's growth? What if we, having invited the world to be with us, have let the life of the feeling die?

> The wind, one brilliant day, called
> to my soul with an odor of jasmine.
>
> "In return for this jasmine odor,
> I'd like all the odor of your roses."
>
> "I have no roses; I have no flowers left now
> in my garden. . . . All are dead."
>
> "Then I'll take the waters of the fountains,
> and the yellow leaves, and the dried-up petals."
>
> The wind left. . . . I wept. I said to my soul,
> "What have you done with the garden entrusted to you?"

When we have finished the book, we are aware that Machado has found certain passageways that lead inward or certain paths that lead downward, and they are not collective paths; and because he has found those paths, on his own, it doesn't matter so much if he is successful or not, if his life is full or not.

Kabir ended one of his poems:

If you want the truth, I'll tell you the truth;
Friend, listen: the God whom I love is inside.

Kabir says that simply and flatly, with his entire culture behind him. Machado calls out in a magnificent poem, parallel to Kabir's, a similar vision, and calls his vision a "marvelous error."

Last night, as I was sleeping,
I dreamt—marvelous error!—
that I had a beehive
here inside my heart. . . .

Last night, as I slept,
I dreamt—marvelous error!—
that it was God I had
here inside my heart.

The Westerner, after centuries of extroverted science, and determined philosophical attempts to remove soul from conversation, architecture, observation and education, sees inside himself, and sees what the ancients saw, but can hardly believe it. He confesses that he must be seeing wrong.

In 1917, when Machado put together his *Selected Poems,* he wrote an introductory piece for *Soledades,* and this is what he said:

The poems of this first book, which was published in January of 1903, were written between 1899 and 1902. Around that time, Rubén Darío, whom the critics then in fashion attacked with mockery, was the idol of a small minority. I too admired the author of *Prosas profanas (Worldly Stories),* the great master of form and feeling, who later revealed the depth of his soul in *Cantos de vida y esperanza (Poems of Life and Hope).* But I tried—and notice I do not boast of results, but only of intentions—to follow a quite distinct road. I thought that the substance of poetry does not lie in the sound value of the word, nor in its color, nor in the metric line, nor in the complex of sensations, but in the deep pulse of the spirit; and this deep pulse is what the soul contributes, if it contributes anything, or what it says, if it says anything, with its own voice, in a courageous answer to the touch of the world. And I thought also that a man can overtake by surprise some of the phrases of his inward conversations with himself, distinguishing the living voice from the dead echoes; that he, looking inward, can glimpse the deep-rooted images, the things of feeling which all men possess. My book was not the systematic realization of this proposal, but such were my artistic intentions at that time.

This book was republished in 1907, with the addition of new poems which added nothing substantial to the original work, under the title *Soledades, galerías y otros poemas.* The two volumes in effect made up a single book.

ANTONIO MACHADO
Madrid, 1917

3.

"Only in lazy moments does a poet concentrate on interpreting his dreams, picking things out of them he can use in his poems. Dream study has not yet produced anything of importance in poetry. The poems written while we are awake, even those less successful, are more original and more beautiful, and sometimes more wild than those made from our dreams. I can say this because I spent many years of my life thinking just the opposite. But a part of wisdom is changing one's opinions."

Machado wants the conscious mind to take part, even more vigorously than it did in *Soledades*, while the poem itself remains mysterious and committed to depth. This idea marks a big shift from the aims of *Soledades*. During the five years that he spent in Soria, from 1907 to 1912, he wrote *The Countryside of Castile (Campos de Castilla)*, first version, and I'll mention five areas in which I've noticed shifts, turns, changes, increases in depth. He responds, in this book, to his mother's question: "What have you done with your eyes?"

Living in Soria, he tries to see the countryside and to describe what a dawn in Castile is like, rather than to remain content with a dreamy or poetic version of dawn. He understands that being spiritually awake and keeping the eyes open are connected. "One has to keep the eyes well open in order to see things as they are, and still more open to see them as other than they are, and open them still more widely in order to see things as better than they are."

One also senses that he experienced something entirely new in his love for Leonor. We could say that Machado, with his marvelous introversion, had met years before his feminine self, or feminine soul, far inside himself, at the end of some passageway in a dream. He experienced that acquaintanceship; knew "her." But when he met Leonor he experienced that feminine soul in another person. Isn't a man's feminine soul younger than he is? The soul that was once inside him, or only inside him, is now outside as well, and what once tended to separate him from others now draws him close to one human being, bonds him. His faith in the surprises of the universe deepens.

Third, he continues to search in his work for "the things of feeling that all men possess." He moves to bring the private close to the public, or, more exactly, to embody his private introverted perceptions in poetic forms so available they could be called public, for even the people in Spain that can neither read nor write know the coplas (the popular songs) and ballads. He compared the coplas to a common earthen jug that he once saw lying beside a spring which people could drink from. In this deepening he resembles Yeats, who, shortly before he died, referring to a recent article, said that the greatest honor anyone could pay him was to use the word "public" about his language.

In accordance perhaps with his determination to write with eyes open, he takes a step few twentieth-century poets have taken: he asks thinking to enter his poems. He is not afraid that thinking will evict feeling, and it doesn't; and he recognizes it as a power, a life energy. Thinking often shows itself in the willingness to break the hoped-for unity. Yeats says:

> The intellect of man is forced to choose
> Perfection of the life or of the work.

Machado says:

> There are two sorts of consciousness:
> one involves light, one patience.

He opposes the church because it depresses thinking:

> Make noise, anvils; be silent, you church bells!

He brings the widest possible poles into a small poem. For example: Does everything pass away? Or is what passes away only a veil, and behind that is there something that lasts forever?

> All things die, and all things live forever;
> but our task is to die,
> to die while making roads,
> roads over the sea.

His thinking is sprightly, and he takes risks with it.

Finally, one senses in *The Countryside of Castile* that he has passed through some intense burning, some testing, a cooking of some kind, which has changed some of his slow lead into gold. He no longer has a bushel-basket over his candle, but allows his light to radiate, and is very clear about what sort of light it is.

> I never wanted fame,
> nor wanted to leave my poems
> behind in the memory of men.
> I love the subtle worlds,
> delicate, almost without weight
> like soap bubbles.
> I enjoy seeing them take the color
> of sunlight and scarlet, float
> in the blue sky, then
> suddenly quiver and break.

Here are the words he wrote about *The Countryside of Castile:*

> In a third collection I published my second book, *Campos de Castilla* (1912). Five years in and around Soria, which is now sacred to me—there I married and there I lost my wife, whom I adored—drew me, my vision and my feelings, into what was deeply Castillian. Moreover, my set of ideas had changed very much. We are victims, I thought, of a double hallucination. If we look outward, and concentrate on entering things, our external world begins to lose solidity, and if we conclude that it exists not

in and for itself, but exists because of us, it ends by dissolving. However, if moved by our private reality, we turn our eyes inward, then the world pushes in on us, and it is our interior world, our being, that disappears. What to do then? Weave the thread given to us, dream our dream and live; it is the only way we can achieve the miracle of growth. A man attentive to himself and trying to overhear himself drowns the only voice he could hear—his own; but other voices confuse him. Are we then doomed to be merely observers? But when we see, reason is present, and reason analyzes and dissolves. The reason will soon bring the whole theater down, and finally, our shadow alone will be projected against the background. As for the poet, I thought that his job was to create new poems out of what is eternally human, spirited stories that have their own life, even though they came from him. I considered the old narrative *romance* the supreme expression of poetry, and I wanted to write a new book of them. *La tierra de Alvergonzález* came from this longing. The last thing I want is to resuscitate the genre in its traditional sense. Working up of old-style ballads—chivalrous or moorish—was never to my taste, and all imitations of archaic things seem ridiculous to me. It's true that I learned to read in the *Romancero general* which my uncle Agustín Durán collected; but my own narratives did not spring from heroic tales, but rather from the people who composed them and the parts of the country where they were sung; my narratives look to what is fundamentally human, to the Castilian countryside and to the first book of Moses, which is called *Génesis.*

You will come on many poems in this book a long way from the propositions I have just mentioned. Many of the poems spring from a preoccupation with the nation; others from a simple love of nature that in me is far stronger than the love of art. Finally, some of the poems show the many hours of my life spent—some would say wasted—thinking about the puzzles of the human being and the outer world.

ANTONIO MACHADO
Madrid, 1917

4.

Antonio Machado published his third book, *Nuevas canciones (New Poems)*, in 1930. Eighteen years had passed since the first version of *Campos de Castilla*, and thirteen years since the enlarged edition. Such patience! Some of those years he spent in Baeza, and then, until 1932, in Segovia. The small room he occupied is still there; his old landlady showed it to me a few years ago.

We notice two advances in *New Poems*. He masters the peculiar union he longed for of introverted subject matter and public form; he brings his substance to the copla form and the folk stanza. The proof of his advance lies in the masterpiece beginning "The huge sea drives / against the flowering mountain." It is one of the most beautiful poems of the twentieth century, derived from a highly developed sensibility, and yet is in no way inaccessible. It resembles in its shape "Thirteen Ways of Looking at a Blackbird."

Machado still believed deeply that the true poem is language caught in time. He developed a sentence he loved to repeat: "Hoy es siempre todavía," which we could translate as "What we are living is a continuation," or "Today is always still," or "There is no separation between past and present," or "Pythagoras and Christ are still alive."

> "I hear old stuff now."
> "Good, sharpen your ears then."

The physicist David Bohm has remarked that when we talk with each other, the words we say are unfolded or explicate, but the meaning of those words is implicate or folded everywhere into the universe. In a similar way, what we experience, instant by instant, appears unfolded, and what has led to this instant also exists, though folded up everywhere in space.

It is as if the past were folded up into the outer world, which Machado goes on struggling to see; and he suggests that if the human being does not learn to see, he will remain a narcissist. Machado mentions in his new series of "Moral Proverbs and Folk Songs" that we are worse off now than in the nineteenth century: the narcissist at that time, associated with the dandy, obsessively looked into a mirroring pond to see his face. The modern narcissist doesn't bother to look in the pond, because he has replaced nature with his own consciousness.

> This Narcissus of ours
> can't see his face in the mirror
> because he has become the mirror.

Machado's disciplined efforts to see bring many original details into his great poem "Passageways." The invention of the stereoscope excited him, and in "Passageways" he tries to bring in both lobes of the brain, as we would say now, and by this double presence create a three-dimensional vision. Heraclitus' praise of lightning comes up in the third poem, and the mystery of the spectrum, of colors that unfold in a certain order, appears in the sixth poem of the series.

Machado wants in his new book first, to see the outer world, and, second, to converse with "the other who walks by my side." As early as 1908 he had expressed the concept of the "other one" in "Portrait."

I talk always to the man who walks along with me.

In the second series of "Moral Proverbs and Folk Songs" he writes:

Look for your other half
who walks along next to you,
and tends to be what you aren't.

To find this one, we should look in the mirror, and we will see the other half of us looking back.

Now a wonderfully complicated idea appears: the more we try to see, the more our "other eyes" can see us. The more we try to see, the more we encourage the "other eyes" to see us.

The eyes you're longing for—
listen now—
the eyes you see yourself in
are eyes because they see you.

This kind of seeing does not make us feel self-conscious, as when we imagine that other people are looking at us, but on the contrary it calms us down, makes us feel seen.

The eye you see is not
an eye because you see it;
it is an eye because it sees you.

Our job is to stitch ourselves and the world together. This is particularly necessary after the appearance in Europe of the Cartesian split by which one usually means the separation of mind and body, or consciousness and the world. A gap develops between the westerner and the world, and he falls in. It is as if the western man or woman sees, but nothing looks back.

I notice also in this book a powerful advance in thinking. If Antonio Machado in *Campos de Castilla* invited thinking to enter the poem, we could say that he takes a further step now, and invites philosophical thinking to enter. He is not afraid that it will kill feeling, and it doesn't.

To do philosophical thinking implies that one takes the old philosophical arguments seriously, as if the old philosophers were still alive, and then one takes a stand on them. "With old Heraclitus we believe that the world is ruled by lightning."

Machado takes up several philosophical problems, and one is this: If God is absolute Being, then how could He have created, in us and the world, something incomplete? It can also be put this way: Since creation, like thought, always proceeds by opposites, then God, who is absolute Being, would of course create absolute Nothing, or Nada. But the world partially at least exists, so there we are again. Verlaine expressed the paradox, saying: "The universe amounts to a flaw / in the purity of non-existence." The medium Michael MacMacha once said to me that this idea is the essence of the insanity that the Aryans brought down with them from the mountains around 1500 B.C.—in its accent on purity it is a little insane. And I like it that Machado when he thinks does not reject this philosophical problem passed on to us by the Aryan past, but instead takes it in his arms; one could say that if these old problems are old clothes, he washes them. He brings the problems down to the river, and spends years washing them.

The washing he does in two places: the new series of "Moral Proverbs and Folk Songs" (I have translated forty of the ninety-nine in the series) and in the "Abel Martín" poems.

"Moral Proverbs and Folk Songs," with swift thinking and elegant poetry mingled, is a genre Machado invented. The genre derives from four distinct models. One is the popular Spanish copla, the second the sayings of Pythagoras, the third the Japanese haiku, and the fourth the wisdom quatrains of Muslim and Jewish literature. Machado refers several times to Sem Tob, the fourteenth-century doctor and rabbi whose book of seven hundred quatrains he read. Machado points out that not-thinking is no guarantee that you exist:

Now someone has come up with this:
Cogito ergo non sum.
What an exaggeration!

But his late masterpieces are the "Abel Martín" poems. Abel Martín, his invented poet-philosopher, helped him to say certain things, and he composed for Abel Martín a small book of about sixty pages, made up of literary criticism, remembrances of Martín by his student Juan de Mairena, poems by both men, and commentary on the philosophical implications of these poems. "In the theology of Abel Martín," Mairena says, "God is defined as absolute Being, and therefore nothing which exists could be his work."

> When the I AM THAT I AM made nothing
> and rested, which rest it certainly deserved,
> night now accompanied day, and man
> had his friend in the absence of the woman.

Nada, or Pure Nothing, Machado imagines in this poem as the zero or empty egg. Reason, which is able to abstract, and so approach this empty circle, now appears, or breaks out, in man.

> And the universal egg rose, empty,
> pale, chill and not yet heavy with matter,
> full of unweighable mist, in his hand.

Only the "standing animals" can see zero, and so only they are capable of conceptual thought, on the one hand, or "olvido" on the other, which literally means "forgetting," but which implies letting something fall out of the conscious mind.

> Since the wild animal's back is now your shoulder,
> and since the miracle of not-being is finished,
> start then, poet, a song at the edge of it all
> to death, to silence, and to what does not return.

"Siesta," Juan de Mairena's elegy for Abel Martín, I think is one of the most powerful brief poems of the century. So much of Machado returns here: time passing returns as the goldfish, the Roman and Greek past returns as Cupid, who "flies away in the white stone," art that is accessible returns as the ivory copla of the green cicada, and God's creation of nothing returns as the siesta, which amounts to a short time of silence in the midst of noise.

> let us give honor to the Lord—
> the black mark of his good hand—
> who has arranged for silence in all this noise.

Faith does not give birth to human thought, but human thought is hidden inside faith, as a sculpture is hidden inside a block of stone.

> Honor to the God of distance and of absence,
> of the anchor in the sea—the open sea—
> He frees us from the world—it's everywhere—
> He opens roads for us to walk on.

Because "Hoy es siempre todavía," all that has lived is still living. Machado is now in his fifties, but his childhood is still within him, perhaps even events that took place before he was born. I'll end my commentary on his work with a memory he let Juan de Mairena tell.

> Another incident, also important, took place before I was born. There were some dolphins who lost their way, and riding the tides, ascended the Guadalquiver River, arriving at last as far up as Seville. People came down to the river from all over the city, drawn by the extraordinary sight, young girls, lovers, and among them my parents, who wanted to see this sight they had never seen. It was a bright afternoon. I recall that afternoon now and then . . . or perhaps I imagined it or dreamt it.

William Stafford and the Golden Thread

William Stafford is a master. He belongs to that category of artists the Japanese have named "national treasures." He offers the work of art, as well as sharp ideas about the craft. One of his most amazing gifts to poetry is his theme of the golden thread. He believes that whenever you set a detail down in language, it becomes the end of a thread . . . and every detail—the sound of the lawn mower, the memory of your father's hands, a crack you once heard in lake ice, the jogger hurtling herself past your window—will lead you to amazing riches.

William Blake said,

> I give you the end of a golden string,
> Only wind it into a ball,
> It will lead you in at Heaven's gate
> Built in Jerusalem's wall.

I asked Stafford one day, "Do you believe that every golden thread will lead us through Jerusalem's wall, or do you love particular threads?" He replied, "No, every thread." In "Views on the Author's Vocation" (1978), he said, "Any little impulse is accepted, and enhanced. . . . The stance to take, reading or writing is neutral, ready, susceptible to now. . . . Only the golden string knows where it is going, and the role for a writer or reader is one of following, not imposing."

If every detail can by careful handling, through association, sound, tone, language, lead us in, then we live in a sacred universe. Stafford remarked, however, that "purposeful writers" may pull too hard. One has to be careful not to break the thread.

By following the tiny impulses through the meadow of language, the writer may find himself or herself closer to "the self most actually yours." It would be too much to claim that art, the practice of it, will establish a good, a serene, a superior self. No. But art will, if pursued for itself, bring into realization the "self most centrally yours." Writing poetry, then, doesn't make a poet such as Stafford a better person, only a more genuine *William.*

We note that following the thread is not a passive act. It actually means elaborate mental activity—the longer the line, the more choices we have to make as we near the right margin. The choices are how to follow the thread but not pull it, how to treat associating sounds, emphasize them or let them go, how much assertion is appropriate at each moment. Whether we stay close to the known voice or stretch toward a new voice, whether we come down on the side of aggression or quietism, rebellion or service, we take actions as we follow the thread, or more accurately, as we follow the thread, we immerse ourselves in a flood of action.

Animals are pious, it is said, because they obey their gorgeous limitations. The hawk is always a hawk, even the moment before his death. Hungers remain consistent, such as the owl's for the mouse. The owl does not hanker after the lion's roar, nor does the blue heron hanker after the octopus's elaborate nervous system in his many-minded cave. William Stafford is pious in this wild way. He returns again like a swallow to the barn of yielding, to the little spark of light given off by the end of the thread. We work within limitations, like the owl. "We must accustom ourselves to talking without orating, and to writing without achieving *Paradise Lost.*"

2.

New light falls on some of William Stafford's poems when you realize that he is part Indian. This helped me understand an odd quality I had often felt in his poems: his mind almost coincides with the tenets of the white man's world, but not quite. There's even a sense that the fast-moving European way may be only a passing thing. Here is a poem called "Indian Caves in the Dry Country."

> These are some canyons
> we might use again
> sometime.

We begin to notice the several poems in which he speaks to Crazy Horse or Ishi; in another he prays for the frozen dead at Yellow Knife. He speaks of the Crees as "we"; talks of the Apache word for love; writes "Sioux Haiku."

> On a relief map
> mountains remind my fingers:
> "Where Crazy Horse tried."

Bill's father used to tell the children they were part Crowfoot, a tribe historically known from upstate New York. There is something in his wide ranging, lively, narrow-lidded way of seeing the world that is not European. It feels prudent, informed, patterned by earth facts, very old.

> The chokecherries along our valley
> still bear a bright fruit. There is good
> pottery clay north of here. I remember
> our old places. When I pass the Musselshell
> I run my hand along those old grooves in the rock.

There is anger at society and its moral stupidities underneath Stafford's poems, and yet one doesn't feel the anger directed at the self that is so much a part of establishment poetry or confessional poetry or leftist poetry. He sees what was lost and what was saved; what was rejected by the Indian community and what was accepted; there's a little distance. No one is wholly at fault, but no one is innocent. "Justice will take us millions of intricate moves."

3.

Many contemporary writers, usefully, study their mothers' and fathers' psyches and feel the weight of these invisible forces pressing them into something smaller than they wished. Stafford in these matters looks to the palpable or hearable. For example, he hears his mother's sharp and sarcastic voice:

> Our mother knew our worth—
> not much. To her, success
> was not being noticed at all.
> "If we can stay out of jail,"
> `she said, "God will be proud of us."
>
> "Not worth a row of pins,"
> she said, when we looked at the album:
> "Grandpa?—ridiculous."

Stafford remarks, "My mother would say abrupt things, reckless things, liberating things. I remember her saying of some people in town, 'They are so boring you get tired of them even when they're not around.'" The poems feel like an extension of family gossip, trenchant statements made to people listening with a little more care than usual. "Something of the tonality of my mother's voice . . . recurs to me now; and I feel the bite of her disappointment in life, and a wry angle of her vision." We can feel that tonality of disappointment in Stafford's voice. Sometimes he'll end a poem with it:

> "Yes" means
> "Maybe."
>
> Looking like this at you means
> "You had your chance."

Stafford experienced his father in a very different way. His father once said to a high school child:

> "No need to get home early;
> The car can see in the dark."

184

His father seemed to hear voices from far out in the night. He is described as a listener who encouraged. When William was nine or ten, his father, walking with him in his alert, bird-glimpsing way, remarked, "You know, Billy, if you watched carefully, you could see one first." That's astonishing in this world where so many fathers compete with their sons: "Give me that wrench . . . you're ruining everything."

> My father heard so much that we still stand
> inviting the quiet by turning the face,
> waiting for a time when something in the night
> will touch us too from that other place.

Stafford has written many poems about his father, who belonged apparently to that rare group who let their faults be discussed, a great gift to a son. What he heard from his father was: "Your job is to find what the world is trying to be." The father's lack of blaming was remarkable. When Stafford's sister wrecked the family car during high school and called home, the father said, "Are you all right?"

We notice that William Stafford never apologizes for a weak poem, but he can easily offer his own poems up for scrutiny or side looks. Talking of his piece on the Sequoia seed, he remarks, "I gave you the poem, mostly just a little evasion, or excursion, then a payoff."

The most helpful advice I ever heard for beginning writers came from Bill during an interview with Cynthia Lofsness, when she was inquiring about his habit of writing a poem every day. She said something like, "What do you do if you're not so good that day?" He said, "Well, then I just lower my standards." The important thing is to adventure you way through language each day, and let blame for weak poems go.

Some critics talk of a poet's body of work as being a conversation between the living poet and some dead person such as Emerson or Milton. When we read Stafford, we glimpse the possibility that we're hearing two voices, both of which he valued and treasured: his mother's voice and his father's. Perhaps only their child could get them into the same poem.

4.

Of all the American poets of the last thirty years, I think William

Stafford broods most about community—the "mutual life" we share, as black people and white people, pacifists and militarists, city people and small town people.

> If you don't know the kind of person I am
> and I don't know the kind of person you are
> a pattern that others made may prevail in the world. . . .

This talks to the value of "inclusiveness," including many people in your world, to the encouragement of diverse voices, listening to the powerful and powerless. Why is it important that we listen?

> For there is many a small betrayal in the mind,
> a shrug that lets the fragile sequence break
> sending with shouts the horrible errors of childhood
> storming out to play through the broken dike.

He refers to the abuse that children take from adults—which Alice Miller wrote of so cogently in *For Your Own Good*—and remarks that this "small betrayal" can be a "shrug," but it is powerful enough to destroy the mutual agreements on which a just society depends.

Then he offers an astonishing image. He notes that elephants parade each holding the other's tail:

> but if one wanders the circus won't find the park.

I would have thought "they won't find their way home," but for Stafford it's "the park," the place near the center of town where the whole community plays. When the Staffords lived in Hutchinson, Kansas, their house was only a couple of blocks away from the state fairgrounds.

He offers his idea that the root of all cruelty lies in refusing to recognize what we all know as facts—that others are different from me, that we need to speak who we are, that one person "wandering" can have enormous harmful results. He says we should "consider"—slow down and see what is occurring—"lest the parade of our mutual life get lost in the dark."

He has already covered an immense amount of ground in this poem, and then he goes on to cover more:

For it is important that awake people be awake,
or a breaking line may discourage them back to sleep;
the signals we give—yes, no, or maybe—
should be clear: the darkness around us is deep.

Suddenly we realize another characteristic of William Stafford's work: he wants to talk to people who are awake. When Milton shouts, in a line Stafford has quoted in another context,

Avenge, O Lord, thy slaughtered saints, whose bones
Lie scattered on the Alpine mountains cold,

we could say Milton is shouting to those who are asleep, here a "Lord" who is asleep. Much leftist poetry, as well as didactic poetry, is directed to people who are asleep; see Mayakovsky, Robinson Jeffers, Pound's usura canto. Stafford dislikes shouting. "We must accustom ourselves to talking without orating."

We could say that Stafford's calmness, then, flows from his confidence that at least some of us who read him are awake. That confidence probably evokes the courtesy we notice in his poems, to follow him as he follows the golden thread we have to be awake. If we aren't awake, like so many critics who have—sadly and mistakenly—labeled him as simple, we will complain that we want stronger medicine. By contrast, I like the honor he gives to the intelligence of those who read poetry: "It is important that awake people be awake."

5.

Because William Stafford believes in talking to people awake, he doesn't offer enormous oppositions—Christianity vs. paganism—and then come down heavily, with full artillery, on one side. His habit and his discipline is to think ethically, but he likes to present arguments from both sides, so the poem balances precariously, like a high-wire walker standing on one hand.

If you're driving on a mountain road at night and come on a dead deer, what should you do, go around or stop? Stop only a moment or stop to take action?

Traveling through the dark I found a deer
dead on the edge of the Wilson River road.
It is usually best to roll them into the canyon:
that road is narrow; to swerve might make more dead.

He stops and walks back to the deer, and now the ethical problem becomes more vivid, pulls in emotion. There is a live fawn inside.

By glow of the taillight I stumbled back of the car
and stood by the heap, a doe, a recent killing;
she had stiffened already, almost cold.
I dragged her off; she was large in the belly.

My fingers touching her side brought me the reason—
her side was warm; her fawn lay there waiting,
alive, still, never to be born.
Beside that mountain road I hesitated.

At this moment, he could "swerve," or follow the wrong elephant. "To swerve might make more dead," as a car swerving around his parked car could injure strangers. To be an artist means to discriminate. The artist owes language to the human community, but owes his or her breathing body to the animal community. Every poem we write, every day we live, we think about what we owe to each. By knowing what to take from the world of culture and what to give back, what to take from the world of animals and what to give back, we become adults. That awake people are aware of the two communities—the human beings and the animals—is assumed, and the decision between those two is not easy,

The car aimed ahead its lowered parking lights;
under the hood purred the steady engine.
I stood in the glare of the warm exhaust turning red;
around our group I could hear the wilderness listen.

Ah, yes. The wild things *are* interested in the discriminations a human being makes standing beside his car.

I thought hard for us all—my only swerving—
then pushed her over the edge into the river.

6.

William Stafford looks mild, but actually he is quite fierce. I heard a story about a week he spent as teacher at the Bread Loaf Writers' Conference. The staff emphasized "finding your voice," which turned out to be a study of what the poetry establishment wanted at the moment. Every teacher gave one craft lecture. Stafford began, "I want to say that I don't agree with anything that has been said here this week. You already have a voice and don't need to find one." He hasn't been invited back.

Stafford made a decision in 1942, when he was twenty-six, to refuse induction in the U.S. Army. Clearly it was a fierce decision. Such refusal brought more consequences in the Second World War than in the Vietnam era. Patriotism ran high in 1942, and the four years Stafford spent working in various objectors' camps put him in danger sometimes from local citizens. His fine prose memoir called *Down in My Heart* decribes those four years. And he doesn't apologize, decades later.

In camps like that, if I should go again,
I'd still study the gospel and play the accordion.

He says, in "For my Young Friends Who Are Afraid,"

What you fear
will not go away: it will take you into
yourself and bless you and keep you.
That's the world, and we all live there.

He didn't take that decision—to refuse violence—as a calm man, either. In a disturbing poem called "Clash," he begins

The butcher knife was there
on the table my father made.
The hatchet was on the stair;
I knew where it was.

He locates the knife and the hatchet not among evil people or in some other country, some other tribe, but in his own house. His mother, it seems, had the hatchet; he had the knife.

> If she taunted, I grew still.
> If she faltered, I lowered the knife.
> I did not have to kill.
> Time had made me stronger.
>
> I won before too late,
> and—a man by the time she died—
> I had traveled from love to hate
> and partway back again.

He is not describing any particular family incident here, I think, but a relationship with knife and hatchet that extended over decades. Yet there was one important moment.

> Now all I have, my life,
> strange, comes partly from this:
> I thought about a knife
> when I learned that great word—"Choose."

Stafford is not an eccentric thinker who makes up positions as he goes along. Eliot's intellectual matrix was Augustine's certainties around depravity. Wallace Stevens's matrix was Emersonian and Nietzschean certainties around the disappearing gods. Stafford's matrix is clear. He draws from two sources: the rebellious certainties of the Brethren and the pacifists, those who do; and the introverted philosophers, those who think and say.

> Our vows
> cross: never to kill and call it fate.

He vows he will not kill; he does not call it fate. He compares these vows with every set of impulses that crosses his line of vision. He lays the ideas up next to tiny human events; like a philosopher he is willing also to extend the idea into God's realm and see what happens. When his thought reaches into God's realm, his poetry brushes tragedy:

> Animals full of light
> walk through the forest
> toward someone aiming a gun
> loaded with darkness.
>
> That's the world; God
> holding still
> letting it happen again,
> and again and again.

7.

Stafford's decision in 1942 when he was twenty-seven to refuse to be drafted, to refuse to follow the old aggressive patterns, started his adult life. This life—so different in that way from most of ours—began with a right decision. Many began their lives with what was for them a wrong decision. These decisions return one way or another every day. Stafford—distinctively among contemporary poets—faces decisions about aggression in every poem. All those slyly named "decisions" he talks of when he follows the golden thread to the center of the poem amount to refusals to adopt instinctive pressures. "As far as I can assess my own attitudes . . . I have an unusually intense distrust of language." He doesn't want to be led by habit. He wants to make up his own mind whether to mention parking lights or the moon, whether to honor General Patton by bringing him into a poem, or Pascal.

> . . . around our group I could hear the wilderness listen.

And the wilderness is interested in what human beings will do—for example, if they pause to think before they respond, and how long they pause. When we give up "orating," we forego collective truths and adopt adventuring in language. When we "decide," we are doing the only possible thing to protect ourselves from interior aggressive patterns.

The reason why William Stafford is such an important poet is that he deals in every poem with discerning, discriminating, particularly how to discriminate between the various responses in us to our own aggressive impulses. We could say that despite his playful titles, his secret subject is aggression.

A brief glance at infants raging makes clear that the human species is an aggressive species. The human being is aggressive just as water is wet. We know animals—stags or cranes—thrive by a ritualized aggression that ritual controls confer. We abandoned ritual control long ago. Tribal and city culture, human culture as we know it, attempts instead to dampen the aggressive drive in children by taboos, rules, parental tyranny, religious doctrine, by threats of exile or hellfire, by beatings that usually take place in the family or the school.

Many of the taboos have recently been abandoned. During the last few decades, more and more barriers to aggression fell away. During the period when Mao, through the Red Guards, actively ordered citizens in China to throw away discrimination and indulge denunciation, violence, destruction of treasures, and the beating of cultured persons, increased shootings, murders, dismemberments, revenge, and mindless killings were being shown on family television in the United States. We could say that mass culture no longer stands in the way of aggression.

How can aggression be controlled? The only other possibility is for each individual member of society to renounce instinctual aggression and chooses a peaceful life inside society. "The most stubborn enemies of civilization are its individual members," so the German psychologist Alexander Mitscherlich says. The "driver" inside each human being can, by weighing, balancing, reflecting, pausing, examining, and discriminating, keep his or her own aggressive drives from moving forward into action. Stafford writes in his poem called "Lit Instructor" of his work as a teacher:

> Day after day up there beating my wings
> with all of the softness truth requires,
> I feel them shrug whenever I pause:
> they class my voice among tentative things,
>
> And they credit fact, force, battering.
> I dance my way toward the family of knowing,
> embracing stray error as a long-lost boy
> and bringing him home with my fluttering.

Every quick feather asserts a just claim;
it bites like a saw into white pine.
I communicate right; but explain to the dean—
well, Right has a long and intricate name.

And the saying of it is a lonely thing.

This realization that each word we "adventure toward" in a poem involves either giving in to aggression or finding a new way is a weighty one. Poetry is the most playful art of all, and here we see a man bringing serious decision into all this playfulness. That is a wonderful triumph. I believe William Stafford will be read with even greater attention in the next hundred years, because this subject of restraining aggression is the most important problem we face.

Some Rumors About Kabir

No one knows much about Kabir. A few life details and a few stories are told over and over. He was evidently not a monk or an ascetic, but was married, had children, and made his living by weaving cloth at home. Some say he was the son of Moslem parents, others that he was found on the streets and brought up by a Moslem couple. There may have been in the house books of the great Sufi poets of two hundred years before, such as Rumi. So it is possible Kabir knew the eccentric energy of the Sufis, the heretic or rebellious branch of the Mohammedans, by the time he was sixteen or seventeen. It is said he then asked Ramananda, the great Hindu ascetic, to initiate him. Ramananda had experienced the ecstatic power of the male god Rama and took "the glad joy of Rama" as his name. Ramananda refused Kabir, saying, "No, you're a Moslem." Kabir knew that Ramananda went down to the Ganges each day before dawn, and Kabir lay down on the steps. Ramananda walked out in the half dark and stepped on the boy's body. Astonished, he leapt up and cried, "Rama!" Kabir then jumped up and said, "You spoke the name of God in my presence. You initiated me. I'm your student!" Ramananda then, it is said, initiated him. Kabir became a powerful spiritual man and poet. His poems are amazing even in his wide tradition for the way he unites in one body the two rivers of ecstatic Sufism—supremely confident, secretive, desert meditation, utterly opposed to orthodoxy and academics, given to dance and weeping—and the Hindu tradition, which is more sober on the surface, coming through the Vedas and Vishnu, Ram, and Krishna.

Here is another Kabir story. At one time about fifteen hundred meditators came down from the hills and sat together in a big hall in north India. The number of people doing hard inner work in that century was large. They asked Kabir to read to them, but they had not asked Mirabai. Mirabai composed ecstatic bhakti poems; her whole life flowed in the stream of Radha-Krishna intensity. She walked from village to village with holy men singing her poems "for the Dark One," and dancing; she was much loved. Kabir entered the hall and said, "Where is Mirabai? You know what I see in this hall? I see fifteen hundred male egos." He refused to read until Mirabai came. So someone went for her—she was miles away—and they waited in silence, maybe one day or two. Mirabai at last arrived. She read for thirty-five minutes. At the end of that time it was clear that her bhakti was so much greater than anyone else's in the room that the gathering broke up, and all the meditators, reminded of how much they had to do, went back to their huts.

Mirabai wrote her poems in Rajasthani, and about two hundred of them have survived. This story of Mirabai and Kabir is lovely and, as the Sufis would say, in the spiritual world it happened. In chronology there is a problem. When my first small group of Kabir versions was printed in Calcutta, the publisher set down firmly the birth date of Kabir as 1398, and the death date as 1518. That means he lived one hundred twenty years. That's possible. Most scholars guess Mirabai's birth date as 1498. That means Kabir was a hundred years old the day she was born. So if both dates are true, then she could have been eighteen when she arrived at the hall, and he would have been one hundred eighteen years old. That's possible; anything is possible. Or, since dating is difficult, both birth dates may be wrong. We do know that both poets lived—accounts of people who met them have survived. Mirabai does mention Kabir in one of her poems, as well as another poet, Namdev, born earlier, around 1270. Mirabai says, speaking to Krishna,

> Oh you who lift mountains, stay with me always!
> You brought a full ox to Kabir's house,
>> and mended the hut where Namdev lived.

So there was a flow between the two, and the story suggests that very well.

✳   ✳   ✳

Most of the observations a critic could make about Kabir's poems you can deduce by reading them. He does mention several times that his poems belong in the bhakti tradition, and I've decided to leave their word as it is. There's very little one can say about the bhakti tradition that doesn't diminish it. Perhaps we could see it more clearly by comparing it with a contrasting road. Some of the European saints of the Middle Ages, such as Tauler, walked the opposite path, they said no to the body and meant it. On this path, the link between the ego and the body is emphasized, and the ego is then dispersed through humiliation of the body. The humiliation is a long process associated with hatred of the senses. The practicer tries to imagine how disgusting his or her body will be when it's dead, hair shirts and whips re used to humiliate the skin, attachments are dispersed, the practicer tries to free his spiritual energy from sexual energy by repulsion. Blake wrote the most powerful criticism of this path: "Better murder an infant in its cradle than nurse unacted desires." "Priests in black gowns are walking their rounds, And binding with briars my joys and desires." The road was called the "via negativa," and Eliot in his religious life consciously followed it.

The bhakti path is not peculiar to India, is no one's invention, and I'm sure it existed in Ras Shamra and among the Etruscans. Some of the Odin myths and Babylonian myths that seem to us quaint will be seen to refer to it. In the Indian subcontinent a vast rise of bhakti energy began in the eighth or ninth century, as if ocean water had suddenly reappeared in the center of a continent. Sometime during those centuries an alternative to the Vedic chanting began. The Vedas were in Sanskrit, and the chanting done for others by trained priests, by what we might call religious academics. The new bhakti worship involved heart-love, feeling, dancing—Mirabai evidently used castanets and ankle rings—love of color, of intensity, of male-female poles, avoidance of convention, a discipline which is shared by Tristan and Isolde. Bhakti worship involves the present tense, and in contemporary language, rather than the old "classical" tongue, as when Dante decided to write *La Vita Nuova* in Italian rather than in Latin. The poets of India began to write ecstatic poetry in their local languages, and so refreshed the bhakti experience "from underneath." Some poems were written specifically for the long bhakti sessions, which lasted three or four hours in the middle of the night, and the sessions were guided through their stages by chanted and sung poems.

In north India, the bhakti experience became associated with Krishna as a visualization of the right side of the body, and with Radha as a visualization of the left. Jayadeva gave a great gift around 1200 with his *Gita Govinda* and its ecstatic passages of Radha and Krishna's lovemaking. "Great circle" dances appeared, and marvelous paintings, where Radha and Krishna look at each other with enormous eyes. "The joy of looking for him is so immense that you just dive in and coast around like a fish in the water. If anyone needs a head, the lover leaps up to offer his. Kabir's poems touch on the secrets of this bhakti." The male poets usually describe Radha and Krishna from outside or evoke her feelings when separated. Mirabai never mentions Radha just as Christ never mentions the Essenes because he is the Essenes, just as she is Radha. Kabir sometimes speaks as a man, sometimes as a woman.

> This woman weaves threads that are subtle,
> and the intensity of her praise makes them fine.
>
> Kabir says: I am that woman.
> I am weaving the linen of night and day.
>
> When my lover comes and I feel his feet,
> the gift I will have for him is tears.

The ecstatic meditator Shri Caitanya traveled occasionally between 1510 and 1530 from village to village in Bengal, teaching the villagers what bhakti experience looked and felt like, bringing dances with him, and the intensity rose higher. Namdev, Jnaneshwar, Chandidas and Vidyapati wrote marvelous poems, all virtually unknown to us, in the years before Kabir. Mirabai, Kumbhandas, and Surda are a few of the intense poets that followed.

✳ ✳ ✳

Kabir in his joyful poems delivers harsh and unorthodox opinions. He enters controversies. For example, when Christ says, "The Kingdom of the Spirit resembles a cottonwood seed," the translators of the time found themselves dealing with three sets of opposites, familiar also to Chinese thought, of Spirit-Body, sky-earth, and Heaven-this world. The translator must choose among them. St. Paul, with other early fathers, committed the Church to translating the phrase as "the Kingdom of Heaven." The opposite state, then, is this life. Salvation is then driven into the next life. Kabir says a simple error of translation like this can destroy a religion. This throwing of intensity forward is a destructive habit of both Hindus and Moslems, and Kabir, attacking both, writes of that in his terrifying poem:

If you don't break your ropes while you're alive,
do you think ghosts
will do it after?

What is found now is found then.
If you find nothing now, you will simply end up
with an apartment in the city of death.

The best-known religious poetry in English, of Vaughn and Traherne, for example, contains rather mild and orthodox ideas. Such harsh instruction as Kabir gives we are unprepared for. In Vaughn the thought and feeling swim together under the shelter of a gentle dogma. In Kabir one leaps ahead of the other, as if jumping out of the sea, and the reader smiles in joy at so much energy. It is as if both thought and feeling fed a third thing, a rebellious originality, and with that tail the poem shoots through the water. We feel that speed sometimes in Eckhart also. Kabir says that when you do interior work, the work is not done by the method, but by the intensity. "Look at me, and you will see a slave of that intensity." The word "intensity" widens to its full range here. We understand that such intensity is impossible without having intense feeling, intense thinking, intense intuition, and intense love of colors and odors and animals. He hears the sound of "the anklets on the feet of an insect as it walks."

In Kabir's poems, then, you see the astonishing event—highly religious and intensely spiritual poems written outside of, and in opposition to, the standard Hindu, Mohammedan, or Christian dogmas. Kabir says, "Suppose you scrub your ethical skin until it shines, but inside there is no music, then what?" He also attacks the simple-minded Yoga practices and guru cults, such as we see growing up all around us in the United States. It's valuable to have these practices discussed by an Indian, not a Westerner. Kabir says, "The Yogi comes along in his famous orange. But if inside he is colorless, then what?" To Kabir, the main danger is spiritual passivity. Kabir is opposed to repeating any truth from another teacher, whether of English literature or Buddhism, that you yourself have not experienced.

> The Sacred Books of the East are nothing but words.
> I looked through their covers one day sideways.

> Kabir talks only about what he has lived through.
> If you have not lived through something, it is not true.

Kabir mocks passivity toward holy texts, toward popular gurus, and the passive practice of Yoga, but we must understand that he himself is firmly in the guru tradition and that he followed an intricate path, with fierce meditative practices, guided by energetic visualization of "sun" and "moon" energies. In poems not translated here—I don't have the language for it, nor the experience—he dives into the whole matter of Sakti energy, ways of uniting right and left, and going upward with "the third." These labors have not been experienced yet in the West, or have been experienced but discussed at length only in alchemy. He has, moreover, enigmatic or puzzle poems that no contemporary commentator fully understands. I love his poems and am grateful every day for their gift.

A Note About My Versions

My versions are based on poems in *One Hundred Poems of Kabir*, translated by Rabindranath Tagore, assisted by Evelyn Underhill (Macmillan). The English of the Tagore-Underhill translations is hopeless, and I simply put a few of them, whose interiors I had become especially fond of, into more contemporary language, to see what they might look like. In one poem I violated chronology, putting "a loaded gun" where Tagore says "deadly weapon." I noticed that we have defenses against the general and the nostalgic, but not against the specific and the contemporary. That doesn't excuse the change, but it explains my motive. I believe translations should be as accurate as possible. Kabir wrote the originals in Hindi; Tagore was working from a Bengali translation of that. Many errors may be built in, but I have done my best.

The Surprises in Ghalib

As I read the literal versions that Sunil Dutta prepared of Ghalib's poetry, it was clear to me that some fresh substance was appearing that I hadn't seen before. I have been fond for years of Kabir's delight in God and the soul:

> Inside this clay jug there are canyons and pine mountains, and the
> maker of canyons and pine mountains!
> All seven oceans are inside, and hundreds of millions of stars. . . .

> If you want the truth, I will tell you the truth:
> Friend, listen: the God whom I love is inside.

Rumi is equally sure:

> This moment this love comes to rest in me, many beings
> in one being.
> In one wheat grain a thousand sheaf stacks.
> Inside the needle's eye a turning night of stars.
> *(translated by Coleman Barks)*

This enthusiasm, this surety, so far beyond the hopes we usually have for change, widens the boundaries of our soul in a way they are not used to, moving them toward ecstasy and joy. It's as if when Kabir writes a letter to God, God always answers. We could say that when Ghalib writes a letter to God, God doesn't answer. Ghalib says:

> When I look out I see no hope for change.
> I don't see how anything in my life can end well.

Ghalib's lines, so elegant and sparse, do stretch the muscles a little that we use for truth, muscles we don't use very often.

> My destiny did not include reunion with my Friend.
> Even if I lived a hundred years, this failure would be the same.

Ghalib's tart, spicy declaration of defeated expectations ranges over many subjects:

> Heart-sorrow eventually kills us, but that's the way heart is.
> If there were no love, life would have done the trick.

This change from the buoyant confidence of Kabir, Rumi, and Mirabai to the disappointment of Ghalib, what could that mean? Perhaps the turn to failure is a natural change six centuries after Rumi and four centuries after Kabir. Perhaps spiritual achievement is harder now than it was in the thirteenth century. It's possible this change in tone has nothing to do with history at all. Perhaps Ghalib writes only six letters a day to God, instead of forty; perhaps he's distracted from the Road by the very love affairs that are to him the essence of the Road. He is a truth-teller around losing the Road. Awareness of this change was my first surprise.

The second surprise I felt as we worked lay in finding out that in Urdu there are no pronouns to distinguish gender. Some of Ghalib's poems are highly flavored and elaborate love poems declaring that the one he loves doesn't answer his letters or is capriciously cruel or generally inaccessible. There is no way of knowing from the "you" or from objective pronouns whether this person he is addressing is a woman or a man. Moreover, one can't tell whether it is a divine personage or a human personage.

A gift given by such pronouns is that the question of whether the divine is male or female is bypassed at the start. We are free at one stroke of this situation of God's gender which has so bedeviled Western religion.

When the word "you," moreover, can refer either to a divine or human "you," it is easy for a description of a love affair on the human plane to resonate as well on the divine plane.

> Others in your poetry gathering kiss the wine cup,
> But we remain thirsty even for the invitation.

Ghalib says in one ghazal:

> I'll write this letter even though I may not have a message.
> I'll send it just because I'm a lover of your name.

An Indian friend recently said to me, "At the University I loved Ghalib. I memorized his poems. He described all my experiences in love affairs. Now that I'm older, I read some of the same poems but I now experience them as written to God."

Some of Ghalib's poems are, in essence, pure love poems to a human lover, or so they seem to me; and others are clearly poems to God. But many hold both possibilities in reserve.

> My message hasn't received a reply, so I guess I'll write another.
> I think I know what the Great One would have said anyway.

Such a poem does seem to want to be read in two senses simultaneously.

> Why shouldn't I scream? I can stop. Perhaps
> The Great One notices Ghalib only when he stops screaming.

Sometimes, where a pronoun such as "he" or "she" would be called for in English, we have used the phrase "the Great One" if it seems clear that the poem is one of those addressed at least partially to God.

When a certain poem is clearly addressed to God, we sometimes use the word "You":

> Since nothing actually exists except You,
> Why do I keep hearing all this noise?

202

Our perception that "things" are real doesn't quite fit with the idea that they don't actually exist. One view held in Muslim religious circles is that the universe we know is a mixture of the Existent and the Non-Existent. Such things as trees, streets, people and clouds all belong to Non-Existence in that they're only shadows thrown by a genuinely existent Sun.

> These magnificent women with their beauty astound me.
> Their side-glances, their eyebrows, how does all that work? What
>   is it?

> These palm trees and these tulips, where did they come from?
> What purpose do they serve? What are clouds and wind?

I think this is a marvelous poem. He ends the poem by saying:

> The abundant objects of the world mean nothing at all!
> But if the wine is free, how can Ghalib hold back?

This last poem lets us see the amazing way that the thoughts of Ghalib's ghazals are put together. No clear thread unites all the couplets. For example, if we return to the poem mentioned above, called "My Spiritual State," which begins,

> When I look out, I see no hope for change.
> I don't see how anything in my life can end well.

we see it as a statement of theme. But a fresh theme arrives in the next stanza, a little explosion of humor and sadness:

> Their funeral date is already decided, but still
> People complain that they can't sleep.

The third sher embarks on a third theme:

> When young, my love-disasters made me burst out laughing.
> Now even funny things seem sober to me.

It becomes clear that we are dealing with a way of adventuring one's way through a poem which is utterly distinct from our habit of textual consistency in theme. Most of the poems we know, whether written in English or French or German or Hausa, tend to follow from an idea clearly announced at the start. "Something there is that doesn't love a wall." And the poet then fulfills the theme, often brilliantly, by drawing on personal experience, and by offering anecdotes, dreams, other voices ("Good fences make good neighbors.") so that by the end the theme is fulfilled. The ghazal form we are dealing with here—there are others—does not do that. It invites the reader to discover the hidden center of the poem or the hidden thought which ties it all together, a hidden center which the poet himself or herself never expresses. I find this delicious. Moreover, when we arrive at the final sher, where, according to our typical expectations, the poet should clinch his argument, Ghalib often does exactly the opposite. He throws everyone off the scent by making a personal remark.

> Your talk about spiritual matters is great, Oh Ghalib.
> You could have been thought of as a sage if you didn't drink all the
>   time.

Over the centuries, the ghazal writers have found a way of keeping the mystery of the poem intact, or perhaps it is a way of asking the reader to do more work than Western poets ask the reader to do. This ghazal way refuses to accommodate our felt need that the windows should be lined up so that one beam of light goes straight through all of them. It's as if, in such a ghazal, the writer throws a group of handsome bones onto the field, and the reader has to put them together to make a dog, or if he or she prefers a larger companion, perhaps a horse. The holding of mystery we feel especially in the poem called "When the Day Comes." It begins:

> One can sigh, but a lifetime is needed to finish it.
> We'll die before we see the tangles in your hair loosened.

The second stanza says:

> There are dangers in waves, in all those crocodiles with their jaws
>   open.

The drop of water goes through many difficulties before it becomes
   a pearl.

The third embarks on a different thought:

> Love requires waiting, but desire doesn't want to wait.
> The heart has no patience; it would rather bleed to death.

The fourth stanza goes back to answers than do not come:

> I know you will respond when you understand the state of my soul,
> But I'll probably become earth before all that is clear to you.

Then he mentions that the dawn sun makes the dewdrop disappear:

> When the sun arrives the dew on the petal passes through existence.
> I am also me until your kind eye catches sight of me.

He calls up the delight of the poetry readings that were held in private houses
in his time.

> How long is our life? How long does an eyelash flutter?
> The warmth of a poetry gathering is like a single spark.

The last thought is this:

> Oh Ghalib, the sorrows of existence, what can cure them but death?
> There are so many colors in the candle flame, and then the day
>   comes.

I want to take this opportunity to thank Sunil Dutta for the hundreds
of hours of labor he has put into these translations. Our work would begin
as he wrote out each couplet in Urdu script; that was followed by a word-
by-word version in English, which would be awkward and virtually incomprehensible. Then he would abandon the Urdu word order and create two
lines in English that hint at the content of the Urdu. But so many ambiguities
would be omitted in this version that each sher then required several para-

graphs of prose in which the hidden cultural or religious or philosophical questions were brought out into the open. At that point I would enter the process and make a try at composing a couple of lines that would resonate with each other a little. Imposed meanings would stick out here and there like burrs on a dog, and we would have to painstakingly remove those burrs.

Perhaps other people will be able to do better in the future with Ghalib poems than we have done; we know that our versions have many flaws. But each of us has worked out of our own separate delight in Ghalib; and as Ghalib says: "This poem has come to an end, but my longing to praise hasn't."

III
Opinions and Judgments

A Wrong Turning in American Poetry

I

American poetry resembles a group of huge spiral arms whirling about in space. Eliot and Pound are moving away at tremendous speeds. Marianne Moore and Jeffers are driving into space also. This island universe is rushing away from its own center.

Let me contrast this picture with another. Spanish poetry of this century is moving inward, concentrating. Antonio Machado stands at the center of Spanish poetry, standing at the center of himself as well. His poems are strange without being neurotic. His thought is abundant and clear, near the center of life. The younger Spanish poets can judge where they are from where he is. They can look in and see him standing there.

In American poetry, on the other hand, a young poet cannot take Pound, Eliot, or Moore for a master without severe distortion of his own personality. They whirled about so far out that anyone who follows them will freeze to death. If American poetry has a center it would seem to be William Carlos Williams. His poetry however shows a fundamental absence of spiritual intensity. He is in fact as much caught up in destructive expansion as the others.

II

Eliot, Pound, Moore and Williams, all born within five years of each other, form a poetic generation we might call the generation of 1917. They support certain ideas with great assurance. Eliot's support of the idea of the "objective correlative" is an example. His phrasing of the idea is as follows: "The only way of expressing emotion in the form of art is by finding an 'objective correlative'; in other words, a set of objects, a situation, a chain of events which shall be the formula or that *particular* emotion." The tone is authoritative, but the statement is not true. With "objective" here, we stumble onto a word we will find over and over again in the work of the 1917 generation. These men have more trust in the objective, outer world than in the inner world. As poets, they want to concern themselves with objects. The word "formula" above suggests the desire to be scientific, to study things. Eliot says in essence that *objects* are essential in a poem. He wants to arrange them in a formula, as a scientist would, so that the controlled experiment can be repeated any number of times.

As a program, the search for the objective correlative merely obstructs poetry. What does the search for this formula result in? The impulse for the poem does not flow forward into the language. Instead the impulse is stopped: the poet searches about for the proper formula in the public world. This means working up the poem as an idea—for example, in terms of the lower classes ("Sweeney Erect") or in terms of Greek myth ("Sweeney Agonistes"). Greek myths and the lower classes are thought to be very objective. However, the impulse to the poem is broken. True freshness and surprise are impossible. The poet's eyes are not on the impulse but are constantly looking over the public world for reliable sets of objects. Finally, the poet's own mind becomes objective: he becomes the public.

Modern Spanish poetry—to continue our contrast—denies Eliot's thesis of the relevance of the objectivizing process. Ricardo Gullon, for example, has said that the purpose of poetry "is to transfer an intuition." How is an intuition to be transferred? Guillaume de Torre, the greatest contemporary Spanish critic, holds up the personal, even the intimate poem. Intuition is embodied in experiences private to the poet (which the reader can nonetheless share) "and not in common experiences from the public domain masquerading as unique and vital. T. S. Eliot's 'objective correlative' and other vulgarities dressed up in cryptic terms are nothing but so many frauds."

Lorca has a poem describing his emotions while walking on the streets of New York, feeling that he is aging, being rapidly killed by the sky. He does not talk of Circe or the clothes of bums sleeping on the sidewalk. He says:

> Among the forms which are moving toward the serpent,
> And the forms which are searching for the crystal,
> I'll grow long hair.
>
> With the tree of amputated limbs which does not sing,
> And the boy child with the white face of the egg.
> With all the tiny animals who have gone insane,
> And the ragged water which walks on its dry feet.

Lorca conveys his emotion not by any "formula" but by means that do not occur to Eliot—by passionate spontaneity. The phrase "objective correlative" is astoundingly passionless. For Lorca there is no time to think of a cunning set of circumstances that would carry the emotion in a dehydrated form to which the reader need only add water.

Pound said in 1911, "I believe that the proper and perfect symbol is the natural object." Pound considers poetry to be fundamentally a repository of wisdom. He wishes to put into the *Cantos* as many important thoughts and conversations and fragments of the classics as he can, so that should a man be able to own only one book he could own the *Cantos* and thereby possess the truth about economics and government as well as culture. The poem is thus defined with no reference to the unconscious. Instead of the unconscious there is economics. Relations between parts of the outer world take the place of inner relations and of the inner world. The book takes what it needs by force. As a poem, the *Cantos* annexes other people's ideas, facts, other languages. The poem is like an infinitely expanding metropolis, eating up more and more of the outer world, with less and less life at the center. The personality of the poet is driven out of the poem. The expanding poem, like the expanding city, has no personality. The idea of the poem as the essence of the author's personality—Yeats believed this is what a poem was—is entirely lost. How can the personality be present if the unconscious is pushed out?

Marianne Moore's poetry also represents a treasure-house—a feminine one. The objects in the poem are fragments, annexed, and the poem is a parlor full of knickknacks carefully arranged. Melville leaves such a room and goes to sea: there he sees whales moving about in the sea their whole lives, winds thrashing freely, primitive forces that act out their own inward strength. Returning to land he becomes a revolutionary because in society he sees such elementary forces curtailed; he asks why they must be checked and lamed. The purpose of Marianne Moore's art is exactly opposite: it is to reconcile us to living with hampered forces. She brings in animals and fish, but only fragments of them—beaks of birds, single wings of dragonflies, the dorsal fin of a whale, the teeth of snakes, the forepaw of an otter—all adopted to domestic life. Everything is reduced in size, reduced to human dimensions, as in old New England parlors, where there was "a shark's backbone made into a walking stick." The poem becomes a temporary excursion into the dangerous world of nature, with an immediate and safe return already envisioned—a kind of picnic. The fragments of animals that appear are separated from their inner force, their wildness, and turned from living things into objects. A poem is conceived as an exercise in propriety.

William Carlos Williams's work reflects a similar attachment to objects. "No ideas but in things!" he said. His poems show great emotional life mingled with the drive of the intelligence to deal with outward things—but no inward life, if by inward life we mean an interest in the spiritual as well as psychological intensity. Williams was a noble man, of all the poets in his generation the warmest and most human. Still, his ideas contained something destructive: there is in them a drive toward the extinction of personality. Williams's "No ideas but in things!" is a crippling program. Beside the ideas in things there are ideas in images and in feelings. True, bits of broken glass are preferable for poetry to fuzzy generalities such as virtue or patriotism. But images like Lorca's "black horses and dark people are riding over the deep roads of the guitar" also contain ideas and give birth to ideas. Williams asked poetry to confine itself to wheelbarrows, bottle caps, weeds—with the artist "limited to the range of his contact with the objective world." Keeping close to the surface becomes an obsession. The effect of Williams's thought, therefore, was to narrow the language of poetry—to narrow it to general remarks mixed with bits of glass and paper bags, with what Pound called "natural objects." Williams says, "The good poetry is where the vividness comes up true like in prose but better. That's poetry."

BETWEEN WALLS

The back wings
of the

hospital where
nothing

will grow lie
cinders

in which shine
the broken

pieces of a green
bottle

In that Williams poem, the personality and the imagination are merely two among many guests. The imagination has to exist as best it can in a poem crowded with objects. In the bare poems of some of Williams's followers the personality of the poet is diffused among lampposts and match folders, and vanishes. The poet appears in the poem only as a disembodied anger or an immovable eye.

The point in contrasting Lorca's language with Williams's is not that Lorca's poems are richer but that Lorca approaches his poetry with entirely different artistic principles—among them the absolute essentiality of the image. These ideas bear fruit in the poems. Lorca's poems have many things in them sharply observed ("black doves puttering the putrid waves"), but they also have images, also passion, wild leaps, huge arsenic lobsters falling out of the sky.

Charles Olson, about fifty, is generally considered the main transmitter of the ideas of Williams and Pound to the present generation. In Olson's prose, their outward direction is set down even more programatically, as in "Projective Verse"—an essay that echoes T. E. Hulme—in which Olson says,

Objectivism is the getting rid of the lyrical interference of the
individual as ego, of the "subject" and his soul, that peculiar pre-

sumption by which western man has interposed himself between what he is as creature of nature (with certain instructions to carry out) and those other creations of nature which we may, with no derogation, call objects.

In demanding that the poet get rid of himself as a subjective person Olson is simply restating Eliot's belief in the desirability of "extinguishing the personality." To Olson the poet's inwardness is "lyrical interference." Some Zen teachers use language like this, but their meaning is exactly the opposite. The aim of Zen, as of a poet like Rilke, is to make men more and more inward until they stop admiring objects, at which point they will be able to see them clearly, if they wish to.

The ideas of the 1917 generation are quite consistent. Eliot and Pound conceive maturity as a growth of outwardness. Eliot's later plays are naturally more outward than his earlier plays, the *Cantos* are more outward than *Lustra*. The opposite is true of Yeats and Rilke. Rilke was more inward at thirty than at twenty; more inward at fifty than at thirty.

In this country we have a great reluctance to admit that directions can be incompatible. We want to follow both the Pound-Olson direction and the Rilke direction. Yet in *Letters to a Young Poet* Rilke writes, "Give up all that. You are looking outward, and that above all you should not do now. There is only one single way. Go into yourself." And he tells Kappus that poetry will come "from this turning inward, from this sinking into your private world." Rilke believes that the poet actually experiences the soul, does not share the mass's preoccupation with objects.

If we are to develop clear principles in our poetry we must honestly say that we cannot reconcile the inward direction of Rilke with the outward direction of the Williams-Pound-Olson movement. This is why Pound talks of Rilke so little. A man cannot turn his face at the same moment toward the inward world and the outer world: he cannot face both south and north at the same moment.

III

I have tried to point out that the 1917 generation had a rather unified set of ideas centers on objectivism—shared by all the major poets of that gen-

eration despite their other differences. All later poetry has been written, necessarily, under the influence of these ideas. Now how can we describe our
poetry since the twenties in a way that will include Winters as well as Lowell,
Eberhart as well as Ciardi?

It is first of all a poetry without spiritual life. The beginning of spiritual
life is a horror of emptiness that our people feel every day, but it is Rilke
who has described such a state, not one of us.

> Already the ripening barberries are red,
> And in their bed the aged asters hardly breathe.
> Whoever now is not rich inside, at the end of summer,
> Will wait and wait, and never be himself.
>
> Whoever now is unable to close his eyes
> Absolutely certain that a crowd of faces
> Is only waiting till the night comes
> In order to stand up around him in the darkness—
> That man is worn out, like an old man.
>
> Nothing more will happen to him, no day will arrive,
> And everything that does happen will cheat him.
> Even you, my God. And you are like a stone
> Which draws him daily deeper into the depths.

Our recent poetry is also a poetry in which the poem is considered to
be a construction independent of the poet. It is imagined that when the poet
says "I" in a poem he does not mean himself, but rather some other person— "the poet" — a dramatic hero. The poem is conceived as a clock that
one sets going. This idea encourages the poet to construct automated and
flawless machines. Such poems have thousands of intricately moving parts,
dozens of iambic belts and pulleys, precision trippers that rhyme at the right
moment, lights flashing alternately red and green, steam valves that whistle
like birds. This is the admired poem. Richard Wilbur, for all his ability, fell
a victim to this narrow conception of the poem. His earlier "Water Walker,"
written before this oppressive concept of the poem penetrated him, remains
his most personal and freshest poem. Robert Lowell in *Lord Weary's Castle* con-
structed machines of such magnitude that he found it impossible to stop

them. Like the automated, chain-reacting tool of the sorcerer's apprentice, the poems will not obey. The references to Jesus and Mary that end several of them are last-minute expedients, artistically dishonest and resembling a pile of cloths thrown into a machine to stop it.

The great poets of this century have written their poems in exactly the opposite way. In the poems of Neruda, Vallejo, Jiménez, Machado, and Rilke, the poem is an extension of the substance of the man, no different from his skin or his hands. The substance of the man who wrote the poem reaches far out into the darkness and the poem is his whole body, seeing with his ears and his fingers and his hair.

Here is a poem of Machado's, written before the death of his wife; here the "I" *is* the poet.

> From the doorsill of a dream they called my name. . . .
> It was the good voice, the voice I loved so much.
>
> —Listen. Will you go with me to visit the soul?
> A soft stroke reached up to my heart.
>
> —With you always . . . And in my dream I walked
> Down a long and solitary corridor,
> Aware of the touching of the pure robe,
> And the soft beating of blood in the hand that loved me.

Next, the poetry we have had in this country is a poetry without even a trace of revolutionary feeling—in either language or politics.

It is startling to realize that in the last twenty years there have been almost no poems touching on political subjects, although such concerns have been present daily. The *Kenyon Review*, under Ransom, and the *Southern Review*, under Tate, have been effective forces here. The guiding impulse in both Ransom's and Tate's minds is fear of revolution. As Southerners they act to exaggerate the fear felt by even Northerners. This kind of Southerner thinks of himself as a disinherited aristocrat. Their holding position in poetry has more resemblance to the attitude of Governor Ross Barnett of Mississippi than most people would be willing to admit. Laforgue says, "The only remedy is to break everything." Ransom says, in effect, that the only remedy is to keep everything. This is why there is so much talk of Donne and New

Criticism in the *Kenyon Review*—such concerns tend to damp down any tendencies toward revolution. Ransom remarked that he never published poems by Dylan Thomas because Thomas didn't know how to behave in a drawing room. Neruda and Brecht were not welcome in the *Kenyon Review* either.

If revolutionary thought is put down, revolution in language also dies. The absence of any interest in fresh language in literary magazines shows up in the thirties and forties. Compared with that of Hart Crane or Cummings, the language of Nemerov or Ciardi or Jarrell is inexpressibly dull. Jarrell, for example, opens a poem:

> One looks from the train
> Almost as one looked as a child. In the sunlight
> What I see still seems to me plain.

There is almost no contrast inside the line. A poet who has higher standards in language can put together inside a line words that have different natures—like strange animals together in a wood. Mallarmé uses this kind of contrast as a foundation for his poems. Awareness of the different kinds of fur that words have is instantly apparent in Lorca's poems:

> One day
> The horses will live in the saloons
> And the outraged ants
> Will throw themselves on the yellow skies that have taken refuge in
>   the eyes of cows.

Compare this with a typical stanza of ours:

> Youth comes to jingle nickels and crack wise;
> The baseball scores are his, the magazines
> Devoted to lust, the jazz, the Coca-Cola,
>   The lending library of love's latest.
>   —Karl Shapiro, "The Drug Store"

In Shapiro's stanza, the words are all one color: gray.

The poetry of the thirties and forties moves backward. Art Buchwald once described the scene he imagined could take place as a Fly Now-Pay Later plan collides with a failure to make a payment on time. A man from the travel agency comes to your house with a curious electric machine. You sit down in it, the current is turned on, and the machine removes all your memories of Europe. In the poetry of the thirties and forties we are supposed to forget that there were even any ideas of a different language for poetry—forget that the German expressionist poets ever lived, forget the experiments in language represented by French poets, and later by Alberti and Lorca. Poetry is forgotten, if by poetry we mean exploration into the unknown, and not entertainment; an intellectual adventure of the greatest importance, not an attempt to teach manners, an attempt to face the deep inwardness of the twentieth century, not attempts to preserve the virtues of moderation. The forties generation succeeds in forgetting both the revolution in language and any revolutionary feeling toward society.

Our postwar poets defend the status quo. Nemerov, Ransom, and Ciardi, for instance, by their examples, urge poets not to make too much trouble in the universities. Ransom urges us to have a "civilized attitude." Most of these men are merely accepting the ideas of T. S. Eliot, who supports the Establishment. Hölderlin wrote a short poem on this subject, which has great common sense.

> Deep down I despise the herd of leaders and ministers,
> But I despise even more the genius who takes their side.

The poetry we have now is poetry without the image. The only movement in American poetry that concentrates on the image was imagism, in 1911-1913. But "imagism" was largely "picturism." An image and a picture differ in that the image, being the natural speech of the imagination, cannot be drawn from or inserted back into the real world. It is an animal native to the imagination. Like Bonnefoy's "interior sea lighted by turning eagles," it cannot be seen in real life. A picture, on the other hand, is drawn from the objective "real" world. "Petals on a wet black bough" can actually be seen.

We have merely to glance at a typical American stanza of the last years to see that the image is destroyed before birth by pressure of the direct statement or the picture. John Ciardi writes,

> Now mist takes the hemlocks and nothing

stirs. This is a gray-green and a
glassy thing and nothing stirs. A plane
to or from Newark burrs down idling on
its flaps or grinds full-rich up its
airy grade, and I hear it.

But if there is no image how is the unconscious going to make its way into the poem? Let us consider the typical "form" poem. Suppose there is no image: then such a statement in a poem a "I must perfect my will" is composed by the conscious mind, rhymes searched for and found by the conscious mind. The efficient workaday conscious mind creates the entire poem. The important thing about an image, on the other hand, is that it is made by both the conscious and the unconscious mind. This is true of Yeats's image of the beast of the "Second Coming" and of Lorca's "the glasses of the dawn are broken."

Finally, then, our poetry has been a poetry essentially without the unconscious.

This is not surprising. Two of our strongest traditions have been puritanism (our so-called religious tradition) and business (our secular tradition). The mind of the puritan shows fear of the unconscious—a belief that only ugly and horrible images and ideas come from it. All animal life and sexual life are met with fear and disdain. These are the impulses behind the poetry of Eliot and Pound and that of the neoclassic school as well. The impulses do not describe the poetry of Hart Crane and Theodore Roethke, exceptions of almost all the points I have been making.

Max Weber showed that the apparent asceticism of the puritan had a secret purpose: to adapt the man to an efficient life in business. Working in business "ascetically" fifteen hours a day is the mark of a man who has resisted Satan; success in outward things becomes a proof of religious virtue. The drive toward outward things in the 1917 generation and in recent poets is essentially obedience to business traditions.

These two strains—puritan fear of the unconscious and the business drive toward dealing in outer things—meet in our poetry to push out the unconscious. The 1917 poets tried to adapt poetry to business and science. They looked for "formulas." They tried to deal efficiently with natural objects. They studied to develop "technical skill"—like engineers.

Then, brandishing their technical skill, the poets of the thirties and forties evict the unconscious. And poetry sinks—plunges, sometimes—into the outer world. Titles of books indicate this in an interesting way. Richard Wilbur's third book is called *Things of This World*. Shapiro titled his first book *Person, Place, and Thing*, and his new one *The Bourgeois Poet*.

IV

Ortega y Gasset in *Man and Crisis* suggests that the intellectual history of a nation hinges on the difference between generations. Members of the younger generation, when they get to be about thirty years old, find that the ideas of the older men do not seem to describe the world accurately. As the young man "meditates on the world in force" (the world of the men who in his time are mature) he finds "his problems, his doubts, are very different from those which the mature men felt in their own youth." The ideas of mature men seem false or at least no longer adequate. The men of the younger generation therefore advance their own ideas and attack the ideas of the older generation. In this debate—in which all can take part—the old ideas are examined, ideas themselves are made real, new ideas hammered out. A nation's intellectual life depends on this struggle between generations.

I have discussed briefly the generation of 1917. (Frost and Stevens, considerably older men, belong to an earlier group.) After the 1917 generation a group of this country's poets appeared who might be called the metaphysical generation. Not only were these poets of the twenties and thirties profoundly influenced by the English metaphysical poets, but their basic attitude was detached, doctrinaire, "philosophical." Eberhart's poetry is destroyed, in most poems, by philosophical terms used with fanaticism. Poetry becomes abstract. The poet takes a step back and brings doctrines between himself and his experience. The presence of doctrines, metaphysical or political, marks both the puritan metaphysicals and the left-wing radicals—Eberhart and Tate as well as the *New Masses* poets. The interest in doctrine is all taken from the 1917 poets. Tate, for example, is a disciple of Eliot, a man nearly a decade older.

The next clearly defined generation is that of 1947—the war generation, including Karl Shapiro, Robert Lowell, John Berryman, Delmore Schwartz, Randall Jarrell, and Howard Nemerov. Their convictions about poetry are so impersonal and changeable that it would be truer to say they have no convictions at all. Ortega remarks, "Imagine a person who, when in the country, completely loses his sense of direction. He will take a few steps in one direction, then a few more in another, perhaps the exact opposite." We are reminded of Shapiro, who in his first book has a vicious attack on D. H. Lawrence; this is followed by wholehearted praise of Lawrence; his worship of New Criticism is followed by pointed disgust for it; he pursues the academic style in his own poetry, and then discards it for the Ginsberg style. Both styles are for him equally bankrupt.

The generation of 1947 might very well be called the hysterical generation. Its response to the question of literary style or content is hysterical. In fact, hysteria itself is often a subject matter of these men's poetry, as in Berryman's *Homage to Mistress Bradstreet*. The history of Lowell's style shows the same pattern as Shapiro's. Accepting Tate's ideas, Lowell adopts a fanatically formal verse only to abandon it abruptly for the prose style of *Life Studies*. The sad fact is that he is not really fitted for either of these styles, and his own style remains undiscovered.

The progress of the generations since 1917 might then be described as the progress from the objectivist generation to the metaphysical generation to the hysterical—three clearly marked psychic steps. They are not steps toward irrationality but toward dullness and lack of conviction. They are states that succeed one another in a process of disintegration of personality. After the initial step away from inwardness, and toward the world of things, this country's poets increasingly lose touch with their own inward reality and become less and less sure of themselves. They no longer stand firmly inside their own convictions.

The outstanding characteristic of the generation of 1947 is its reluctance to criticize ideas handed to them. That new generation did not create an idea of its own. Randall Jarrell's criticism is occupied with praise of Marianne Moore and others, without any serious discussion of ideas. If Richard Wilbur has any criticism of the ideas or poetry of men older than himself, he doesn't mention it. Robert Lowell reviewed Yvor Winters's collected poems for *Poetry* and reported that the reason Winters had been left out of so many anthologies was that he is "so original and radical," an "immortal poet." In the *Hudson Review* Lowell later gave a similar blanket endorsement of William Carlos Williams. There is something intellectually shameful about his accepting the standards of both of these men, because their standards are not only different but contradictory. Such acceptance of the ideas of older men by younger men is unnatural as well as unhealthy.

What is the result of this strange lack of intellectual struggle between the generations? Ortega remarks,

> Entire generations falsify themselves to themselves; that is to say, they wrap themselves up in artistic styles, in doctrines, in political movements which are insincere and which fill the lack of genuine convictions. When they get to be about forty years old, these generations become null and void, because at that age one can no longer live in fictions.

V

I have been putting forward general ideas about poetry. Let us see if these ideas hold up when poems are in front of us.

Here is an entire poem by Juan Ramón Jiménez, which has an inner intensity.

> Music—
> Naked woman
> Running mad through the pure night!

And here are lines in which the intensity is all on the surface:

> Would you perhaps consent to be
> The very rack and crucifix of winter, winter's wild
> Knife-edged, continuing and unreleasing,
> Intent and stripping, ice-caressing wind?
> (Delmore Schwartz, "Will You Perhaps")

This is the opening of a poem by Rafael Alberti, translated by Anthony Kerrigan:

> By the side of the sea and a river in my early days
> I wanted to be a horse.
> The reed shores were made of wind and mares.

I wanted to be a horse.
And here are lines from a recent American anthology:

> The old man accepts a Lucky Strike.
> He was a friend of my grandfather.
> We talk of the decline of the population
> And of codfish and herring.
> While he waits for a herring boat to come in.
> (Elizabeth Bishop, "At the Fishhouses")

In the Bishop poem we can feel the outer world driving in, invading the poem. The facts of the outer world push out the imagination and occupy the poem themselves. The lines become inflexible. The poem becomes heavy and stolid, like a toad that has eaten ball bearings.

Here are lines from *Life Studies:*

> Father and Mother moved to Beverly Farms
> to be a two-minute walk from the station,
> half an hour by train from the Boston doctors.
> (Robert Lowell, "Terminal Days at Beverly Farms")

And from Jarrell:

> "In a minute the doctor will find out what is wrong
> And cure me," the patients think as they wait.
> They are patient as their name, and look childishly
> And religiously at the circumstances of their hope,
> The nurse, the diplomas, the old magazines.
> (Randall Jarrell, "A Utopian Journey")

In this country's poems the facts are put in because they happened, regardless of how much they lame the poem. *Life Studies* is a very important book on the development of the outward poem, because it shows that the outward poem moves inevitably toward sociology. Here is a poem by Juan Ramón Jiménez, which makes an interesting contrast with the American sociological poem:

> I am not I.
>> I am this one
> Walking beside me whom I do not see,
> Whom at times I manage to visit,
> And at other times I forget.
> The one who remains silent when I talk,
> The one who forgives, sweet, when I hate,
> The one who takes a walk when I am indoors,
> The one who will remain standing when I die.

And one of ours:

> whenever he left a job,
> he bought a smarter car.
> Father's last employer
> was Scudder, Stevens, and Clark Investment Advisors,
> himself his only client.
> While Mother dragged to bed alone,
> read Menninger . . .
>> ("Commander Lowell")

This is seriously reviewed as poetry, because U.S. critics demand very little from our poets. And the poets demand very little from themselves.

Apollinaire insisted on the presence of poetry, even in four lines. His poem "Flies":

> Our flies know all the tunes
> Which they learned from the flies of Norway—
> Those giant flies that are
> The divinities of the snow.

The poem devoid of any revolutionary feeling, in politics or language, has no choice but to become descriptive prose, sociological prose—or worse, light verse. Often in recent American poetry the poet adopts a genial, joshing tone, indicating that what he is saying doesn't seem to be of any importance to him. To point up the difference between real poetry and what passes among us for poetry, let me quote a stanza by the Peruvian poet Vallejo, followed by a stanza in the joshing tone.

> The anger that breaks a man down into small boys,
> That breaks the small boy down into equal birds,
> And the birds, then, into tiny eggs;
> The anger of the poor
> Owns one smooth oil against two vinegars.

And this is the opening of a poem by Howard Nemerov in *Fifteen Modern American Poets:*

> Her laughter was infectious; so, some found,
> Her love. Several young men reasonably
> Regret inciting her to gratitude
> And learning of her ardent facility.

Poetry without inwardness or revolutionary feeling has no choice but to end in a kind of fabricated grossness. Poetry on this level of imagination must become more and more coarse to achieve sensation. Poets like Karl Shapiro are convinced that if they can only make a poem gross or outrageous enough it will be a great poem. A poem, then, becomes defined as something more prosy than prose.

> New York, killer of poets, do you remember the day
> you passed me through your lower intestine? The troop
> train paused under Grand Central. That line of women
> in mink coats handed us doughnuts through the smutty
> windows. They were all crying. For that I forgave New
> York. (We smuggled a postcard off at New Haven.)

In this Shapiro passage the senses are completely dead. In fact, there has been a steady deadening of the senses in our poetry since 1918. There were fewer odors and colors in new poems in 1958 than there were in 1918. The absence of the senses in our poems at times is astonishing.

Here is a medieval Arabic poem called "Storm":

> Each flower in the dark air opens its mouth,

Feeling about for the breasts of the abundant rain.
Meanwhile armies of the black-skinned clouds, loaded with water,
      march by
Majestically, bristling with the golden swords of lightning.

Here are some lines by Stanley Kunitz that are typical of our time:

The compass of the ego is designed
To circumscribe intact a lesser mind
With definition. . . .
              ("Lovers Relentlessly")

Abstraction is merely another form of the flight from inwardness; the objectivist takes flight into the outward world, and the rationalist into the efficient intellect. Rationalists try to convince us that the atrophying of the senses is a good thing, and they describe it as the development of abstract language in poetry.

In this country intellectual statement about passion is thought to be superior to passion—or at least equal to it. Yvor Winters urges us to be sure our rational mind is present when we write a poem:

A poem is good in so far as it makes a defensible rational statement about a given human experience (the experience need not be real but it must in some sense be possible) and at the same time communicates the emotion which ought to be motivated by that rational understanding of the experience.
              ("In Defense of Reason")

Passion cannot be trusted unless taken apart and put together again by the reason. The mind will tell us what we ought to feel. Rilke has an entirely different vision of poetry:

O Lord, give each person his own personal death.
A dying that moves out of the same life he lived.
In which he had love, and intelligence, and trouble.

Here are Winters's lines:

This passion is the scholar's heritage.
The imposition of a busy age.
The passion to condense from book to book
Unbroken wisdom in a single look.

The program is quite mad. If all the senses died, all images die, all association with the unconscious dies, all revolutionary feeling dies, then, it is believed, we are near poetry. Let me quote as a final contrast a medieval Arabic poem—a true poem—followed by some lines of Louise Bogan.

Never have I seen or heard of anything like this:
A pearl that changes out of modesty into a red jewel.

Her face is so white that when you look at its beauty,
You see your own face under its clear water.

and Bogan:

I burned my life that I might find
A passion wholly of the mind,
Thought divorced from eye and bone,
Ecstasy come to breath alone.

Under the influence of objectivism and abstraction, not only does our poetry become mediocre but our criticism also. When the senses die, the sense within us that delights in poetry dies also. And it is this sense of delight that tells us whether a given group of words contains genuine poetry or not. A great poet and a great critic are like the mule who can smell fresh water ten miles away. There is a sense that tells us where the water of poetry is, abroad or at home, West or East, even under the earth.

When this sense is dead, critics have to decide whether certain books of poetry are poetry by the presence of forms, or of "important statements," or of wit, or even of length. The longer a poem is the more poetry it is thought to contain. The American lines I have quoted are often very bad and I chose them partially with that in mind. Yet in each case they show the direction of the quoted poet's work as a whole. Moreover, the very fact that the poet wrote them, printed them in a book, and allowed them to stand is evidence of the atrophying of the sense of poetry. It is possible that the American lines I have quoted are bad poetry, but another possibility is that they aren't poetry at all.

A human body, just dead, is very like a living body except that it no longer contains something that was invisible anyway. In a poem, as in a human body, what is invisible makes all the difference. The presence of poetry in words is extremely mysterious. As we know from the Japanese experience of the haiku, as well as from the experience of many brief poems in the Western tradition, poetry can be present in fifteen words, or in ten words. Length or meter or rhyme have nothing to do with it. Ungaretti has a poem of four words ("m'illumino / d'immenso") which is unquestionably a poem.

> Everyone stands alone on the midpoint of the earth
> pierced by a ray of sunlight;
> and suddenly it's evening.

This poem of Quasimodo's manages to slip suddenly inward.

A poem is something that penetrates for an instant into the unconscious. If it can penetrate in this way, freshly, several times, then it is a poem of several lines. But if it does not do this it is not a poem at all—no matter how long it is.

The outward poem is like a pine tree made half of tin and half of wood. The poem of things conceives itself to be describing the world correctly because there are pieces of the world in it. This poetry cannot sustain the poet or itself because the imagination has no privacy in which to grow. In the last thirty years in America the intelligence of the poet runs back and forth hurriedly between the world inside his head and the world outside. The imagination meanwhile is thinking in its chamber. The intelligence knocks at the door, demanding some imagination to put between a flat statement and a piece of glass, and rushes out with the gift. Then it hurries back to get a little more imagination to prevent two subway cars from rubbing together. The imagination is continually disturbed, torn away bit by bit, consumed like a bin of corn eaten gradually by mice.

The imagination does not want to hear these constant knockings on the door. It prefers to remain in its chamber, undisturbed, until it can create the poem all of one substance—itself. The imagination out of its own resources creates a poem as strong as the world that it faces. Rilke speaks of *"die Be-*

freiung der dichterischen Figur," which may be translated as "the liberation of the poetic image," "the releasing of the image from jail." The poet is thinking of a poem in which the image is released from imprisonment among objects. The domination of the imagination is established over the entire poem. When this happens the poem enters the unconscious naturally.

Our poetry took a wrong turning years ago. Some centuries have a profound spiritual movement: poetry, when vigorous, always is a part of it. We know that ours is a century of technical obsession, of business mentality, of human effort dissipated among objects, of expansion, of a destructive motion outward. Yet there is also a movement in the opposite direction that is even more powerful. The best thought in this century moves inward. This movement has been sustained by Freud, by great poetry of Europe and South America, by painting, by the most intelligent men. This is the important movement. The weakness of our poetry is that it does not share in this movement.

Most of our poetry so far has nothing to give us because, like its audience, it drifts aimlessly in the world. A country's poetry can drift outward, like the lives of most of its people, or it can plunge inward, trying for great intensity. Inward poetry deepens all life around it. Other poets have given their countries this gift. If we fail in this, of what use is our life? As Lorca says, life is not a dream.

1963

When Literary Life
Was Still Piled Up in a Few Places

I first came to Iowa City in 1954, driving an old '42 Dodge which I had bought from a German exile in Boston for $65. I spent a couple of weeks on the way at the famous literary summer school in Bloomington, Indiana. John Crowe Ransom gave a talk on "A Litany in Time of Plague" by Thomas Nashe. One stanza reads:

> Beauty is but a flower
> Which wrinkles will devour;
> Brightness falls from the air,
> Queens have died young and fair,
> Dust hath closed Helen's eye.
> I am sick, I must die.
> Lord have mercy on us!

He noted that most teachers describe this poem as iambic, but if you speak the poem passionately, your voice will tell you the meter is not iambic at all. Powerful beats come in at the start of each line, so the meter is an imitation of the old Greek and Roman rhythms.

> Strength stoops unto the grave,
> Worms feed on Hector brave,

Swords may not fight with fate,
Earth still holds ope her gate.
Come! come! the bells do cry.
I am sick, I must die.
Lord have mercy on us!

This marvelous lecture gave hints of new possibilities beyond the iambic mode I had been taught. I also saw William Empson with his long beard riding down the street on a bicycle. I mention these details only to give a sense of what high or elegant literary life was like in those days. It wasn't spread all over the country, so to speak, to a depth of one or two inches as it is now. Instead it piled up in separate places such as Gambier, Ohio, or Bloomington, Indiana, or even Iowa City, at a height of six or seven feet. I remember hearing that Robert Lowell, on his first honeymoon, pitched his tent on Allen Tate's lawn. He had a fine instinct for where the water was high. Jean Stafford later complained that he kept leaving her alone in the tent; he was always inside talking with the Tates.

When my $65 dollar car finally approached the center of Iowa City, I was astounded. The buildings were two stories high only. I guess I must have had in mind some sort of image as that I've just given, an image that associates literary intensity with physical heights, which may have translated itself into high buildings. I felt dismayed. I knew Robert Lowell had been teaching in Iowa City, and I said to myself, "What kind of country is this in which a poet that great is teaching in a town with two story buildings?" There's a lot wrong with my perception, but I was so self-centered and full of fantasies that there's not much use going into the inaccuracies. One could say that it wasn't as if Lowell had been exiled. Paul Engle, with his useful and intelligent impulse toward concentration of literary intensity, had called him there, and Lowell understood. Lowell's acceptance was a compliment to Paul's grasp of the way literature proceeds. A year or two later Engle brought in John Berryman; and Phil Levine's marvelous essay about Berryman's teaching in *The Bread of Time* suggests perfectly the way the physical presence of one superb writer, in this case Berryman, can change the life, and restructure the body cells, so to speak, of a younger writer ready to be made more intense.

I had come to Iowa hoping for a writing grant from the Rockefeller Foundation, but when I arrived, I heard it had gone to another, and so there I was in Iowa City with no money and no life. I went to see Paul Engle, and after some conversations with Ray West, and the head of freshman English, I was allowed to come into the workshop and given two classes to teach, one in freshman English and one called "Greeks and the Bible." The salary was $100 a month for each, as I recall, so there I was. I could get by on $200 a month, living in a tiny room and eating at a boarding house. Paul was generous, straightforward; he loved poetry, knew good poetry when he saw it, and was no slouch at building a program.

My only other workshop had been at Harvard with Archibald MacLeish. Among the participants were John Hawkes, Kenneth Koch, Don Hall, Mit Hughes, Bob Crichton, Bill Emerson. Most were World War II veterans, just now back in college, and all we did was attack Archibald MacLeish and belittle his friends such as Ezra Pound and Ernest Hemingway. We rarely discussed our own work. Our behavior was outrageous, and it took MacLeish a long time to get over it. So when I sat down in Paul Engle's workshop, it was the first time I had ever seen that strange thing, blue dittoed poems. I was amazed. It seemed beneath the dignity of art to mimeograph poems. We didn't attack the teacher this time; in general, the aggression went against each other. Everyone knew that W. D. Snodgrass, the graduate of an earlier workshop and still hovering in the neighborhood somewhere, had done something introspective and important in poems later called *Heart's Needle*. But he had to be careful if he turned up, because knives seemed to be out for him. That's the way I recall it. I don't recall being aggressive myself, but perhaps my memory is bad. I do remember hearing around 1975 a story of my behavior in the Iowa workshop twenty years earlier. It seems that I regularly brought a snake to class with me in a gunny sack, and whenever someone began to criticize a poem of mine, I would take the snake out and lay it on the table. I was amazed to be imagined as a snake handler. But we can feel several kinds of fear in this story

The workshop discussions were actually a little pedestrian; certain fads among the poets would dominate for a while. That's always the case with workshops. At the end Paul would come in and say rather sensible remarks. Given my history with MacLeish, whose lofty pronouncements floated down from some earlier heaven, this workshop was my first experience of literary democracy, even perhaps of that horizontal and envy-ridden culture which I later called sibling.

This piece will be more a memoir of the time than of Paul himself, but the literary excitement and dedication we all experienced was due to Paul's sagacity. The teaching most of us did made our lives rather hectic, and I commented in my diary, "In such a hectic life no large work can be conceived." I wrote in my diary one day, "I could work today only from 2:45, when I got back from a conference with Paul Engle, till 3:30, when I had to go to Muncie. Then I worked again from 5:30 to 5:45, hardly one hour altogether. I wrote the poem for Paul Engle, or rather attempted it. How wonderful it is to write poems for someone who cares about you!" So it was clear that I felt a lot of affection and support coming from him.

I also found notes from a conversation I had had with Paul, in which I remarked, "Paul's greatest need is precisely to be needed." So he and I were much alike in that way. He gave me advice on a group of poems I showed him, poems full of Ideas for poems and Possibilities for inner life. To me he always talked straight; he warned me about my grandiosity and my tendency to live six lives at once. His advice was very good: "Do one thing, not many." These were warnings that didn't do much good.

Many lively events happened in our workshops, and many able writers came to speak, but I failed to notice most of them. One personality did become vivid to me, a Korean short story writer, Kim Yong Ik, whom Paul had recruited for the fiction workshop. He and I would walk out in the Iowa City cemetery and look at the black-wingéd angel and talk about art. He looked at the creation of art as a marvelous opportunity which in the course of human life, may arrive as a real possibility only once in every ninth or tenth generation. It had come to him. Dostoevsky was our hero, who would talk to himself in his room while he imagined some character in his fiction, and then he would weep over what had happened to that person. "Surely this is what writing really is—to give all," Kim said. And when we parted near dawn, he would say, "Tomorrow morning we must work very hard." He knew a lot. One day I brought to him a poem that I had begun in New York, and it said something like:

> I wander down the streets, not knowing
> Who I am, and I am lost.

Kim said, "Oh no. If you say you're lost, that means you're already partly found. If someone is in the woods and truly lost, he doesn't even know that he's lost."

I was stunned. "Well, what do I do then?"

"You just take out the phrase 'I am lost.' Then you compose some images that seem not to belong exactly, rationally. Then when the reader experiences those images, he will say, 'This kid is lost!'" I've been grateful for that for years.

He didn't believe in Western competition. Sometimes when we walked in the cemetery, he'd say, looking at the large stones and the small ones, "You're still competing." I asked him about Korean graveyards. He mentioned a graveyard with wooden markers in his town that stood on a slope. After a few years, the markers and graves would all wash down the slope. I must mention that Kim who had lived for many years in Pittsburgh, writing well, died only a few months ago, during an emotional trip back to Korea.

I noted in my diary, "William Carlos Williams is coming next Monday." He read his poems in the old Capitol Building on campus. The head of the English department introduced him and said, "Tonight we have William Carlos Williams, one of the finest poets now writing in English." Williams stood up and said, "Goddam it! How many times do I have to tell you, I write in American, not in English!" That's what he was like. I loved him, and had hitchhiked to see him when I was an undergraduate.

Later in the spring, Robert Lowell came back for a visit, though he wasn't teaching at the workshop while I was there. I heard that he was staying at Ray West's house, so I sent a manuscript and, calling, asked if I could talk to him. He replied that he had to leave for the airport at such and such a time, but I could come. Here's how I described the fast glimpse of him in my journal: "He stood there hunched, a weight behind his eyes—gentle, graceful, unburning—wise in adaptation. How I trembled to meet him. How odd a poet is in this housey world, simply growing older among small things and small talk. What graceful hands draped questioningly at his chin . . . Marvelous is the word for him." I didn't describe our actual conversation in the diary. When I arrived, he was chatting with Ray West and Delmore Schwarz's first wife, getting ready to go to the airport. As they exchanged remarks, I was amazed to hear that the subject was William Carlos Williams, and his bad poems, ridiculous attitudes, his provincialism, etc. I began to burn. I knew that Williams had been and still was a sort of foster father to Lowell; Williams acted helpfully to balance the influence of Lowell's other, more conservative foster father, Allen Tate. Finally I spoke from my corner of the room, and said this wasn't a true picture of William Carlos Williams or his poetry. All three turned and looked at me as people look at a cockroach. They went on talking, but moved on to another subject. I waited further. Finally Lowell said, looking at his watch, "All right, come on over." He had in his hand the little manuscript I'd given him; he had picked out a brief poem that I had written the year before while living in New York and virtually as a hobo. After being cooped up in the city for months, I drove with friends in someone else's car down through Maryland and felt amazed by the great trees. The poem goes:

> With pale women in Maryland,
> Passing the proud and tragic pastures,
> And stupefied with love
> And the stupendous burdens of the foreign trees,
> As all before us lived, dazed
> With overabundant love in the reach of the Chesapeake,
> Past the tobacco warehouse, through our dark lives
> Like those before, we move to the death we love
> With pale women in Maryland.

I was uncertain about the poem, uncertain about everything. What he said took me by surprise. He said, "Do you know which county you were passing through in Maryland?" "No," I said. "Well you could find that out," he said, "then go there; or go to a library and find out details of the history of that county. That's what I do," he said. "In that situation, I look up all the historical facts I can, find who founded that county, what sort of crimes took place, who introduced the tobacco farming, and so on. Then as I rewrite I try to get as many of those facts as I can into the poem." He wasn't unkind. At least his advice was clear. But I slumped out and was depressed for two or three weeks, saying to myself, "Well, that's it. If that's how a genuine poem is done, I can't do it. I'm not a poet." I didn't look at the poem again for a long time. Six years later, when I was gathering poems for what was at last to be my first book, *Silence in the Snowy Fields*, I found the poem again and realized that Lowell had been wrong. Some poems don't have historical facts, they just float. This particular poem is a bit elevated and naively romantic in its juvenile love of death, but still it has its integrity like a haiku or a small Chinese lyric. If one puts extraneous, interesting facts into such a poem, it will sink to the bottom of the river. I recalled a poem of Tu Fu's that Kim had often recited to me in Iowa City, a kind of exile's poem:

At the end of the mountain gorge
I hear dark monkeys wail,
In native land a white goose flies over.
Where are my sisters?
Where are my brothers?

This poem could use a few historical facts, perhaps, but if its aim is grief, it's best left as it is.

Paul and Mary would have big parties up at their stone house in Stone City, and I became fond of their children. In the spring of 1956, my wife Carol MacLean and I and Lew Harbison, a student of mine, and his wife went down to the Mississippi River bottoms a few miles south of Iowa City, all wet springiness and tall bare trees and flat ground recently abandoned by the river. High in a tree we saw two young great horned owls. Using a thin movable dead tree, we managed to push the owls along until they fell off the branch. Then we put them in a box and brought them back to Iowa City. I planned to bring the owls north to the Minnesota farm later that week. When Paul heard about the owls, he asked if I would bring them into his daughter's third grade class for the children to see. I did, and the little owls were spectacular, full of feistiness, with huge, intense eyes, like novelists or generals. A few days later, I did drive them up to the farm in Minnesota and let them go, and they were both around there in the draw for years, hooting to each other and wondering what happened to the Mississippi River flats.

When I heard in 1975 or so the story about the gunny sack I would take to class with the snake in it, I realized that it was the same story: the human proclivities for envy, projection and malice had altered the tale of two half-grown owls in a cardboard box in the third grade to a snake in a gunny sack in a graduate school classroom. So it is.

These adventures, these meetings with writers, this gathering place for people sick of small towns, all rose from Paul's sagacity. It was Paul who asked Marguerite Young, that amazing poet, essayist, raconteur, surrealist, fictionalist, to come to town. In my last dip into my diary, I'll put down a few sentences about her:

Tonight I met Marguerite Young and once more the real world returns. Words, vision, meditation, the incredible greatness and sweetness of those on the limb of words. It is all words, and how the whole world dissolves away and leaves in its place the love for those people, and these people, who so love and in return are loved by words. Look into your heart; disregard the world of classes and deadlines and the blue world crossed with red, that entices and takes all away, that one cannot love. Love those who love words, and restrict your friendship to those.

The Eight Stages of Translation

In this essay I will not deal with the theory of translation but I will try to answer the question: What is it like to translate a poem? We'll look mainly at the difficulties. The difficulties are all one difficulty, something immense, knotted, exasperating, fond of disguises, resistant, confusing, all of a piece. One translates a poem in fits and starts, getting a half line here, weeks later the other half, but one senses a process. I'm going to simplify the process into eight stages. I mean by that the stages one goes through from the first meeting with a poem to its recreation, when one says goodbye to it. As I've mentioned above, the stages will often collapse into each other, or a single line will suddenly go through all eight stages in a flash, while the other lines lie about looking even more resistant than before. What I will do then is to pretend that all goes in order; but this is an ancient ploy. When one makes a map, one pretends the earth can be laid out flat. But a map helps us to visualize the territory.

I decided not to choose a poem I had already translated, which I would write about from hindsight, but instead I chose virtually at random a sonnet from Rilke's first series of the *Sonnets to Orpheus,* a poem I did not know well. In preparation for this essay, I took the poem to a seminar in German translation and we all worked through the sonnet. The sonnet is this one:

XXI

Frühling ist wiedergekommen. Die Erde

ist wie ein Kind, das Gedichte weiss;
viele, o viele . . . Für die Beschwerde
langen Lernens bekommt sie den Preis.

Streng war ihr Lehrer. Wir mochten das Weisse
an dem Barte des alten Manns.
Nun, wie das Grüne, das Blaue heisse,
dürfen wir fragen: sie kanns, sie kanns!

Erde, die frei hat, du glückliche, spiele
nun mit den Kindern. Wir wollen dich fangen,
fröliche Erde. Dem Frohsten gelingts.

O, was der Lehrer sie lehrte das Viele,
und was gedruckt steht in Wurzeln und langen
schwierigen Stämmen: sie singts, sie singts!

I

During the first stage we set down a literal version, we don't worry about
nuances—English phrases that are flat, prosaic, dumpy are fine. We only
want the thrust.

Spring has returned again. The earth
is like a child that knows poems;
many, oh many. For the burdens
of her long study, she receives the prize.

Her teacher was hard. We liked the white
in the old man's beard.
Now, how the green [things] and the blue are called,
we dare to ask: she knows it, she knows it.

Earth, on vacation, you lucky one, play
with the children now. We'd like to catch you,
happy earth. Success goes to the happiest.

Oh what the teacher taught her, so many things,
and what is imprinted [or pressed] into roots and the long
difficult stems: She sings it, she sings it!

That is the literal. We notice immediately a problem with the gender of the child. Because Rilke is speaking of earth and a child at once, he is committed, *die Erde* being feminine, to a feminine pronoun, and we'll have to live with that, though we see the child could just as well be male. Earth is "it" in English, so we are already in trouble, and we'll have to face this issue sooner or later.

As we read the literal, our first reaction is: What happened to the poem? Where did it go? So we read the original again and it's still marvelous; so evidently something has been left out—probably the meaning. Before we go farther with a translation then, we have to deal with the issue: What does the poem mean?

2

To find that is what I call the second stage. Some translators just print the literal version; they turn away from this stage. If we enter it, we will need everything we have learned in literature courses, or from our own writing, and all the German we can scrape up in order to penetrate the "problems." Often friends are helpful at this stage, to bring up quirky details that we haven't noticed. Here, for example: Why is this child brought in? And if the earth has to be compared to a child, why a child "*das Gedichte weiss*"? It calls up a typical European schoolroom scene, memorization of poetry; the student who memorizes best, sometimes a girl, wins a prize that the principal perhaps awards her in public at Student's Day. The scene contains the strenuousness and tension of European grade school education. What does that have to do with the spontaneity of spring? That's the first problem.

If we read over our own literal versions, the poem appears to be a sort of depressing testimony to the way school experiences persist in the European adult. It says the earth memorizes poems, gets a prize, and is good at identifying flowers. Then a game at recess appears involving a game of tag, and the poem closes with the child or the earth singing something, no doubt in a school recital. That is what the literal says. If we read over the German, we realize that something else or something more is being said, but what?

We go back to the first question. What does grade school education have to do with the spontaneity of spring? In line with that, we ask: Who is this teacher with a white beard or with white in the beard? The white has to be snow, and he winter. Apparently earth knows her own trees and flowers from some memorization work done in winter, the same time school is in session. That's odd. In this stage, it's important to follow every eccentric branch out to its farthest twig—if one doesn't, one pulls the poem back to the mediocre middle, where we all live, reasonably.

The third stanza continues to compare or associate earth and school-work. Earth is described now as *"frei,"* which in the context means "out of school." During this stage a native born speaker is most helpful—the ambiguous meanings that surround *"weiss"* in line two, *"frei"* in line nine, and *"gedruckt"* in line thirteen, a dictionary will not settle. A native born speaker can shorten the floundering time. Spring apparently resembles the recess time, or perhaps the "play day" some schools have in May. After that we are called immediately back to the teacher. It has been mentioned how strict he is, and now, how many things he teaches. As Americans we tend to get uneasy when our convictions that earth-life and poetry are spontaneous become challenged. The whole mood of American assumptions, of which Whitman is a part, leads us to associate growth—of which the growth from winter to spring is exemplary—with spontaneity, perhaps the spontaneous writing of poetry. But Rilke does not agree with this; he connects growth in the poem— earth growth at least—with discipline, difficulty, routine memorization. This discipline he embodies in the major metaphor: the discipline of learning poems by heart. There is something un-American here, whether by American we mean Whitmanic gladness or the easy stages the "human potential" movement believes in. We don't find our hopeful prejudices supported by Rilke.

A German-born speaker will tell us that *"weiss"* in the second line does not only mean "know" but "memorize," and the context tells us the second meaning is the one used here. *"Beschwerde"* which is related to "burden," "heaviness," "pain," and "difficulty" emphasizes the painful labor involved in growth, as does *"langen"* ("long") before "study," also the word *"streng"* applied to the teacher, and particularly the adjective *"schwierigen"* in the last line, surprisingly given to tree trunks or plant stems. A native speaker will tell us this is not a usual adjective for these nouns at all; so we guess by that that Rilke is laying a special emphasis on the difficulty. Whatever the earth achieves therefore she does not achieve through spontaneity. When a poet from another culture contradicts our assumptions, we tend to fudge his point; therefore to struggle with each eccentricity we see is extremely important. Americans are merely twentieth-century readers. Rilke obviously is aware what we, as twentieth-century readers, think, and he violates our expectations consciously. What can it mean that the earth has a teacher? This detail connects to the idea of the evolution of the earth which Rudolf Steiner and others in Germany have written of. If earth has a teacher, it means earth learns gradually as a child does: the whole thing implies the earth has consciousness; one cannot learn and change without consciousness. We feel ourselves drawn here into areas we do not feel confident in, even to ideas we cannot accept. If we cannot accept them, we will resist them as a translator and do a poor job translating the poem. During this stage, then, we test how far we are willing to go. It's clear that the poet is ahead of us, otherwise the poem would not be worth translating; it would have nothing "to say." So we need to estimate how much resistance we have or we need to sense inside whether we believe, say, in growth by disciplined labor, though it contradicts most cultural assumptions, and whether we believe the earth has a teacher. If we don't, we should let the poem alone and not translate; we'll only ruin it if we go ahead.

Let's continue with this pursuit of problematic detail. A small problem arises with the ball game. The earth is *"frohliche,"* which Cassell's lists as "joyous, joyful, gay, blithesome, jovial, merry, frolicsome, gladsome." We gather the earth is not repressed, not hard-nosed, not "puritan," to use a cultural term. When Rilke suggests who will win in this game of tag with earth, we would expect it to be "the speediest child" or "the most competitive child." But it isn't so. He uses the same root *"froh,"* and the most joyful child wins, and so "catches" the earth. Here again I feel him violating our expectations, perhaps Christian expectations this time, as opposed to pagan. The Greeks, not much given to sin and savior, always taught that the most joyful child, the most joyful sculptor, the most joyful runner would win. Who gains earth? If the translator believes it is the most repentant, the most sorrowful, the most obedient, he or she should not translate this poem—something will go wrong.

The final problem we notice centers around the curious word *"gedruckt"* in line thirteen, which is placed next to "roots" or "trunks." *"Gedruckt"* means impressed, pressed on, laid on, stamped, imprinted. This word belongs to the world of factory presses, work, levers, human forces multiplied, offices, copiers, printing presses, drill presses. What is it doing here? In what sense can a root be "pressed" or "imprinted"? We have to answer it; if we don't, the poem will not be clear. There is enough ambiguity given by the forced movement to another language without additional uncertainty caused by a pious trust in ambiguity which amounts to a refusal to think the question through or risk an answer. What will we do with *"gedruckt"?* We might guess that the imprinting is genetic, as when biologists talk of an animal being "sexually imprinted" at a certain age. But if we accept that, we can't relate it to the singing or the difficulty. Is it possible some words are actually imprinted on the roots? No. Did earth's teacher *impress* this on the plants? I don't think so. Is this some sort of raised lettering, a reference to bark? I don't think so. It is pressed, not raised. How did a sheet-metal press get into this line? We could rephrase the question: How did a printing press get into this line. We see instantly its link with schoolwork because "printed" is exactly how the schoolchild finds the poem which she memorizes. It has been *printed.* After some debate, I adopted this solution, which may or course be wrong, but it allows me to put the details together into a meaningful whole for the first time.

Earth's teacher knows what discipline is, and so earth does. Plants cannot blossom all by themselves. They need earth before they flower. So earth is related to flowers as a human being is to a poem. A poem cannot blossom without a human being; that suggests we should not let a poem lie on the page but should learn it by heart. So out of discipline this enormous blossoming comes and that blossoming from labor lies beneath the excitement that shows itself in the exclamations ending the second and fourth stanzas. It is wonderful to know something, but that is not enough; it also has to be sung, that is, carried by the human body into sound and music, delivered to others, so to speak. Just knowing a poem is not enough. This is quite a different meaning than we arrived at by reading the literal version.

In a good poem, which violates certain secret assumptions, this second stage may take several hours. I spent a long time on this stage alone, some of it arguing over the text with other students and translators. When working with a poem as complicated as this one, the translator can easily get pulled off into a bypath for half an hour; but none of the time is wasted. The more one talks, the more clear Rilke's beliefs become, and so his meaning. He is certain of it, and so the German has a lovely enthusiasm, expressed in lifting, joyful rhythms. If that store of feeling is beyond the translator, he or she should leave the poem be. At the end of this stage, the translator should ask himself whether the feelings as well as the concepts are within his world. If they are not, he should stop. I've had to abandon a number of poems at this point. I remember a Vallejo translation for example; in it I felt Vallejo's feelings toward his own images enter the violet, or grief, range of the spectrum, where I could not follow him. At the age I was, the violet range was not accessible to me, and these feelings can't be faked. In the second stage, we decide whether to turn back or go on.

3

If we decide to go on, we return to our literal version and see where it lost the meanings just found. We redo the literal and try to get it into English this time. We think of the genius of the English language, what its nature is. I'll call that the third stage.

During this stage, we use all we know about the structure of the English language. During the composition of the literal version we followed the word order of the original German, and by doing that found ourselves drawn into the whirlpool of the delayed verb. German gains energy at times by delaying the verb, and even the main noun, so it appears late in the sentence. English gains energy the opposite way, by embarking the main noun immediately and the verb soon after. Most sentences in English that begin with prepositions, with "into" or "upon the" or "for the" tend to be weak in practice; this is not a doctrine but something we observe in reading or writing English. We have to face the issue of the delayed verb immediately, with the third sentence:

Für die Beschwerde
langen Lernens bekommt sie den Preis.

If we say:

For the burden
of her long study, the prize comes to her.

we can feel how dead and flat the lines are. Making the last phrase "she receives the prize" helps, but the lines still feel supine. If we take the main noun and main verb and move them to the front, we can say:

> She receives the prize
> for her long and strenuous study.

It sounds more like English now, and "strenuous" has added considerable energy to the line.

The delayed verb appears again in the green and blue passage of the second stanza. The line: "Now, how the green and blue are called" is not English at all; it belongs to "translatorese," a language never spoken but a language translators know and laugh about.

Anything we try will be an improvement.

> So for blue things and green things, we dare
> to ask their names, and she knows them!

That's not marvelous, but it is English, and some of the passive, dead mood has disappeared. We feel more confident; we are back in our own language. Leaving the word order of the original poem behind is often painful; beginning translators especially resist it. They feel disloyal if they move the verb, but each language evolves in a different way and we cannot cancel a thousand years of language evolution by our will. Moreover, if we are disloyal to German, we are at the same moment loyal to English. The word order of Spanish is closer to that of English, and this stage is usually less painful when translating from Spanish. So then, after redoing later lines, thinking solely in this stage of the sentence and clause structures natural to English, we would arrive at a new draft. We ignore the sentence structure of the German original, and try to move all sentences bodily into the genius of English. Along the way, we rephrase all other lines as well, so as to avoid being caught in the first phrases that have come to mind. The new version might look something like this:

> Spring has returned once more. The earth
> is like a child who has memorized her poems,
> many, many poems. She receives the prize
> for her long and strenuous learning.

Her teacher was strict. We were fond of the whiteness
in the old man's beard.
As for blue things and green things, we dare
to ask their names, and she knows them!

Earth, now out of class, lucky being, play
now with the children. We want to catch you,
happy earth. Only the happiest succeeds.

How many things the teacher taught her,
and what has been pressed into the roots
and long wiry trunks: she sings it, she sings it!

4

We translated the poem into English in the third stage. In the fourth
stage we translate the poem into American . . . that is, if we speak the American language. In England, we would translate it into spoken English. It's the
spoken quality that this stage aims at. The idea that a great poem should be
translated freshly every twenty years is rooted in an awareness of how fast
the spoken language changes. We need the energy of spoken language as we
try to keep a translation alive, just as we need the energy of written.

Rilke's poems, like those of every great poet, mingle spoken language
and written in the most delicate way; the poem balances informal tones and
formal. But his poetry is never without the electrifying power that spoken
rhythms bring. Rilke's group of ten "Voices" ("*Die Stimmen*"), in which a
blind man speaks, a suicide speaks, and a drunkard speaks, carry astonishing
and cunning rhythms, picked up by his ear with its immense feeling for the
rhythms of intimate confession, the accents of desperate conversation, and
the dying fall of street language. The aim is not street language, not slang as
such nor the speech rhythms of half-educated people, but rather the desperate living tone or fragrance that tells you a person now alive could have said
the phrase. Robert Frost believed in such rhythms and wrote of them brilliantly; he called the fragrance "sentence sound." Perhaps one in one hundred
sentences we hear or read has "sentence sound." Frost gives a few examples:
"The thing for me to do is to get right out of here" or "Never you say a

thing like that to a *man*"—in this decade it would be, "You can't say that to a *man*." Another example might be: "John, you come on right down here and do your work." We might end a poem: "And a lot of the changes in my life go back to that decision," and that line would be English but it would lack sentence sound. The phrasing with sentence sound would be: "And that has made all the difference." As Frost correctly says, it isn't the rational mind that understands these distinctions but the ear and the ear's memory.

So during the fourth stage we begin to need the ear. As we read it over, the opening phrase, "Spring has returned again," which seemed adequate for both first- and third-stage drafts, doesn't sound so good anymore. Suppose we met a friend one day as we left our house. Could we imagine him or her saying, "Spring has returned again"? I don't think so. It doesn't sound right. We may not be able to move this phrase from written English to spoken American, but we can try.

What do we remember people saying to us? I remember: "It's spring!", "Spring is back," "Spring is here again," "It's spring again," "Spring has come again" (not likely, that one). How about "Spring is here, baby" or "My God, it's spring!" The German definitely has the idea of a cyclical return in it, but we're not sure how important that detail is. For the moment we'll try "It's spring again."

"Viele, o viele," partly because of the "ee" sounds, does not sound bookish in German, but "many, oh many" does sound bookish in American. Suppose a friend comes from the grocery store and says he bought some potatoes. You want to know how much, and he says, "Many, oh many." It doesn't sound right. His answer would be humorous, but the German here is not. What might he say? How many potatoes? "Lots of potatoes!", "Tons of potatoes!", "Potatoes and potatoes!", "Oodles of potatoes!", "Sacks and sacks!", "More than enough!", "A lot of them!", "A ton, a roomful!", "A lot, a lot . . .!" The American language is so astoundingly abundant now in possibilities, that one always ends up with more phrases than one can use, but there's great fun in that too. For the moment we'll choose: "A lot, a lot . . ."

"She receives the prize for her long and strenuous learning" doesn't sound as if it were spoken language anymore. Rarely in speech these days do we let a sentence go so long without a pause. "Receives" doesn't sound right either. We'll try "gets."

And she gets the prize,
gets it after study, hard work.

My ear feels better now; it remembers sentences like this, spoken hundreds of times. The sequence is two three-beat phrases, followed by one two-beat phrase, "hard work." That sequence is characteristic in spoken American English.

The next two lines sound all right, but the naming passage I don't like anymore. We'll move the "daring to ask" concept to the front of the sentences:

We feel able to ask what the names of green
and blue things are, and she knows all of them!

Or

We feel able, looking at green shades and blue, to ask
what their names are, and she knows them!

Or

Asking what this is, so green, and that, so blue,
seems all right. And she knows the names!

Or

Asking about the blue, and about the green
seems right to do, and she knows. She knows!

I'm sure it's clear to the reader now the sort of work one does during this step, and I won't go over the rest of the poem in detail.

Asking the ear about each phrase, asking it, "Have you ever heard this phrase spoken?" is the labor of this draft. The ear will reply with six or seven new phrases, and these act to shake up the translation once more and keep it from solidifying. The language becomes livelier, fresher, lighter. Many translators stop before this stage; some of them have an exalted idea of the poet and think Rilke uses written German; others associate literature with a written language, with written English—many academic translators have this habit—and it never occurs to them to move to the spoken. Nineteenth-century translators in general rarely took this step; it was Whitman, Pound, and William Carlos Williams who sharpened everyone's sense for spoken English and spoken American. The marvelous translation that is now being done in the United States, work that has been going on for thirty years or more, is partly a gift of these three men and their faith that poetry can be composed in spoken rhythms.

The new draft then might look something like this:

It's spring! The earth
is like a child who's learned poems by heart,
a lot, a lot! And she gets the prize,
gets it after study, hard work.

Her teacher was strict. We were fond of the white
we saw in the old man's beard.
Asking about the green—how about that blue—
seems all right, and she knows all the names!

Earth, now out of school, born lucky, play
now with the children. We want to play catch,
glad earth. The most glad catches you.

The teacher managed to teach her so much.
Astonishing! And what the roots and the long
strenuous stalks hold in printed form, she sings!

5

We haven't thought about tone yet. Does this last draft have the tone of the German? In what I'll call the fifth stage we need the ear again—not the ear turned outward toward human speech but the ear turned inward toward the complicated feelings the poem is carrying. Each poem has a mood. Harry Martinson remarked that to him a poem *is* a mood. A poem did not come to him out of an idea, but a poem marked a moment when he was able to catch a mood.

To succeed at this stage I think it is important that the translator should have written poetry himself. I mean that he or she needs the experience of writing from mood in order to judge accurately what the mood of a stranger's poem is. We need accurate judgment on mood now because in finding spoken phrases to replace the written we may have thrown the tone off. We may have the wrong "tone of voice" in the new phrases. The spoken language has dozens of tones available; sometimes in American, hundreds. The reason that "Spring is here, baby" doesn't sound right for the opening sentence is not because it isn't *spoken*—it carries a wonderful fragrance of the spoken— but rather because the mood of the original poem is quite different. Many translators stop before this stage; they translate a poem into spoken American and then quit. Pope put Homer into eighteenth-century spoken English and ignored the problem of mood. When in America we force Catullus into hip language, it means we have stopped before struggling with this problem. Catullus likes mischievous words and obscene phrases, but he will lay them in among measured Latin rhythms. Overall Catullus's mood is a tender, complicated grief that resembles the mood of Celtic art.

The younger we are, the easier it is to make mistakes in tone. During my late twenties, I translated over sixty poems of Rilke's. A few years ago when I went back to look at them, I had to throw away virtually every line I had done because I had confused Rilke's mood with certain violent moods I had at the time. I had made almost every line more extroverted than it was. I may still be doing that.

Rilke is especially difficult in the matter of mood because German in one of its levels is high-flown. All language has two levels at least: an upper and a lower. We recognize the "upper" in Shakespeare's sonnets; language high-flown, ethical, elaborated, capable of concept, witty, dignified, noble in tone.

We might speculate that in the American language now only the "lower" level is alive. It flows along on earth; it is a physical language that everyone contributes to, warm, intense, with short words, well connected to the senses, musical, capable of feeling. This sensual language is the only one we have; William Carlos Williams used this language by principle when he wrote, and Brecht used the lower level by choice in his German poems. In America the "noble" stream dried out around 1900, against the will of Henry James, and since that time, as Williams declared, the writer has had no choice.

What we have to do then in Rilke is use our one level to carry his two.

The problems of tone are tremendous. Pablo Neruda's *Odas Elementales* go into American so much more easily because by 1956, when he wrote them, Neruda too was using only the sensual language. But Rilke in 1920 found both the "upper" and "lower" languages alive, and the presence of both in his work is a part of his greatness. Rilke not only invited in the "noble language" with its immense garden of associations, but he carried it brilliantly. Rilke's richness became especially noticeable during World War II when the Nazis were destroying the resonance of the German language by inserting brutal bureaucratic jargon. A German professor sympathetic with the Resistance told me that in his city the word "Rilke" was a secret password for their Resistance and became so precisely because of Rilke's rich language.

We notice that this problem of "noble language" causes a lot of trouble to translators in their effort to translate Rilke into English. Rilke translations have frequently been nobly dead. The translator, in the effort to rise to the upper or resonating level he senses in Rilke, abandons our living language and resorts to old cloudlike phrases that are now only scenery. He tries, from the best intentions, to retrieve and revive dusty clauses and high-flown diction and stuff them into the poem, with the result that the living language dies, both languages die, and Rilke seems ridiculous. J. B. Leishman, speaking of a palace in one Rilke translation, says:

> And, dazzlingly from all points manifest
> (like pale sky with diffused illumination),
> by weight of fading portraiture possessed
> by some deep interior contemplation,
> the palace, in unfestal resignation,
> stands taciturn and patient as a guest.

It is hard to recognize these lines as Rilke's. The vividness is gone and the senses have evaporated. Mr. Leishman is not inaccurate, but the translation fails in tone, and that comes from pretending that the aristocratic stream of language is still alive in English. We have to use the feeling stream only; it is grievous, but we have no choice. As I mentioned, Rilke used both languages, but interestingly the simple or feeling language grows stronger as he grows older. Each poem he wrote in the ten years before his death moves toward its own tone fragrance, in contrast to the poems from *A Book for the Hours of Prayer* in which a whole group of poems carry a single tone, often high-flown.

To return to our sonnet, if we read the sonnet that comes just before it in the *Sonnets to Orpheus* and the sonnet just after, we notice great distinctions in mood. The sonnets in each side plunge into memory; number 22 for example sinks into a sort of deep Gothic memory, with slow heartbeats. The sonnet we have, by contrast, is light-hearted, gay, and enthusiastic—the exclamation marks alone indicate that—but the light-heartedness is one that comes after long brooding or long thoughtfulness. The point is not only that "It's spring" but that "It's spring again." So the simple statement "It's spring!" doesn't seem quite right now, in mood. Moreover, the topped sounds in "a lot A lot!" create a pugnacious mood, even though enthusiastic, that "*viele, o viele*" doesn't have. Moreover we notice that changing the word order of the sentence about receiving the prize has changed the mood of the stanza. In German the prize represents the close of a learning process; but we, by moving the prize to the middle, interrupted the process. The prize interferes with the grief of learning, so to speak. So we'll have to change that.

> It's spring once more. The earth
> is like a child who's learned poems by heart,
> many of them . . . and after hard work
> and long study, she gets the prize.

That's better. Studying the next stanza, I have become uneasy with the tone of "how about that blue." Perhaps we should aim for a softer tone.

> Her teacher was strict. We were fond of the white
> we saw in the old man's beard.
> And we can ask the blue flower's name
> and that green bush—she knows all the names!

I'm a little dissatisfied also with "glad" earth or "happy" earth. Both are too light. Something is wrong with their mood. Neither "glad" nor "happy" carries the dark side, as one feels "*fröliche Erde*" does. The adjective "*fröliche*" may be related to the word Freya, the ancient Germanic Great Mother. Her joy has a lot of darkness in it. Perhaps Freya's darkness is connected to the luck she brings.

> Earth, now out of school, lucky inside, play

now with the children, we want to touch you,
deeply glad earth. The deepest catches you.

"Deeply glad" may be wrong but we'll try it; and I feel better about the mood
of that stanza now; it has a little more darkness in it.

But I don't feel the next line is right—there is a lovely enthusiasm in the
German "O, was der Lehrer sie lehrte, das Viele." We could try: "The teacher she
had, he taught her so well."

We could try leaving out "he":

The teacher she had taught her so well!
So much!

The problem is that we're getting caught in the human part of the poem
now. Rilke's German, because "Erde" is feminine, is able to hold our attention
evenly divided between what the *earth* learns, and what the *school girl* learns;
we see with two eyes at once. But because "Erde" is "it" in English, we've lost
one eye. We're forgetting the earth. By repeating "she" we're losing some of
the deep earth mood, and veering too far toward the more human mood we
feel in the girl student. For the sake of tone, we may have to replace that
"she" with "earth."

The teacher earth had taught her so well!
So much! And what nature printed in roots
and knotty, slender trunks, she manages to sing!

Summing up, then, in this stage we move to modify errors that may have
come in with the emphasis on the spoken. Most of all we open ourselves
for the first time to the mood of the poem; we try to be precise about what
its mood is, distinguishing it from the mood of nearby poems. We try to
capture the poem's balance high and low, dark and light, seriousness and
light-heartedness.

6

In the next stage, which I call here the sixth, we pay attention to sound.
The question of tone has led to this. If we wonder whether the poem's tone

is enthusiastic or melancholic, there is only one thing to do: memorize the poem in its original German and say it to yourself, to friends, to the air. No one can translate well from a poem he or she hasn't learned by heart: only by reciting it can we feel what sort of oceanic rhythm it has, which is a very different thing from analyzing the meter.

When we recite Rilke's German, free from the page, we notice immediately that there is a powerful beat on the opening syllable of the first, third, and fourth lines. This is a rhythm characteristic of pagan poetry; almost all Greek poems begin with this resolute firm stroke on the first syllable, and much of *Beowulf.* Christian poetry gradually evolved toward iambic rhythm, in which the first syllable is somewhat ingratiating, softer, more modest, and prepares the way for the heavier second stroke. Throwing the energy toward the start of the line hints again at the poem's nature, which is more pagan than Christian. A number of phrases: *"viele o viele," "Streng war ihr Lehrer," "dürfen wir fragen," "Erde, die frei hat," "fröliche Erde"* start the line with a stroke, a confident assertion, causing a rocking motion.

What's wrong with "a lot! a lot!" as an opening to line three is that it doesn't have this initial stroke. "Many, o many" is better, but the crest doesn't rise high enough. *"Viele, o viele"* resembles a high rising wave, and the sound "ee" in *"viele"* helps it to rise. "Ee" is high. The "an" in "many" does not carry the line far enough up.

In our last draft the opening lines read:

> It's spring once more. The earth
> is like a child who's learned poems by heart,
> many of them . . .

We can only get a higher wave in line two by going to an open vowel. We'll try this:

> so many poems . . .

The opening phrase:
> Frühling ist wiedergekommen
also has a rocking motion, and our versions of that sentence so far, though spoken and all right in tone, feel a bit flat: "It's spring," or "It's spring once more." I'd favor trying to pick up some sort of rocking motion.

> Spring is here, has come! The earth
> is like a child who's learned poems by heart,
> so many poems. . . .

We're getting there.

We can distinguish in a poem between two sound energies, one in the muscle system and one in the ear. That is very roughly stated. The rocking motion we have spoken of is a body motion, which Donald Hall calls "goat foot" because of its associations with the Greek drum and dancing. Similarly, in a recent essay Robert Hass struggles to separate certain rhythms felt in the muscle system from meter. "I have already remarked that meter is not the basis of rhythmic form." The body motion alerts the mind and builds tension which is later released. Most nineteenth-century translators, ignoring the distinction, imagined that by following the meter of the original poem precisely they would arrive at the rhythm. But it didn't happen. The translator's job is to feel the body rhythm of the line, but that may or may not lead to the meter. The rocking motions, or body motion, is primary, not meter. Using Donald Hall's metaphor, we can speculate that we can understand the meter in a poem without necessarily experiencing the goat's foot. A flat line, in metered or free verse, may have human feet but not goat's feet.

I've mentioned a second quality of sound—sound calling to sound, which is related to internal rhyme. I don't feel right in talking about that one yet because I'm just learning it myself. But if the reader will memorize the Rilke poem in German and say it over many times, he will understand sound calling to sound without my help.

Keeping these two aspects of sound in mind, and saying the German over many times, I decide to make the following changes in the first stanzas:

> Spring is here, has come! The earth
> resembles a child who has learned her poems.
> So many poems! Her study long,
> strenuous, earns it. . . . the prize comes to her.

In the next stanza I decide, for the sake of internal rhyme, to change "strict" to "*stern*." The rhythmical wave in German rises at the left wall with "*Nun, wie das Grüne,*" so we have to do some work with the English rhythm at that point. "And we ask the blue flower's name" is too flat. There's no heavy stroke at the start.

> What names to give to green patches, and blue
> occurs to us, we ask! Earth knows it by heart!

The change helps.

Let's go on to the third stanza. I see that by altering the ninth line I can shift the rhythm over to the left. We had:

> Earth, now out of school, lucky inside, play
> now with the children. We want to touch you,
> deeply glad earth. The deepest catches you.

Now the "deeply glad" earth passage bothers me. None of the phrases we've tried please me. "Happy earth," "glad earth" . . . "deeply glad earth." The last seems closest. So separating *"fröliche"* into an adverb and an adjective may be a solution. Rilke uses two words from the same root, *"froh,"* and we should follow him if we can. "Happy" and "happiest," "glad" and "gladdest" do that, but they are too light. Listening to the German sound, we notice that Rilke uses here the open "oh" sound for the first time in the poem. *"Wir wollen dich fangen . . . Dem frohsten gelingts."* It's possible that the "aeh" sounds we have been using in "happy" or "glad" are wrong for his mood. I decide to try this:

> Earth, free from school now, joyful, come
> play with the children. We want to catch you,
> wholly glad earth. The most whole gets you.

One can never be sure, when helped by sound to a solution, if the solution is reasonable, justifiable, within Rilke's area of meaning. After brooding about it, I decide the emphasis on "whole" as opposed to "happy," "glad," or "perfect" is all right. Some associations that cluster around *"froh"* are carried in our culture by "whole." We notice for example that becoming whole, whole earth, whole-wheat bread, resonate with certain associations around the earth mother. I have to trust my sense of it. I may be wrong, but the line now seems to me more in focus than it was.

The German of the next line has a strong opening beat with *"O was der Lehrer. . . ."* If I want something like that I'll have to abandon my old line, even though I like it:

> The teacher earth had taught her so well.

I'll try "Earth's teacher," and rephrase also the final two lines of the poem:

> Earth's teacher taught her things, so many!
> And the sounds that lie printed inside roots
> and long entangled stalks: she carries and sings them!

I'll set down here, then, a draft worked out after brooding over Rilke's rhythm, which has a strong rocking motion, and the dominant vowel sounds of the poem, and internal and external rhymes.

> Spring is here, has come! The earth
> resembles a child who has learned her poems.
> So many poems! Her study long,
> strenuous, earns it. . . . The prize comes to her.
>
> Her teacher was stern. We loved the white
> that showed in the old man's beard.
> What names to give to the green patch and the blue
> comes to us, and we ask: earth knows it by heart!
>
> Earth, free from school now, joyful, come
> play with the children. We want to catch you,
> wholly glad earth. The most whole gets you.
>
> Earth's teacher taught her things, so many!
> And the sounds that lie printed inside roots
> and long entangled stalks: she carries and sings them!

7

We are nearly finished now. During what I will call the seventh stage we ask someone born into the language to go over our version. Perhaps we go back to the native speaker who helped us in the first draft; if we did not get such help then, we do now; we ask him or her to find errors that have crept in.

For beginning translators, this stage is very painful. As beginners, we tend to give ourselves permission to veer away from the poem's images, pulled away in fact by our private mental horses, and dismay sets in when we realize that some of our best solutions are simply wrong. Hardie St. Martin has always performed this reining-in function when I, or James Wright with me, translated from Spanish. Once I remember he found in a single Jiménez poem that I had already worked over for months, and that contained only twenty lines to start with, twenty-two errors that could not be allowed to stand. The error was sometimes in tone, sometimes in image, or slant of image, or I had picked up a South American coloring the word had rather than its Castilian coloring, or I had gotten the rhythms or vowels wrong. None of us can learn a foreign language well enough up to pick all these things up.

During this new stage we also have a second chance to ask about the implications of certain words that have begun to bother us. I want to check out my sense of *"fröliche"* and *"Frohsten"* and talk some more about *"gedruckt."* I didn't notice *"schwierigen"* so much at first, but now I see it as an unsolved or entangled knot of associations, and I want to know what its German root is. Almost all words that seem abstract now once, as Owen Barfield makes so clear in his book on the history of words, carried a physical motion at the start, perhaps pulling or cutting or lifting. Sometimes knowing the German root helps to choose an English word. If one has a German friend nearby then the labor of this stage can be done gradually, as the problems come up, and that is probably best. But if not, we should take on this stage by will, and consider it as important as any of the earlier stages. We have been slowly possessing the poem and making it ours—we have to do that to bring it alive—but it is possible that we have kidnapped it instead.

8

Our last stage is making the final draft. We read back over all our earlier drafts—perhaps a half line was said better in one of them. We have to make our final adjustments now. I decide to change the blue and green clause once more, but I won't make many substantive changes. As a result of the conversation around *"schwierigen"* I've decided to use "involved," and I notice that the *n*'s are coming along well in the final stanza, and "involved" will help that. During this stage we allow ourselves, at last, the pleasure of examining other people's translations of the poem. That is fun we can't deny ourselves after all the work, and we can sympathize with each translator. We don't expect much from J. B. Leishman, and he doesn't give much.

> Spring has come again. Earth's a-bubble
> with all those poems she knows by heart,—
> oh, so many. With prize for the trouble
> of such long learning, her holidays start.

One can see he has had trouble with his rhymes. I believe in working as much as possible with internal rhymes, but I think it's best not to insist on reproducing end rhymes. Nineteenth-century translators often felt obsessive about end-rhyming, and usually did it in exactly the same pattern as in the original poem. Leishman's version shows a common outcome: the translator has to add images that destroy the poem's integrity. There is no mention of earth bubbling in Rilke's poem, and the "start of the holidays" interferes with the learning process he is evoking. Leishman's third stanza reads:

> Eager to catch you, Earth, happy creature,
> play with the children now pouring!
> Conqueringly foremost the happiest springs.

Leishman is helpful, in a way, because reading his translations one grows determined to retranslate.

Al Poulin, who published *Duino Elegies* and the *Sonnets to Orpheus* in 1977, is a much better translator. We could look at his first two stanzas:

> Spring has returned again. The earth
> is like a child who's memorized
> poems; many, so many . . . It was worth
> the long painful lesson: she wins the prize.

> Her teacher was strict. We liked the white
> in the old man's whiskers.
> Now when we ask what green or blue is, right
> away she knows, she has the answer!

This is not so bad; good work on the spoken. But rhyming causes trouble again. He wanted to rhyme "earth," and ended up with "worth." Rilke's doesn't say whether the prize was worth all the effort or not. Possibly a half-rhyme with "answer" pulled him into "whiskers," which loses some dignity and some feeling of the snow. In general, though he is translating with considerable accuracy, we feel that he stopped in his labors after the spoken stage. He does not work on sound. His lines are not joyful in sound. In fact, the *s* sounds dominate: "lesson," "memorized," "prize," "strict," "whiskers," "ask," "answer." The *z* and *s* sounds produce a kind of hissing that encourages anxiety.

His third stanza goes:

> Earth, lucky earth on vacation,
> play with the children now. We long
> to catch you, happy earth. The happiest will win.

He uses "happy" and "happiest" so the "oh" sound doesn't have a chance to enter. Of course one might say that if a translator is doing all the sonnets, he has no time to pay so much attention to one. We understand that, but it is perhaps better to do one carefully than to do the whole fifty-five.

The French translation by J. F. Angelloz, which he did with Rilke's knowledge, is accurate and clear. We notice that in the third stanza he uses the word "*compliques*" to translate "*schwierigen*":

> O, ce que le maître lui enseigna, l'innombrable,
> et ce qui est imprime dans les racines et les longs
> troncs compliques: elle le chante, elle le chante!

To my surprise, I found a commentary on this poem by Angelloz at the back, which I hadn't known of before. Now that we have gone over the poem so carefully, Angelloz's commentary is extremely interesting, and I'll translate it here, roughly, from the French.

> . . . Here spring blazes up and fills the poem. Holthusen says that the true season of the *Sonnets to Orpheus* is summer, the season of fullness and possession. But that is a misconception. Rilke had a predilection for transitional times and, especially during the final

years of his life, for that transitional time the Germans call, so happily, "*Vorfrühling.*" He saw such transitional times are the creative periods. It was, in fact, at the start of February 1922 that he completed the *Elegies* and the *Sonnets*; it was on the 9th that he wrote "Children's Spring Song" (*Frühlings-Kinder-Lied*) which he sent to Madame Oukama-Knoop to replace the sonnet beginning "*O das Neue, Freunde, ist nicht dies*" (published in *Späte Gedichte*, p. 97), and to serve as a counterpart to the horse poem (Letter to Madam Oukama-Knoop, February 9, 1922). And, finally, it was at a similar time of the year, in 1913, that Rilke experienced, at Ronda in southern Spain, the incident that inspired this sonnet.

In a convent church he heard a mass accompanied by music, as by bouquets of joyful sound; it was a remarkable music, with a dance rhythm; to it children were singing an unknown text to the sound of a triangle and a tambourine. Rilke considered this sonnet as an interpretation ("*Auslegung*") of that mass, and he found in it "the mood of spring at its most luminous." He starts, in essence, with a cry of joy that greets the return of spring. Moreover the earth is compared to a child, who knows numerous poems; she receives the prize for assiduous work. But it is wrong to talk of a comparison; in fact, there is an identification going on of the springtime earth, the children singers, and the Orphic poet himself, who, in the second stanza, uses "we." There is a parallel identification of winter, an old man with a white beard, a singing master, whom Rilke does not mention again, and Orpheus, who teaches the art of distinguishing the main springtime colors (green, blue), as he also teaches all creatures to listen. And now, the earth freed from winter, the children, who have learned their poems by heart, and the poet himself, who takes part in the awakening of nature, play tag with the earth, source of all joys; the victory goes to the most joyful of them. The sonnet closes in a magnificent harmony: the universal impulse of Dionysius expresses itself in singing; and all of it—we can think also of the early sonnets—all of it is Orpheus singing.

I am encouraged by this story. And our interpretation of the poem is supported by his comments, and what I called "pagan" he calls "Dionysian." It is possible that the mysterious teacher of the earth is Orpheus.

Well, then, after studying once more all our earlier drafts, and making our final sound and rhythm adjustments, and after taking in what we can from other people's translations and commentaries, we are ready to set down the final draft. We know that we haven't captured the original: the best translation resembles a Persian rug seen from the back—the pattern is apparent, but not much more. The final version, then, so far, is this:

Spring is here, has come! The earth
is like a child who has learned her poems—
so many poems! . . . Her study, long,
strenuous, earns it . . . the prize comes to her.

Her teacher was stern. We loved the white
showing in the beard of the old man.
What is blue and what is green have distinct names—
What are they? Earth knows all that by heart!

Earth, free now of school, lucky one, come,
play with the children. We want to tag you,
wholly glad earth. The most whole catches you.

Earth's teacher, how much he taught her!
So much! And what lies printed inside roots,
inside long, involved stalks: earth carries that and sings it!

IV
Thoreau and Wildness

Thoreau and Wildness

1.

The Bug in the Table

Thoreau was sure that we could have an original love affair with the universe, but only if we decline to marry the world, and he suspected that the divine man is the man uncontrolled by social obligation. He believed that the young man or young woman should give up tending the machine of civilization and instead farm the soul. We can sense the boundaries of our soul, whose stakes are set thousands of miles out in space, only if we disintegrate property boundaries here on earth. When we fight for the soul and its life, we receive as reward not fame, not wages, not friends, but what is already in the soul, a freshness that no one can destroy, that animals and trees share.

The most important word is *soul.* All of the ideas referred to above are really a single idea, one massive truth, and we can call that truth the Truth of Concord, the Green Mountain Truth, the truth believed in the Bronze Age, the truth of the soul's interior abundance.

To many Americans in the generation of the 1840s it felt as if the United States had fallen into mesmeric attention to external forces, and a shameless obedience to them. The swift development of the Northeast, with its numerous factories, its urban workshops for immigrants, its network of free-acting capitalists, its centralized industry, showed that external forces can and do overwhelm forces of soul and conscience, changing everyone's life for the worse. To many in New England it felt as if some sort of Village King had been killed; the ancient, grounded religious way was passing; new dispensation had arrived. The sovereign of the new administration was not a king or a human being, but what Blake called "a ratio of numbers," and this ominous, bodiless king lived in the next county, the next state, the next planet. Living under the power of the bodiless king is a bad way to live.

A man who lived in the Concord area, fourteen years older than Thoreau and with a fierce, bold and reckless mind—I mean Ralph Waldo Emerson—introduced his statement of the truth of the soul's abundance in this way in his essay "Nature":

> To go into solitude, a man needs to retire as much from his chamber as from society. I am not solitary whilst I read and write, though nobody is with me. but if a man would be alone, let him look at the stars. . . .
>
> . . . In the presence of nature a wild delight runs through the man, in spite of real sorrows. . . . Crossing a bare common, in snow puddles, at twilight, under a clouded sky, without having in my thoughts any occurrence of special good fortune, I have enjoyed a perfect exhilaration. I am glad to the brink of fear. In the woods, too, a man casts off his years, as the snake his slough, and at what period soever of life is always a child. In the woods is perpetual youth.

The direction could not be clearer. We don't expect this man to urge the establishment of vocational schools, or to praise the trickle-down philosophy of heavy industry, or to believe that amassing wealth is evidence of divine favor. These words move toward the soul, not toward manipulation of matter, and when we have arrived within the soul the motion is not lateral, but downward and upward:

> Standing on the bare ground,—my head bathed by the blithe air and uplifted into infinite space,—all mean egotism vanishes. I become a transparent eyeball. ("Nature")

The metaphor, though well known, remains astonishing: the transparent eyeball. The emphasis on transparency tells us that Emerson does not intend to occupy the castle of sorrow and the kingdom of melancholy, nor to descend into the dungeon of the body, but that he wants to recruit an army for a charge into the infinite, desperate as the Light Brigade's. He wants inside him an army disciplined, ascetic, single-minded; an army with few baggage trains, living in floorless tents on dried food. His quest will be to marry nature for vision, rather than for possession. His aim is not to live more but to see more.

Emerson, in "Nature," goes on: "I am nothing; I see all; the currents of the Universal Being circulate through me." As he says that, it is clear he is not talking of a narrow or tribal god, and he finishes the passage by saying, "I am part and parcel of God."

The truth that we have been circling around with images of journey, similes of battle, metaphors taken from the history of love, amounts, as suggested, to one essential truth. It is a lucky generation that hears it, because it is one of the few truths on which a young person can ground his or her life.

Many young men and women want to marry nature for vision, not possession. Some, having accomplished by their late twenties no deed worthy of praise, feel insignificant and scorned. The world scorns football players who make no yardage, writers who do not publish, fishermen who catch no fish. But the soul truth, which young people, when lucky, pick up from somewhere—perhaps in Emerson's phrasing, perhaps in someone else's—sustains them. If the world doesn't feed them, they receive some nourishment from this truth. The substance of the truth goes to their paws, and they live through the winter of scorn and despicability in the way hibernating bears were once thought to live, by sucking their own paws.

The soul truth assures the young man or woman that if not rich, he or she is still in touch with truth; that his inheritance comes not from his immediate parents but from his equals thousands of generations ago; that the door to the soul is unlocked; that he does not need to please the doorkeeper, but the door in front of him is his, and intended for him, and the doorkeeper obeys when spoken to. It implies that nature is not below the divine, but is itself divine, "perpetual youth." Most important of all, the soul truth assures the young man or woman that despite the Industrial Revolution certain things are as they have always been, and that in human growth the road of development goes through nature, not around it.

I think one reason that the Thoreau-Melville-Hawthorne generation wrote so much great literature is that this fundamental soul truth, well phrased by Emerson, Horace Bushnell and other writers, and untainted yet by mockery, came through freshly to mind and body. Forty years later Yeats was fed by this truth, phrased this time by Blake and Edwin Ellis, and supported by old Celtic stories. Yeats expressed the truth in a very different way, but if we listen we can hear it throughout his poem "Paudeen":

> Indignant at the fumbling wits, the obscure spite
> Of our old Paudeen in his shop, I stumbled blind
> Among the stones and thorn-trees, under morning light;
> Until a curlew cried and in the luminous wind
> A curlew answered; and suddenly thereupon I thought
> That on the lonely height where all are in God's eye,
> There cannot be, confusion of our sound forgot,
> A single soul that lacks a sweet crystalline cry.

Yeats, like Thoreau, recognized that marrying nature for vision, rather than for possession, creates a luminous place inside that every human being longs for. He calls it "the townland":

> There's many a strange farmer
> Whose heart would break in two,
> If he could see the townland
> That we are riding to;

The truth that nourished Thoreau in 1847 had nourished Goethe a half-century earlier, and he ended his great poem "The Holy Longing" with these two stanzas:

> Distance does not make you falter
> now, arriving in magic, flying—
> and, finally, insane for the light,
> you are the butterfly and you are gone.

> And so long as you haven't experienced
> this: to die and so to grow,
> you are only a troubled guest
> on the dark earth.

In this section there are nineteenth texts—some poems, others passages from his journals or from *Walden*—in which Thoreau, using the bricks of his intricate and precise detail, builds a house for this truth. His walls are more solid than Emerson's. Thoreau wrote a few good metrical poems on the soul truth, but his prose on the subject is exquisite, high-spirited and elegant. The anecdote of the insect egg he tells very well. The egg remained for years inside the trunk of an apple tree, undisturbed even when the carpenter cut down the tree and made it into a table, and rested dormant there until, warmed one day, perhaps by a coffee pot set above it, it hatched out at last. This is a marvelous tale, and by the anecdote Thoreau suggests that inside us, too, there may be a winged life that is not visible to us when we sit at a table, or become a table. The story suggests that there is an unhatched abundance inside us that we ourselves have not prepared. Our psyche at birth was not a schoolchild's slate with nothing written on it, but rather an apple-wood table full of eggs. We receive at birth the residual remains of a billion lives before us.

2.
The Habit of Living Meanly

A great idea is a useful invention, like an eyeglass or a new fuel. A doctrine may be a piece of charcoal left behind by an earlier genius for a token of remembrance, as Whitman said, "designedly dropped," and useful now in our daily lives. When an idea is an eyeglass, details otherwise fuzzy become sharp.

Thoreau understands that we have a winged life inside us, even if people are presently using us as a table. When Thoreau set that idea to his eyes, he saw that most people around him were living meanly.

We hate it when observers notice mean lives, because we are afraid we may be among those being watched. Much of the hostility to Thoreau, which I remember feeling strongly in college—scribbled insults in the margins of my *Walden* remain as testimony—comes from the fear that we are being watched.

What is it to live meanly? We may easily confuse living a mean life with living a low life. Puritan Christians struggled against a low life, which to them meant giving in to instinctual urges, but in Thoreau's understanding many Puritans nevertheless lived mean lives. And the twelfth-century Chinese Taoists—mad about sex, some of them—remind us that though we may spend hours each day balancing yang and yin, we can still live meanly. It isn't a matter of living our sexuality or avoiding it, of embodying animal instincts or rising above them, of eating huge dinners or not eating them. Living meanly, to Thoreau, is the opposite of "living sincerely." To live sincerely is to live your own life, not your father's life or your mother's life or your neighbor's life; to spend soul on large concerns, not to waste your life as a kind of human ant carrying around small burdens; and finally, to live sincerely is to "live deep and suck all the marrow of life," as Thoreau declares in *Walden*. That may require unsociability. Thoreau noticed that at a certain age boys remain in shadows and corners of rooms, look a little wild, make up their minds about a given grownup in a second, and may come to supper or not. Thoreau values that unsociability in both boys and girls. But those moments soon disappear, replaced by an old anxiety to please.

Many women have described the moment when they realized to their dismay that they had spent their lives trying to please others. They had tuned themselves to others' needs while ignoring their own. And men do the same thing wholesale, so to speak; instead of retailing their attention to particular persons, they try to guess the needs of entire generations or congregations, and so end up leading their congregation's life, or their generation's life.

The ancient metaphor for living meanly is sleep. Lovers and writers can be asleep. "A man can make war in his sleep, make love in his sleep, even write books in his sleep, but they will only serve to put other people to sleep." This, a parable that Gurdjieff heard as a youth, would have delighted Thoreau. The state of being awake could then be called "living sincerely." Thoreau's wit is just as sharp as the parable maker's when in the opening passage of *Walden* he says "Moreover, I, on my side, require of every writer, first or last, a simple and sincere account of his own life, and not merely what he has heard of other men's lives; some such account as he would send to his kindred from a distant land; for if he has lived sincerely, it must have been in a distant land to me."

That is the first sentence of Thoreau's that I ever memorized, and I still admire it. At the sentence's end the claws come out, and we realize that though Henry David Thoreau is called a transcendentalist, he has not "transcended his negative emotions," as some New Age transcendentalists long to do; on the contrary, he often expresses anger, contempt and disdain. He stings the unwary. He distinguishes the shallow life from the deep and does not tolerate people who live shallowly.

In our century, Rainer Maria Rilke has written a number of poems that distinguish between his hurried life on the one hand and his deep life on the other. This poem of his is from *Das Stundenbuch*:

> My life is not this steeply sloping hour,
> in which you see me hurrying.
> Much stands behind me; I stand before it like a tree.
> I am only one of my many mouths,
> and at that, the one that will be still the soonest.
>
> I am the rest between two notes,
> which are somehow always in discord
> because Death's note wants to climb over—
> but in the dark interval, reconciled,
> they stay there, trembling.
> And the song goes on, beautiful.

This is how Thoreau said it in prose:

> I love to weigh, to settle, to gravitate toward that which most strongly and rightfully attracts me;—not hang by the beam of the scale and try to weigh less,—not suppose a case, but take the case that is; to travel the only path I can, and that on which no power can resist me. It affords me no satisfaction to commence to spring an arch before I have got a solid foundation. Let us not play at kittly-benders. There is a solid bottom everywhere. We read that the traveler asked the boy if the swamp before him had a hard bottom. The boy replied that it had. But presently the traveler's horse sank in up to the girths, and he observed to the boy, "I thought you said that this bog had a hard bottom." "So it has," answered the latter, "but you have not got half way to it yet." (*Walden*)

Thoreau does not expect that the "sleep" will end today or tomorrow, but he has some hope. It is not clear that nature wants men and women to wake: perhaps nature prefers them to remain asleep, work like oxen or blind mules and then lie down beneath the ground. Thoreau develops a pun around the word "sleepers," which is commonly used for railroad ties: "We do not ride on the railroad; it rides upon us. Did you ever think what those sleepers are that underlie the railroad? Each one is a man, an Irishman, or a Yankee man. . . . I am glad to know that it takes a gang of men for every five miles to keep the sleepers down and level in their beds as it is, for this is a sign that they may sometime get up again."

Thoreau's hope that he may escape such sleep turns into wit, and his fear that he cannot escape it turns into a generalized sorrow such as we hear in the Babylonian epic *Gilgamesh* or in ancient Egyptian laments. He notices how easy it is for us to sentimentalize a trail of smoke rising from a valley farmhouse:

> It suggests all of domestic felicity beneath. . . . When I look down on that roof I am not reminded of the mortgage which the village bank has on that property,—that that family long since sold itself to the devil and wrote the deed with their blood. I am not reminded that the old man I see in the yard is one who has lived beyond his calculated time, whom the young one is merely "carrying through" in fulfillment of his contract; that the man at the pump is watering the milk. I am not reminded of the idiot that sits by the kitchen fire. (*Journal*, October 3, 1859)

The suffering the citizens of Concord go through when living meanly or asleep struck Thoreau as Oriental in its fierceness: "What I have heard of Bramins sitting exposed to four fires and looking in the face of the sun; or hanging suspended, with their heads downward, over flames; . . . or measuring with their bodies, like caterpillars, the breadth of vast empires; or standing on one leg on the tops of pillars—even these forms of conscious penance are hardly more incredible and astonishing than the scenes which I daily witness."

He feels grief for the life wasted around him. The larvae of the Plicipennes, he mentions, eventually will leave "their sunken habitations, and, crawling up the stems of plants, or to the surface, like gnats, as perfect insects henceforth, flutter over the surface of the water, or sacrifice their short lives in the flames of our candles at evening." His grief can lead him to marvelously agile leaps of language, as when he asks why we should "level downward to our dullest perception always, and praise that as common sense? The commonest sense is the sense of men asleep, which they express by snoring."

Thoreau's awareness of the suffering entailed in "living insincerely" commits him to create sentences athletic and daring enough to be worthy of his own nature, and the reader will find a number of these wiry sentences, both in prose texts and in poems here.

3.
Going the Long Way Round

Thoreau's major decision was his decision not to live meanly. The salt of this decision buoyed him up, floated him almost to the end of his life. It was daring because his father lived meanly, and probably his mother too. It was one thing for Yeats to decide on the lofty life of artistic poverty when he saw his father pursuing a similar life, and it was another thing for Thoreau to do so; for by doing so, Thoreau was acting the rebellious son. And that is dangerous.

Thoreau saw early on, in his poem "Though All the Fates Should Prove Unkind," that his own ship would sink. We can't say what the "worm" is that eats the hull, but we should not rule out his guilt over rebellion. The ship embarks, as Thoreau says, with flags raised, and cuts through the water jauntily, but what if, underneath the coppery sheathing, a worm is eating at the wooden vessel?

> Whether she bears Manilla twine,
> Or in her hold Madeira wine,
> Or China teas, or Spanish hides,
> In port or quarantine she rides;
> Far from New England's blustering shore,
> New England's worm her hulk shall bore,
> And sink her in the Indian seas,
> Twine, wine, and hides, and China teas.

I feel that Thoreau's decision to leave his father's way of life was a complicated move, with something careful in it and something reckless, something noble and something destructive. But when he determined on it, he made sure that all of Concord knew, to cut off possibility of retreat.

The radiance that comes from that complicated, ambivalent decision makes the prose of *Walden* shine; the sentences glow with the heat given off by high spirits. If a book is a house, then, as Thoreau might say, the spirits of dried hickory and of a man who is in the right heat a house well.

Thoreau wanted greatness, and he wanted to live greatly, but most of all he wanted not to live meanly. Others have left a record of their decision not to live meanly—I think of Kierkegaard, Juan Ramón Jiménez, Emily Dickinson, Walt Whitman and Robert Frost—but none, I think, have seen so clearly, grasped so keenly, or defended so tenaciously the waiting period that such a decision entails. Agreeing to a waiting period is a part of it.

Jung remarks in one of his essays that some plants grow best out of direct sun, in damp light, or in northern light. When a man or woman determines to leap over the petty life and tries to hatch the egg dormant in the apple wood, he or she needs leisure time, and the courage to take it. Courage is needed to withstand the melancholy and loneliness. He or she learns that for years nothing tangible will come from this inward and invisible swerving. No fruit will appear that his or her family or the surrounding society can eat. Milton describes the grief beautifully in this sonnet:

> How soon hath Time, the subtle thief of youth,
> > Stol'n on his wing my three and twentieth year!
> > My hasting days fly off with full career,
> > But my late spring no bud or blossom shew'th.
> Perhaps my semblance might deceive the truth,
> > That I to manhood am arrived so near,
> > And inward ripeness doth much less appear,
> > That some more timely-happy spirits endu'th.
> Yet be it less or more, or soon or slow,
> > It shall be still in strictest measure ev'n,
> > To that same lot, however mean or high,
> Toward which Time leads me, and the will of Heav'n;
> > All is, if I have grace to use it so,
> > As ever in my great Task-Master's eye.

Thoreau, at twenty-five, writes in his journal (March 22, 1842): "Nothing can be more useful to a man than a determination not to be hurried."

Richard Lebeaux, in his book *Young Man Thoreau*, pays attention to Thoreau's moratorium, adopting a term suggested by Erik Erikson. It took tremendous courage for Thoreau to refuse his town's insistence that he take a job the day after college graduation; there was no place in his townsmen's psyche for the man who waits. Thoreau's ability to endure a moratorium goes to the root of his courage and his accomplishment. He had to agree to change from a rooster to a setting hen, and he asked himself in his journal on March 26, 1842: "Are setting hens troubled with ennui? Nature is very kind; does she let them reflect? These long March days, setting on and on in the crevice of a hayloft, with no active employment! Do setting hens sleep?"

At other times Thoreau adopts the image of moulting: "Our moulting season, like that of the fowls, must be a crisis in our lives. The loon retires to solitary ponds to spend it. Thus also the snake casts its slough, and the caterpillar its wormy coat, by an internal industry and expansion; for clothes are but our outmost cuticle and mortal coil. Otherwise we shall be found sailing under false colors, and be inevitably cashiered at last by our own opinion, as well as that of mankind." (*Walden*)

Erikson observed the value of such a waiting period in the lives of Martin Luther and Gandhi. It is possible that at an earlier time initiation groups, made up of older men or older women, gave the young ones permission for a waiting period. Now each person has to demand, create and defend his or her own. I feel that Thoreau's declaration of the need for a moratorium is his greatest gift to the young. He does not require that each of us go, as he did, to the woods to live alone, as the Basques, Buddhists and some Native American cultures still do:

> I would not have any one adopt *my* mode of living on any account; for, besides that before he has fairly learned it I may have found out another for myself, I desire that there be as many different persons in the world as possible; but I would have each one be very careful to find out and pursue his own way, and not his father's or his mother's or his neighbor's instead. (*Walden*)

But he asks each person to take time early in life for a moratorium, even if only two years. In *Walden* he asks the community members who have read his words to encourage and support their young people in this effort, and testifies to its value:

> Sometimes . . . I sat in my sunny doorway from sunrise until noon, rapt in a revery, amidst the pines and hickories and sumachs. . . . I grew in those seasons like corn in the night.

Thoreau's own moratorium was long. He began it tentatively in 1837, when he was twenty, on graduating from Harvard. The next year he and his brother John established a small school, where both taught for three years. When John became ill, and the brothers dissolved the school, Henry's moratorium began in earnest. On his last day of teaching, Henry wrote a magnificent poem in four lines; after a dull, cloudy day the sun came out in late afternoon:

> Methinks all things have travelled since you shined,
> But only Time, and clouds, Time's team, have moved;
> Again foul weather shall not change my mind,
> But in the shade I will believe what in the sun I loved.

Seeing the faces of students respond, and receiving their affection and gratitude, resembles living in the sun. But Thoreau agrees to leave that sunlight and live in the shade, and he swears that "in the shade I will believe what in the sun I loved." It is an original and powerful line.

It took thirteen years after that day for *Walden* to appear in print; the book was published in 1854, only eight years before Thoreau died. Its appearance meant the end of his moratorium, and he wrote in his journal on September 19, 1854:

> Thinking this afternoon of the prospect of my writing lectures and going abroad to read them the next winter, I realized how incomparably great the advantages of obscurity and poverty which I have enjoyed so long. . . . I have given myself up to nature; I have lived so many springs and summers and autumns and winters as if I had nothing else to do but live them, and imbibe whatever nutriment they had for me; . . . If I go abroad lecturing, how shall I ever recover the lost winter?

One could say that Thoreau had twenty-four years of youth, thirteen years of moratorium and eight years of arrival or visibility. We know from reading *Walden* that his waiting period bore fruit. That book has gathered a sweetness, a groundedness in every sentence, a psychic weight, as if each page were a chunk of maple. Robert Frost, in an introductory essay to his collected poems titled "The Figure a Poem Makes," said of a good poem: "Its most precious quality will remain its having run itself and carried away the poet with it. Read it a hundred times; it will forever keep its freshness as a metal keeps its fragrance." Thoreau kept his mouth shut until it was time to speak. Each sentence in *Walden* is bold, precise and calculated to arouse opposition: "From the desperate city you go into the desperate country, and have to console yourselves with the bravery of minks and muskrats." Each sentence is a stone, and he has consciously shaped edges on it before he puts it in your hand.

Thoreau loved malic acid, that pungent power in small wild apples. When we taste that acid, we know that no one engineered this fruit to please large numbers of people. So in his moratorium Thoreau learned to grow small wild apples. He was also able "to drive life into a corner, and reduce it to its lowest terms, and, if it proved to be mean, why then to get the whole and genuine meanness of it, and publish its meanness to the world; or if it were sublime, to know it by experience, and be able to give a true account of it in my next excursion." (*Walden*) He became acquainted with the night, with the sorrow of the woods and the melancholy of the snow; he found depths and learned to trust them; he lived alone and liked the company. Once a writer has had that experience, he is content to write for the few who understand him, rather than for the millions who might, with the help of a loudspeaker, hear him.

Thoreau made a tart distinction between hearing and understanding. He said, in *Walden,* "The orator yields to the inspiration of a transient occasion, and speaks to the mob before him, to those who can hear him; but the writer, whose more equable life is his occasion, and who would be distracted by the event and the crowd which inspires the orator, speaks to the intellect and heart of mankind, to all in any age who can *understand* him."

We can ask of every writer whether he or she is writing to be heard, or to be understood. One danger of large poetry readings in our time is that in them the poet is urged to speak to those who can hear; those who understand the poet may not yet be born.

Did the moratorium damage Thoreau? I would say that it increased his sense that he was superior to others, of which he already had too much, and it must have increased also the compensatory sense of inferiority. By omitting domestic love, wife, children and community position, he decreased the number of unknowns in his life, and perhaps the number of knowns. I also think his moratorium went on so long that he resigned himself to not being at home in either male or female company. On July 26, 1852, he wrote in his journal:

> By my intimacy with nature I find myself withdrawn from man. My interest in the sun and the moon, in the morning and the evening, compels me to solitude.
>
> The grandest picture in the world is the sunset sky. In your higher moods what man is there to meet? You are of necessity isolated. The mind that perceives clearly any natural beauty is in that instant withdrawn from human society. My desire for society is infinitely increased; my fitness for any actual society is diminished.

The poems and prose pieces in this section center on the decision Thoreau made to move away from the "lives of quiet desperation" and his thoughts about the waiting period that followed, the long time when "no bud or blossom sheweth." Some journal passages suggest the images that he used to nourish him at that period: images of the vivid life that goes on underneath the snow, the picture of a hibernating bear, the story of an artist in ancient India who "made no compromise with Time." One poem, "Among the Worst of Men That Ever Lived," hints at his pride that he had become one of those citizens of Concord and the world who, despite all the elevated talk of spirituality around him, and the availability of high-spirited horses able to clear "riders" or fence poles easily, took the slow way and "went on to heaven the long way around."

4.
Seeing What Is Before Us

Thoreau was capable of true patience in observing the nonhuman world, and he exclaims in one passage, "Would it not be a luxury to stand up to one's chin in some retired swamp for a whole summer's day?" If we've read

Thoreau, we know that he would be perfectly capable of it. He walked two to four hours each day and noted with the most astonishing perseverance and tenacity the exact days on which wildflowers—dozens of varieties—opened in the forest. In 1853 he notes in his journal: "My Aunt Maria asked me to read the life of Dr. Chalmers, which, however, I did not promise to do. Yesterday, Sunday, she was heard through the partition shouting to my Aunt Jane, who is deaf: 'Think of it: He stood half an hour today to hear the frogs croak, and he wouldn't read the life of Chalmers.'"

His neighbors saw him stand motionless for eight hours beside a pond to watch young frogs, and all day at a river's edge watching duck eggs hatching.

Thoreau felt invited to observe the detail in nature, and he did not receive his invitation from Wordsworth or Milton: it came to him as a part of his genius. When he was twenty-one he wrote in his journal: "Nature will bear the closest inspection. She invites us to lay our eye level with her smallest leaf, and take an insect view of its plain." There is something brilliant in the last clause, advising us to take a low-lying, or insect, position when we look. One day, while he lay on his back during a soaking rain, he saw a raindrop descend along a stalk of the previous year's oats. "While these clouds and this sombre drizzling weather shut all in, we two draw nearer and know one another," he wrote in his journal (March 30, 1840). R. H. Blyth declared this sentence to be one of the few sentence in the English language that was a genuine haiku.

Emerson said this of Thoreau's patience in his "Biographical Sketch":

> It was a pleasure and a privilege to walk with him. He knew the country like a fox or a bird, and passed through it as freely by paths of his own. He knew every track in the snow or on the ground, and what creature had taken this path before him. One must submit abjectly to such a guide, and the reward was great. Under his arm he carried an old music-book to press plants; in his pocket, his diary and pencil, a spy-glass for birds, microscope, jack-knife, and twine. He wore a straw hat, stout shoes, strong gray trousers, to brave scrub-oaks and smilax, and to climb a tree for a hawk's or a squirrel's nest. He waded into the pool for the water-plants, and his strong legs were no insignificant part of his armor. On the day I speak of he looked for the Menyanthes, de-

tected it across the wide pool, and, on examination of the florets, decided that it had been in flower five days. He drew out of his breast-pocket his diary, and read the names of all the plants that should bloom on this day, whereof he kept account as a banker when his notes fall due. The Cypripedium not due till to-morrow. He thought that, if waked up from a trance, in this swamp, he could tell by the plants what time of the year it was within two days. The redstart was flying about, and presently the fine gros-beaks, whose brilliant scarlet "makes the rash gazer wipe his eye," and whose fine clear note Thoreau compared to that of a tanager which has got rid of its hoarseness. . . .

. . . His power of observation seemed to indicate additional senses. He saw as with microscope, heard as with ear trumpet, and his memory was a photographic register of all he saw and heard.

We need to understand that Thoreau received through Emerson and Coleridge, through the Eastern spiritual books he read, among them those of the Indian poet Kabir, and through Goethe, Schelling and other German writers, the doctrine that the spiritual world lies hidden in, or moving among, or shining through the physical world. Nature is one of the languages that God speaks. He spoke in Hebrew—New Englanders had always known that—but the truth of the soul's interior abundance, while not denying that, added that He also spoke the local language called nature.

Since the physical world conceals or embodies a spiritual world, if one studies facts in nature, one might be able to deduce or distill from many physical facts a spiritual fact. Robert Frost, who is Thoreau's greatest disciple, hinted at that in his poem "Mowing":

> There was never a sound beside the wood but one,
> And that was my long scythe whispering to the ground.
> What was it it whispered? I knew not well myself;
> Perhaps it was something about the heat of the sun,
> Something, perhaps, about the lack of sound—
> And that was why it whispered and did not speak.
> It was no dream of the gift of idle hours,
> Or easy gold at the hand of fay or elf:

Anything more than the truth would have seemed too weak
To the earnest love that laid the swale in rows,
Not without feeble-pointed spikes of flowers
(Pale orchises), and scared a bright green snake.
The fact is the sweetest dream that labor knows.
My long scythe whispered and left the hay to make.

Thoreau remarked in his journal on February 18, 1852:

> I have a commonplace book for facts, and another for poetry, but
> I find it difficult always to preserve the vague distinction which
> I had in mind, for the most interesting and beautiful facts are so
> much the more poetry and that is their success. They are trans-
> lated from earth to heaven. I see that if my facts were sufficiently
> vital and significant—perhaps transmuted into the substance of
> the human mind—I should need but one book of poetry to con-
> tain them all.

So one can translate certain facts "from earth to heaven." Scientists, because
they do not know Kabir's truth of the double world, do not translate. Scientific study of facts in Thoreau's time did not encourage the scientist to
cross over the threshold between worlds. But Thoreau is able to cross from
earth to heaven: "I see that if my facts were sufficiently vital and signifi-
cant—perhaps transmuted into the substance of the human mind"—they
would become poetry.

We understand that Thoreau's observation is not a simple-minded cat-
aloging of detail. Behind his persistence lies the promise, grounded in his
vast reading, that, in Coleridge's words, "each object rightly seen unlocks a
new faculty of the Soul." What is it like, then, to look at an object rightly?
Suppose one watched ants fighting. Eyes see surprises, polarities, nuances;
the observer's language, if he or she wrote of the battle, would have to contain those nuances, so that the reader could also see rightly. We notice in the
following passage that Thoreau provides "embraces," "sunny valley" and
"chips" as nuances among the violence:

> I watched a couple that were fast locked in each other's embraces,
> in a little sunny valley amid the chips, now at noonday prepared

to fight till the sun went down, or life went out. The smaller red champion had fastened himself like a vise to his adversary's front, and through all the tumblings on that field never for an instant ceased to gnaw at one of his feelers near the root, having already caused the other to go by the board; while the stronger black one dashed him from side to side, and, as I saw on looking nearer, had already divested him of several of his members. They fought with more pertinacity than bulldogs.

How good "pertinacity" is here! The swift changes of mood in animal encounters, the intricacy of instinctual gesture, the mixture of comical and tragical, require a vocabulary that can go from high to low in an instant, that can move from dark to light and back, from metallic word to fragrant word, from a slang phrase to words from the Middle Ages or the eighteenth century. American democracy suggests that good writing about nature requires only a simple heart; but bravery of soul, immense learning and cunning in language—none of them simple—are what nature writing requires.

We recognize that Thoreau's account of the ant battle is not pure observation without human imposition; while he observes detail, he is also declaring that men's proclivity for battle is mechanical and antlike:

Holding a microscope to the first-mentioned red ant, I saw that, though he was assiduously gnawing at the near foreleg of his enemy, having severed his remaining feeler, his own breast was all torn away, exposing what vitals he had there to the jaws of the black warrior, whose breastplate was apparently too thick for him to pierce; and the dark carbuncles of the sufferer's eyes shone with ferocity such as war only could excite.

"Assiduously" is essential here. Long, "unnatural" words suggest the fierce intensity of the insect world, in which no one is "laid back" in the California way. Thoreau places "feeler," a word a child might use, near "vitals," an adult word that evokes complicated feelings, including fear. He mingles with that "black warrior" and "breastplate," words that carry a Middle Ages fragrance, and they prepare for the astonishing phrase "dark carbuncles of the sufferer's eyes."

Thoreau writes with equal cunning when he composes less tendentious description—for example, when he describes a squirrel chewing on successive ears of corn. His language then imposes fewer human analogies, becomes amazingly quick-footed, and his nimble rhythms seem transparent to the animal's consciousness.

Thoreau attempts something new in American literature. He does not agree with earlier New Englanders that the world is fallen, and a dark ruin, but believes by contrast that the world remains radiant from the divine energy that shines through it. A few days before he died, a family friend asked him "how he stood affected toward Christ." Thoreau answered, as reported in the *Christian Examiner* in 1865, that "a snow-storm was more to him than Christ." He is suggesting, I think, that even in the 1860s, so far into the nineteenth century, the snowstorm is still luminous with spiritual energy; and Christ is not needed to lift it back up into radiance. The snowstorm and God have never quarreled.

Thoreau trained himself over many years to see. His training involved a number of disciplines. The first was constant labor. His journals are so immense that they must have required, during his short life, two or three hours of writing each day, over and above the walks he wrote about. Second, he aimed to become just, and in this struggle followed the ancient doctrine, contrary to scientific doctrine, that certain secrets of nature reveal themselves only to the observer who is morally developed. The alchemists founded their penetration of nature on their moral character. Concentrating on a "low-anchored cloud," Thoreau wrote:

> Drifting meadow of the air,
> Where bloom the daisied banks and violets,
> And in whose fenny labyrinth
> The bittern booms and heron wades;
> Spirit of lakes and seas and rivers,
> Bear only perfumes and the scent
> Of healing herbs to just men's fields!

Third, he aimed to diminish the distance between subject and object, to heal the split that intellect in general, and Descartes in particular, opened between man and nature. When Descartes distinguished between "the thing that thinks" and "the thing that has space," he widened the split between human beings and nature. Melville expressed the terror of this gap in a marvelous metaphor given to Ishmael: "If you lean away from the mast," Ishmael says, "over Descartian vortices you hover." Thoreau aimed to heal the Cartesian gap by studying the idea that forms and colors are adapted to the human eye. We do not have, then, two things—an eye on the one side and an incomprehensible, strange, nonhuman object on the other—but rather we have a human eye as natural as and a part of the meadow and the island: "I am made to love the pond and the meadow, . . ." (*Journal*, November 21, 1850) Thoreau grasped that such interchange means that a human being cannot discover his own makeup solely by studying history, or investigating his dreams, or noticing his reaction to other human beings. On the contrary that person will never understand himself or herself until he or she has consciously loved the pond and the meadow.

Thoreau trained himself also to see the darkness of apparently light-filled things. When we see smoke rising from an isolated farmhouse, we idealize the life by the hearth. Thoreau trained himself to see the mortgage and "the idiot sitting by the fire." When he visited Cape Cod, he described a woman he saw there:

> We saw one singularly masculine woman, however, in a house on this very plain, who did not look as if she was ever troubled with hysterics, or sympathized with those who were; or, perchance, life itself was to her a hysteric fit,—a Nauset woman, of a hardness and coarseness such as no man ever possesses or suggests. It was enough to see the vertebrae and sinews of her neck, and her set jaws of iron, which would have bitten a board-nail in two in their ordinary action,—braced against the world, talking like a man-of-war's-man in petticoats, or as if shouting to you through a breaker; who looked as if it made her head ache to live; hard enough for any enormity. I looked upon her as one who had committed infanticide; who never had a brother, unless it were some wee thing that died in infancy,—for what need of him?—and whose father must have died before she was born. (*Cape Cod*)

But he is not satisfied with his ability to see. One of his most magnificent poems is "Smoke":

Light-winged Smoke, Icarian bird,
Melting thy pinions in thy upward flight,

Lark without song, and messenger of dawn,
Circling above the hamlets as thy nest;
Or else, departing dream, and shadowy form
Of midnight vision, gathering up thy skirts;
By night star-veiling, and by day
Darkening the light and blotting out the sun;
Go thou my incense upward from this hearth,
And ask the gods to pardon this clear flame.

Thoreau realized that if he were to succeed in seeing truly, he himself would have to take in more darkness. He noticed that smoke's associations are with dream and midnight vision, and that smoke veils the stars at night and darkens the sun by day, and so he wrote:

Go thou my incense upward from this hearth,
And ask the gods to pardon this clear flame.

We feel in Thoreau's life the presence of a fierce and long-lived discipline, and one reward of that discipline was his grasp of the wildness in nature.

5.
In Wildness is the Preservation of the World

Photographs of Thoreau give a sense of sedateness and sobriety, and they determine our usual view of him; but he also had a grand interior wildness. He remarks in *Walden*, "As I came home through the woods with my string of fish, trailing my pole, it being now quite dark, I caught a glimpse of a woodchuck stealing across my path, and felt a strange thrill of savage delight, and was strongly tempted to seize and devour him raw. . . ."

Rose Hawthorne, in her book *Memories of Hawthorne*, left a lovely description of Hawthorne, Thoreau and Emerson skating. Hawthorne "moved like a self-impelled Greek statue, stately and grave," and Emerson moved as if "too weary to hold himself erect, pitching head foremost, half lying on the air." Thoreau did "dithyrambic dances and Bacchic leaps on the ice." A visitor to the Thoreau house, whose memoir Thoreau's biographer, Walter Harding, found, remembers that one evening Thoreau ran down from his upstairs study and broke into a dance, "spinning airily around, displaying most remarkable lightness and agility, and finally springing over the center table, alighting like a feather on the other side. . . ."

Of the marsh hawk Thoreau said, "There is health in thy gray wing," and he reminded the reader that "in literature it is only the wild that attracts us." We require that all things be mysterious and unchartable, that land and sea be infinitely wild, unsurveyed and unfathomed by us because unfathomable. He associated "wild" with "willed," with what is not passive and indecisive. And he was sure that the civilized nations—Greece, Rome, England—have "been sustained by the primitive forests" that surrounded them, and that these same nations have died and will die when the forests end.

The Spanish poet Antonio Machado, so like Thoreau in many ways, wrote this sentence about his own poems in the introduction to his *Selected Poems:* "Many of the poems spring from . . . a simple love of nature that in me is far stronger than the love of art." Few writers would state this sentiment so baldly, and we would not expect it from writers who love and practice their craft as artists. When Machado—who was, like Thoreau, a great artist—says it, we listen.

Moreover, I think that few men or women, artists or not, love nature and its wildness. Many people understand the truth that nature is a deeper friend of the soul than society. But, just because a person knows and believes this truth doesn't mean that he or she will love nature. We tend to love what is like us: Chaucer found the seasons thrilling, but he loved the Wife of Bath; the Anglo-Saxon poets admired nature as a terrible master, but they loved men who earned fame and had a great civil helpfulness; Jane Austen liked the garden, but she loved the soul's ability to make distinctions in feeling; Milton, when walking with a woman he loved, forgot all time—"all seasons and all change, all please alike"—he liked the wildness of nature, but he loved the rebellious impulse in the human soul.

In 1857 Thoreau wrote in his journal: "How rarely a man's love for nature becomes a ruling principle with him, like a youth's affection for a maiden, but more enduring: All nature is my bride." Five months earlier he had realized that he was about to become a husband: "There was a match found for me at last. I fell in love with a shrub oak."

On December 12, 1851, he also wrote in his journal: "Ah, dear nature, the mere remembrance, after a short forgetfulness, of the pine woods! I come to it as a hungry man to a crust of bread."

For I had rather be thy child
And pupil in the forest wild
Than be the king of men elsewhere
And most sovereign slave of care,
To have one moment of thy dawn
Than share the city's year forlorn.
Some still work give me to do
Only be it near you.

We know the speculation that Thoreau loved nature because he couldn't love a woman, and I'll talk of that a little in the biographical sketch. But his love of nature, to me, is not to be reduced to something else: "I am made to love the pond and the meadow, as the wind is made to ripple the water."

Moreover, if nature is a woman he loves, who is his bride, we see that he is not loving a coarse, mechanistic, dull-headed woman, but rather a woman like Emerson's Aunt Mary, full of intelligence in every cell of her body. I have suggested that Thoreau was one of the first writers in America to accept the ancient idea that nature is not a fallen world, but on the contrary a veil for the divine world, the chest in which God is hidden, an alphabet whose vowels are a beam going straight to the kingdom of light, so that the owl's dark eyelids cover a luminosity our reason cannot grasp, let along reason about.

If we use Blake's terms, the body of Thoreau's bride "is a portion of the Soul discern'd by the five Senses, the chief inlets of Soul in this age," and each part of nature is holy. Blake says in "Auguries of Innocence":

A Robin Red breast in a Cage
Puts all Heaven in a Rage.

Thoreau, like Blake, was training himself to see *through*, not *with*, the eye. When people see only with the practical eye, they will see material beings, objects without light around them, pieces of inert nature, dead rocks, trees no more alive than the gears in a watch. Blake called such vision "single vision," and he said:

. . . May God us keep
From single vision & Newton's sleep!

The contrary way of seeing—seeing through the eye, or through the inner eye—leads us to glimpse the divine energy in each thing we see:

> To see a World in a Grain of Sand
> And a Heaven in Wild Flower,
> Hold Infinity in the palm of your hand,
> And Eternity in an hour.
>   "Auguries of Innocence"

As we read Thoreau's work, especially his prose, we slowly become aware of a light in and around the squirrel, the ant, the woodchuck, the hawk, that belongs to *them* and not to the eyes observing or the brain producing words. The human mind, when it is in its own deeps, shares that light, so that it is not always improper to bring in human feelings when describing an animal or object. When people insist on keeping all human feelings out, they mean to retain single vision.

Blake said:

> For double the vision my Eyes do see,
> And a double vision is always with me.
> With my inward Eye 'tis an old Man grey:
> With my outward a Thistle across the Way.

It isn't that Blake doesn't see the thistle; he sees the thistle with the eye, and then through the eye he sees in the thistle an old man gray. Thoreau does not aim to glimpse imaginary or fantasy figures while ignoring the physical world; on the contrary, he sees with the material eye marvelously; no detail escapes his attention. As Emerson remarked, "His power of observation seemed to indicate additional senses." But he wants to go further.

His journal entry of October 29, 1857, is a good example of his increasing respect for impalpable seeing. A recurrent dream came to Thoreau, and he wrote of it at last in this entry, roughly four and a half years before he died. He saw in his dream a mountain near Concord that did not exist. He "steadily ascended along a rocky ridge half clad with stinted trees, where wild beasts haunted." He did not climb to a European or Christian Mount of Purgatory, but rather arrived at an American rocky mountain plateau, "bare and pathless rock." This bare and rocky peak participates in what the late-eighteenth century poets called Terror, and which they contrasted to beneficent nature, or Beauty. "You know no path, but wander, thrilled, over the bare and pathless rock," Thoreau wrote. "In dreams I am shown this height from time to time." He added that walking on it resembles walking on the face of a god.

Two strange features of the dream strike him. First, the ascent begins where the "Burying Hill" is in ordinary life. "You might go through its gate to enter that dark wood, but that hill and its graves are so concealed and obliterated by the awful mountain that I never thought of them as underlying it." So one goes through the place of the dead to arrive at the wildness and the terror. The dead seem to be a part of that darkness that he, despite his efforts to approach it, had avoided too much in his life. The mountaintop participates in the terror that Goya and others had seen in nature, while he and Wordsworth, to name a writer akin to Thoreau, had seen primarily the beauty and order of nature.

Second, in his dreams he descended the mountain by going through a sunny pasture. That was strange, because he had never ascended that way. "There are ever two ways up: one is through the dark wood, the other through the sunny pasture." His psyche seems to be telling him that a whole new way of writing lies ahead of him. Descending the mountain in his dream, he entered the ordinary world through a sunny pasture, as Odysseus entered his old life in Ithaca through the gladsome swineherd's hut. Thoreau can now see the possibility of climbing the terror through a sunny pasture. He had often begun his books and poems with an image of imprisonment and ended them with an image of light. *Walden* ends with the statement, "The sun is but a morning star." He was about to die of tuberculosis, yet the psyche, as Jung reported from the experience of many dying patients, seems to pay no attention to the impending death. The dream says, "You could write something wholly new now, beginning your ascent the other way." But Thoreau didn't live long enough to write this new sort of poem.

It only remains to say a few words about the qualities I love in Thoreau. I love his fierce and meticulous observation. Most artists begin, as seems right, with interior absorption, introversion and examination of their inner world, and often end there. From much ancient art, we deduce that the next stage involves attention, which goes to the life beyond one's house, beyond one's mind, beyond human obsession to the enormous intertangling that we call the universe. Thoreau got to this second stage, a place reached by very few artists of the last century.

I also love the density Thoreau developed in his own personality. He got rid of the collective expectations projected on him, as the community projects on us all, and filled those spaces with more Thoreau—more likes, opinions and original nature. He was named David Henry Thoreau, but he changed that, and became Henry David Thoreau everywhere in his body, and even in his dense and magnificent sentences. When he was an adult, he was not the sort of tree one cuts down to make a house. Even his old enemy, Daniel Shattuck, president of the local bank, said of him after he died, "Mr. Thoreau was a man who never conformed his opinions after the model of others; they were his own; were also singular. Who will say they were not right? He had many admirers, and well he might for, whatever might be the truth of his opinions, his life was one of singular purity and kindness." An ancient tree, hundreds of years old, once spoke to a Taoist who walked past it, and explained that it had got to its height, with its gnarled branches and bitter bark, by "being useless." Thoreau chose the way of bitter bark and gnarled branches and no one cut him down for a house.

Lastly, I love his genius at metaphorical thinking. All mythological thinking, as Joseph Campbell has so often stated, is metaphorical, and difficult to us for that reason. Thoreau noticed that an insect egg got caught inside an apple-wood table and hatched years after its secretion. Such a physical fact, when seen metaphorically, carries the observer into the soul or the inner world or the invisible world. Thoreau did not throw away the fact of the insect egg and its slow hatching, but loved it as a fact, until it carried him to the soul. He was a master of metaphorical thinking. In "The American Scholar," Emerson hoped that for his generation the ancient precept "Know thyself" and the contemporary precept "Study nature" would become a single precept, a single piece of advice, a single guide. In Thoreau the two joined.

A Brief Biography of Thoreau

Henry David Thoreau was born, and given the name David Henry Thoreau, on July 12, 1817, in Concord, Massachusetts. His father's family went back to French Protestants who had moved to the Isle of Jersey after the Edict of Nantes in 1685; Henry's grandfather, John Thoreau, shipwrecked from a Jersey privateer, settled in Boston and alternated after that between business on land and attacking English ships at sea. Thoreau's father John was one of ten children. His mother's side of the family was lively and given to self-confident actions. Cynthia Thoreau's father, Asa Dunbar, led a rebellion when at Harvard against some inadequacy and became successively a schoolteacher, preacher and lawyer. Her mother, Mary Jones Dunbar, born to a line of Tories and slave owners, supported her Tory brothers when they were in prison during the Revolutionary War, slipped files to them in jail and helped them escape to Canada.

In the household into which Henry was born, Cynthia Thoreau struck all visitors as dominant. She was talkative, hard-working and a sharp-tongued reformer. Henry's father, John, opened several shops early in his life but hesitated to collect debts. Eventually he succeeded in establishing a pencil-making factory. He was a flute player and lover of reading, and both Cynthia and John loved to walk in the woods and fields.

They had four children: Helen, John, Henry and Sophia. Henry was chosen to go to Harvard, though John seemed the more promising. Henry went, but never was enthusiastic about it, and did not rank very high in his class of fifty students. When he graduated in 1837 he walked home rather than stay for the ceremony. Later, when he asked is mother what he should do, she remarked that he could strap on his backpack and go out into the world. His sister Helen noticed that tears sprang to his eyes, and she put her arms around him and said, "No, Henry, you shall not go; you shall stay at home and live with us."

For the most part, that is exactly what he did. He lived for a time in other houses, but invariably returned. Neither of his two sisters married, and maiden aunts also lived in the house. He got a job teaching school, but abruptly resigned when he was required to flog a student. John and Henry started a local school of their own, which lasted three years, closing at last in April of 1841 because of John's tuberculosis. During those years, both John and Henry fell in love with the same woman, Ellen Sewall, who was from Scituate, and Henry waited until John had proposed and been refused before he proposed. Ellen was a father's girl, and her father considered the Thoreau boys too advanced, being aware there was a transcendental taint to their thoughts. Ellen refused Henry as well. Shortly before he died, when his sister mentioned Ellen, Henry said, "I have always loved her. I have always loved her." It is possible that the turtledove he mentions losing in *Walden* was

Ellen Sewall. On New Year's Day of 1842, John cut his finger shaving, and eleven days later died of lockjaw. Henry's care for his brother was extremely tender and his grief so deep that he contracted a sympathetic case of lockjaw eleven days following John's death, but he recovered.

After John died, Ralph Waldo Emerson, with whom Thoreau had first become friends in the fall of 1837, became his most important friend, and his great teacher. Thoreau lived for several periods as a handyman in Emerson's house and became a favorite of Emerson's children. Toward the end of his life, Emerson considered Thoreau to have been his best friend. Hawthorne lived nearby also, but he was never quite so fond of Thoreau. Emerson had bought a plot of ground on Walden shore, and Thoreau began building a cabin there in the early spring of 1845. He eventually moved in on July 4, 1845, and remained there, visiting Concord often, until September 6, 1847.

Leon Edel accuses Thoreau of concealing information about the number of his visits to the Thoreau family house and to Concord, implying that he was almost never alone, but no country person can read the winter sections without realizing that Thoreau experienced long times of winter solitude. Before and after his stay at Walden, he rambled incessantly through the Concord countryside, and eventually knew it so well that he took up part-time work as a surveyor, earning some money that way. Meanwhile he wrote in his journal, recording with intense dedication his observations during his long walks and setting down his thoughts. Writing two or three hours a day he completed fourteen volumes in printed form; it alone is an immense labor. In 1838 he gave his first lecture to the Concord Lyceum and in 1842 published his first major essay, "Natural History of Massachusetts," in the *Dial*. As a memorial to his brother, he turned his notes on their earlier river trip into the book called *A Week on the Concord and Merrimack Rivers,* and it became his first published book in 1849. In the same year his essay "Civil Disobedience" also appeared in print.

In practical life, Thoreau was amazingly able; he could construct, repair and invent with equal skill. When competition to the Thoreau pencil factory developed, he several times entered the business decisively, making improvements. Pencil makers had always split the cedar pencil-wood, put the lead paste into the grooves, and then glued the parts back together. Thoreau discovered a mixture of graphite and Bavarian clay that could be baked; then he invented a machine for drilling holes in the solid pencils into which he could insert the firmly baked graphite, saving the trouble of splitting and reglueing. He also developed pencils of varying hardnesses by increasing or decreasing the amount of clay. Thoreau pencils were considered the equal of English pencils, and Boston art teachers, it is said, required their students to buy only Thoreau pencils. The Thoreau firm received the Silver Medal for the best lead pencils at the Salem Charitable Mechanic Association of 1849, and all of this came about through Henry's practical genius, inventiveness and active interest in the firm.

After he moved out of his Walden cabin in September of 1847, Thoreau continued to work on *Walden*, and that book was published at last in 1854. When his father died in 1859, Thoreau immediately assumed the position of head of the family and manager of the family graphite business. He soon began to use stone rather than iron balls for grinding graphite, and so improved the lead once more. He also made some income by his lectures, traveling around New England on request. In 1859 he began defending John Brown in his lectures. In October of that year he announced a lecture on John Brown at the Concord Town Hall. When the Republican Town Committee and the Abolitionists both advised against it, he replied to them, "I did not send to you for advice, but to announce that I am to speak." When the selectmen refused to ring the bell, he rang it himself. On November 28 he arranged services at Town Hall on the day John Brown was to be executed in the South. Observing John Brown's moral honesty and the State's reaction to it led him to write even more vividly on the importance of resisting the State. His moral personality now became highly developed.

What can we say about his undeveloped side? We could say that even at the end of his life he had not come to any solid peace with his own body. In "Higher Laws" he wrote:

> We are conscious of an animal in us, which awakens in proportion as our higher nature slumbers. It is reptile and sensual, and perhaps cannot be wholly expelled; like the worms which, even in life and health, occupy our bodies. Possibly we may withdraw from it, but never change its nature. I fear that it may enjoy a certain health of its own; that we may be well, yet not pure. The other day I picked up the lower jaw of a hog, with white and sound teeth and tusks, which suggested that there was an animal health and vigor distinct from the spiritual. This creature suc-

ceeded in other means than temperance and purity. "That in which men differ from brute beasts," says Mencius, "is a thing very inconsiderable; the common herd lose it very soon; superior men preserve it carefully."

A little farther on in this passage he attacks sexuality in a way implied by the earlier metaphors:

> The generative energy, which, when we are loose, dissipates and makes us unclean, when we are continent invigorates and inspires us. Chastity is the flowering of man; and what are called Genius, Heroism, Holiness, and the like, are but various fruits which succeed it. Man flows at once to God when the channel of purity is open. By turns our purity inspires and our impurity casts us down. He is blessed who is assured that the animal is dying out in him day by day, and the divine being established.

It was as if he never took his body to be a part of nature. He would never have said, "Any woods is blessed that is assured that the animal in it is dying out day by day."

Yeats declared that every truth has its countertruth. We are given one truth, and the countertruth we have to develop; Yeats worked hard at developing his countertruth. The truth of the soul's interior abundance declared that we can have a love affair with the universe only if we decline to marry the world; that nature is the true friend of the soul; and the divine man is uncontrolled by social obligation. The countertruth might be: society is a deeper friend of the soul than nature; a man or a woman grows only if he or she is willing to give up a solitary affair with a shrub oak; no solitary self can replace society, social sensibility, manners and the institutions of Church and State. Had Thoreau lived longer, he might have developed that countertruth.

We could say also that Thoreau's soul, despite his immersion in nature, began to feel the lack of some moistness. Odell Shepard, in his collection called *The Heart of Thoreau's Journals*, comments: "Thoreau fills hundreds of pages in his last journals with minute notations of things measured and counted, mostly written in the lifeless style of professional scientists against which he had so often railed." Thoreau himself complained of dryness. In

February 18, 1852, he wrote of the snow crust over rivers and ponds: "I can with difficulty tell when I am over the river. There is a similar crust over my heart." His fierce will gave him the power to break away from mean living, and he succeeded at that effort magnificently; but it was difficult for him to take in warmth from other men or from other women besides his mother and sisters, and one feels his soul, while remaining disciplined, grew increasingly isolated and thirsty. His love energy held on to nature, as he himself suggested by calling nature his bride.

But every writer has an undeveloped side. Emerson reported that a young Concord woman mentioned that taking Henry's arm was a little like taking the arm of an elm tree. She chose a slowly growing, tall and long-branched tree, a native American tree, as the image for him.

In February of 1860, Thoreau gave his newly completed "Wild Apples" lecture to the Concord Lyceum, and it turned out to be his last lecture there. On a lecture trip to Connecticut in September of 1860, he developed a cold and bronchitis, which activated his latent tuberculosis, and for the first time he could not take his long winter walks that year. A trip to Minnesota only made his tuberculosis worse, and when he returned in July of 1861 he was seriously ill. When Bronson Alcott visited him on New Year's Day of 1862, bringing cider and apples, he found Thoreau in bed and feeble, but talkative. They discussed Pliny and other rural authors. As long as Thoreau could sit up, he took his chair at the family table, saying, "It would not be social to take my meals alone." He also continued working on his Maine woods paper. Thoreau's last sentence contained the audible words "moose" and "Indian," and he died quietly on the evening of May 6, 1862, at the age of forty-four.

Robert Bly

Robert Bly was born on December 23, 1926, in Madison, Minnesota. He attended Harvard University and received his M.A. from the University of Iowa in 1956. As a poet, editor, and translator, Bly has had a profound impact on the shape of American poetry.

He is the author of more than thirty books of poetry, including *Stealing Sugar from the Castle: Selected Poems* (W. W. Norton, 2013); *Talking into the Ear of a Donkey: Poems* (2011); *Reaching Out to the World: New and Selected Prose Poems* (White Pine Press, 2009); *My Sentence Was a Thousand Years of Joy* (2006); and *The Night Abraham Called to the Stars* (2001).

As the editor of the magazine *The Sixties* (begun as *The Fifties*), Bly introduced many unknown European and South American poets to an American audience. He is also the editor of numerous collections including; *The Soul Is Here for Its Own Joy: Sacred Poems from Many Cultures* (1995); *Leaping Poetry* (1975); *The Rag and Bone Shop of the Heart: Poems for Men* (1992); and *News of the Universe* (1980). Bly is also the author of a number of nonfiction books, including *The Sibling Society* (Addison-Wesley, 1996); *Iron John: A Book about Men* (1990); and *Talking All Morning* (1980).

His honors include Guggenheim, Rockefeller, and National Endowment for the Arts fellowships as well as The Robert Frost Medal from the Poetry Society of America. His most recent books include *Like the New Moon I Will Live My Life* (White Pine Press), *More Than True: The Wisdom of Fairy Tales* (Henry Holt) and *Collected Poems* (Norton).

Thomas R. Smith

Thomas R. Smith is an internationally published poet and essayist living in western Wisconsin. His most recent poetry collections are *The Glory* (Red Dragonfly) and *Windy Day at Kabekona: New and Selected Prose Poems* (White Pine Press). He has also edited three books on Robert Bly's work, most recently *Airmail: The Letters of Robert Bly and Tomas Tranströmer.* He teaches at the Loft Literary Center in Minneapolis and posts poems and essays at www.thomasrsmithpoet.com.

The mystery of the
Seven Holy Vowels
by Joscelyn Godwin

Harmonium - W. Stevens

ESSENTIAL BLY

POETRY

The Chinese-influenced strain of Bly's work with its room for movement, spontaneity and openness is celebrated and showcased in over 160 poems from out-of-print books, chapbooks and uncollected work spanning fifty years.

ESSAYS

For those readers who have followed the incandescent arc of Robert Bly's artistry and thought for the past five or six decades, this book packs the emotional satisfaction of a reunion of beloved friends — so many vivid speakers gathered at table, the conversation by turns fiery, lyrical, prophetic, reckless, intimate, generous, obscure or even esoteric.

Two does stop
between the rock &
a sparagus patch
on the edge
between forest & yard
Both stop to 'look at us
The long gaze
Soon they wander
separately
behind the tall weeds
That curtain the garden
fence
I know they want in
I see one nosing thru the fence
Wild grass & clover not good enough
Longing for the unreachable
bean plants & young corn stalks